WORLD BANK OPERATIONS EVALUATION DEPARTMENT

The Effectiveness of World Bank Support for Community-Based and -Driven Development

An OED Evaluation

2005
The World Bank
Washington, D.C.

http://www.worldbank.org/oed/cbdcdd

1818 H Street, NW
Washington, DC 20433
Telephone 202-473-1000
Internet www.worldbank.org
E-mail feedback@worldbank.org

1 2 3 4 09 08 07 06 05

Cover photo: © Giacomo Pirozzi/Panos Pictures.

ISBN-10: 0-8213-6390-5 ISBN-13: 978-0-8213-6390-4
e-ISBN: 0-8213-6391-3
DOI: 10.1596/978-0-8213-6390-4

World Bank InfoShop
E-mail: pic@worldbank.org
Telephone: 202-458-5454
Facsimile: 202-522-1500

Operations Evaluation Department
Knowledge Programs and Evaluation Capacity Development (OEDKE)
E-mail: eline@worldbank.org
Telephone: 202-458-4497
Facsimile: 202-522-3125

Printed on Recycled Paper

Contents

Figures

Table

Acknowledgments

The report was prepared by a core team consisting of Nalini Kumar (Task Manager), Barbara Pozzoni, Anju Vajja, and George Garner Woodall. Additional team members were Ewa Gradzka, Kavita Mathur, Sonali Moonesinghe, Ridley Nelson, Floribert Ngaruko, Camilo Gomez Osorio, and Peter Whitford. In addition to the core team, data collection was undertaken by Dr. Alberto Coelho Gomes Costa and his team of surveyors in Brazil, the staff and students of the Centre for Development Economics, Delhi School of Economics in India, and Dr. Roch Mongbo and his team of surveyors in Benin. William Hurlbut edited the original report and Caroline McEuen edited the manuscript for publication. Tomas Caspellan, Soon-Won Pak, and Helen Phillip provided administrative support. Julius Gwyer provided technical support for the maintenance of the Web site. Jacintha Wijesinghe and Etsegenet Nigussie advised on the budget. The report benefited considerably from the guidance provided by Alain Barbu, Ajay Chhibber, Nils Fostvedt, Patrick Grasso, Gregory Ingram, and Kyle Peters.

The External Advisory Panel for the review consisted of Dr. Norman Uphoff, Director of the Cornell International Institute for Food, Agriculture and Development and Professor of Government at Cornell University; Mr. Paiboon Wattanasiritham, Chairman of the Community Organizations Development Institute (CODI) in Thailand; and Professor Robert Chambers, Research Associate at the Institute of Development Studies at the University of Sussex (UK).

Colleagues inside the Bank provided comments at various stages. They include: Ruth Alsop, Hans Binswanger, Victor Botini, Ed Bresnyan, Mark Cackler, Robert Chase, Luis Coirolo, Monica Das Gupta, Gershon Feder, Scott Guggenheim, Jeffrey Gutman, Steen Jorgensen, Christine Kessides, Ghazala Mansuri, Alexander Marc, Robin Mearns, Deepa Narayan, Daniel Owen, Vijayendra Rao, Martin Ravallion, John Redwood, Louise Scura, Susan Wong, Mark Woodward, and Michael Woolcock.

We would like to thank the staff of the World Bank Country Offices in Benin, Brazil, Egypt, India, Nepal, and Vietnam for all their support. OED also gratefully acknowledges the input of numerous community members and other stakeholders across various countries who patiently participated in interviews and surveys and provided valuable perspectives.

We are grateful for comments from the following OED staff: Martha Ainsworth, Bill Battaile, Soniya Carvalho, Victoria Elliott, Fareed Hassan, Edoardo Masset, Janardan Prasad Singh, Denise Vaillancourt, and Howard White.

This review was greatly enhanced by the generous support and input of several donors. Substantial feedback and financial support from the Swiss Agency for Development and Cooperation—in particular Laurent Ruedin, Joerg Frieden, Robert Groeli, Walter Meyer, and Ursula Funk—as well as contributions from the Norway MFA Partnership and the Norwegian Consultancy Trust Fund, are gratefully acknowledged.

Acting Director-General, Operations Evaluation: *Ajay Chhibber*
Acting Director, Operations Evaluation Department: *R. Kyle Peters*
Manager, Sector, Thematic, and Global Evaluation: *Alain Barbu*
Task Manager: *Nalini Kumar*

Foreword

This report analyzes the effectiveness of the World Bank's lending support for the growing area of community-based development (CBD) and community-driven development (CDD). The latter supports the empowerment of the poor by giving communities control over subproject resources and decisions, while CBD gives communities less responsibility and emphasizes collaboration, consultation, or sharing information with them on project activities. Since the late 1990s, the focus of Bank-supported CBD/CDD projects has shifted toward CDD, though many CDD projects also include CBD components.

The share of projects that include a CBD/CDD component has grown from about 2 percent in fiscal 1989 to 25 percent in 2003. Over the 1994–2003 period, the outcome ratings of CBD/CDD projects have been better than those for non-CBD/CDD projects. Much more success has been achieved in CBD/CDD projects on quantitative goals such as construction of infrastructure than on qualitative goals such as capacity enhancement. Sustainability ratings for the projects have improved over time, but there is considerable room for improvement. Bank interventions have often failed to provide the consistent, long-term support needed for an activity to become sustainable (for example, in a forestry project, support should be provided until the forest starts yielding adequate returns from timber and non-timber products).

The study finds that Bank-supported CBD/CDD projects have typically performed better on capacity enhancement—an important objective of the projects—when they have supported indigenously matured participatory efforts or when the Bank has provided sustained, long-term support to communities beyond the length of a single subproject.

The distribution of costs and benefits—to the institution, the borrower, or the communities—related to undertaking CBD/CDD projects has not been systematically assessed by the Bank. The OED study finds that CBD/CDD projects are more expensive to prepare and supervise than other Bank projects. Governments also spend considerable resources to put a participatory approach in place. While a participatory approach lowers the cost to the government for service-delivery infrastructure, the communities bear a significant part of this cost burden.

CBD/CDD projects have increased access to service delivery infrastructure such as schools and health centers for remote communities. In addition, several CBD/CDD projects in conflict and post-conflict countries have helped in rehabilitating infrastructure and have provided significant employment benefits to the local population. However, as with other projects, increased access to infrastructure does not always translate into effective service delivery. Further, the poorest may not always benefit from these projects. There is little hard evidence to date on the poverty-reducing and community capacity–enhancing impact of the projects.

Bank-supported CBD/CDD projects have enhanced the capacity of government institutions to implement participatory interventions, but few borrower governments have adopted the approach more widely in their development programs.

Adaptation of operational policies and decentralization of the Bank to field offices have enhanced the Bank's capacity to implement CBD/CDD interventions, but additional changes are needed. Weaknesses in monitoring and evaluation, the need for development of adequate guidelines for staff on safeguards for CDD projects, and the short time span of the Bank's subproject cycle constrain the Bank's capacity to implement CBD/CDD projects. These projects, most particularly CDD, also continue to pose a challenge for both safeguard and fiduciary compliance.

Going forward, the Bank could do a number of things to improve its effectiveness for community-based and community-driven development. The study makes three recommendations:

- In undertaking new CBD/CDD projects, the Bank should analyze whether it is building on existing local initiatives or starting a new program in a country and give priority to the former. In the latter case, the Bank should tailor the initiative to the country and community context and undertake selective, rigorous impact assessments of its projects before scaling up.
- The Bank needs to strengthen operational guidance for the application of safeguard policies and fiduciary oversight of CBD/CDD projects and for cost-benefit analysis and monitoring and evaluation (M&E) systems, and it should commission an audit of the fiduciary aspects of a representative sample of CDD projects to be submitted to the Board within a year.
- CBD/CDD projects need to be integrated with a country's assistance strategy. Future Country Assistance Strategies (CASs) should show how they have analyzed and addressed linkages not only between CBD/CDD projects, but also between CBD/CDD and relevant non-CBD/CDD projects. Such analysis should also address whether arrangements for CBD/CDD project implementation are made at the expense of local government capacity development.

Ajay Chhibber
Acting Director-General, Operations Evaluation

Executive Summary

Participatory approaches that involve local communities in their own development have gained substantial support among international donors over the past quarter-century and have become increasingly important in the work of the World Bank. Community participation is an approach to development that can be used with any Bank lending instrument and across sectors. Projects can involve communities in different ways—by sharing information, consulting, collaborating, or empowering them. The process of involving communities in project activities is also expected to contribute in most cases to community capacity enhancement.

The World Bank's support for community participation has been manifested in the design and implementation of either community-based development (CBD) or community-driven development (CDD) projects. Although the literature does not clearly distinguish CBD from CDD,[1] there is increasing consensus that CDD projects give communities control over resources and decisions in the design and implementation of subprojects. CBD projects, however, give communities comparatively less responsibility and emphasize collaboration, consultation, and information sharing with them. Since the late 1990s, the focus of such Bank-supported projects has shifted toward CDD, although many CDD projects also include CBD components.

Interest in community empowerment emerged in large part because donors, including the World Bank, were impressed by the poverty-reducing effects of local initiatives that developed independently in several countries. In these islands of success, local communities had taken control of their lives as a result of independent forms of social action. In its ongoing effort to reduce poverty, the Bank has emulated these local initiatives by attempting to enhance community capacity by building social capital and fostering empowerment in communities through its projects. Research into the multidimensional nature of poverty has further reinforced the importance of empowerment. Today, the Bank's Strategic Framework identifies empowering poor people to participate in development as one of the two priorities in the fight against poverty.

Interest in a community-based approach is also predicated on a belief that not only

would it lead to better allocation of resources to help communities, but would also lead to reduced corruption and misuse of resources, and thereby more development assistance would reach the poor. Community involvement is expected to increase transparency and accountability by working directly with the ultimate beneficiaries, especially where state capacity is weak or has been weakened by conflict and other factors.

Evaluation Findings

The Bank has not, until recently, systematically identified and tracked its portfolio of CBD/CDD projects,[2] and therefore has lacked a comprehensive understanding of

Table ES.1: Overview of CBD/CDD Strengths and Weaknesses[3]

Strengths of Bank CBD/CDD projects	Weaknesses of Bank CBD/CDD projects
Outcome ratings are generally better for CBD/CDD than for non-CBD/CDD projects. Much more success has been achieved in CBD/CDD projects on quantitative goals, such as the construction of infrastructure, than on qualitative goals, such as capacity enhancement or quality of training.	The Bank's project M&E systems do not allow systematic assessment of the capacity-enhancing impact of CBD/CDD interventions. It is often assumed that meeting the quantitative goals will automatically fulfill the qualitative goal—for example, holding a certain number of training courses is expected to enhance capacity.
Borrower officials believe that a participatory approach can contribute to poverty alleviation.	Borrower officials do not necessarily believe that community control over decisions and resources in a subproject is the best means of engaging communities.
CBD/CDD projects help lower the cost to government of delivering infrastructure.	Communities bear an increased share of the burden for service delivery infrastructure.
They have increased access of remote communities to service-delivery infrastructure such as schools, health centers, and the like.	But the poorest may not always benefit from CBD/CDD projects.
Capacity-enhancement effort in a CBD/CDD project has been more successful when a Bank project supports indigenously matured efforts or provides sustained, long-term support to communities beyond a Bank subproject cycle.	The individual subproject cycle is too short to sustainably enhance community capacity where it is weak or does not exist.
Sustainability ratings have improved over time.	Infrastructure and services have been difficult to sustain beyond the Bank presence because of a lack of resources from the government and communities to ensure their operation and maintenance.
CBD/CDD projects have enhanced government capacity to implement participatory interventions.	Few governments appear to have adopted the CBD/CDD approach more widely in their own development programs.
Adaptation of Bank policies and decentralization to field offices have enhanced Bank capacity to implement CBD/CDD projects.	More changes are needed to improve fiduciary and safeguard compliance in CBD/CDD projects.

the evolution and scope of its work in this field. Although the Bank has been supporting such projects for more than a quarter-century, it has no database that has tracked these projects since their inception. It is only recently (for projects approved from fiscal year 2000 onward) that the Bank has started maintaining a database.

Despite a rapid increase in lending, most Bank-supported CBD/CDD projects have not yet been subjected to rigorous evaluation.[4] The share of projects in the Bank's portfolio that include a CBD/CDD component grew from about 2 percent in fiscal 1989 to 25 percent in 2003. However, as yet there is very little hard evidence on the impact of these projects in reducing poverty or enhancing community capacity. This is because of: (i) the Bank's failure to include baseline surveys in most of the projects completed thus far and (ii) inadequacies in the design of the Bank's project monitoring and evaluation systems to systematically assess changes in community capacity resulting from the Bank intervention. Some recent CBD/CDD projects are setting up baselines, but the results will not be available for several years. To fill these gaps, in the absence of baseline data, this evaluation used a pragmatic approach based on household surveys to assess the association between CBD/CDD projects and change in communities' capacity and drew on a variety of sources for insights into the projects' poverty impact.

Outcome

Outcome ratings of Bank-supported CBD/CDD projects were, on average, better than those for non-CBD/CDD projects between 1994 and 2003. The education sector has had the highest percentage of projects rated satisfactory on outcome, followed by projects in the transport, urban development, and social protection sectors. The rural development sector, with the largest CBD/CDD portfolio, is a below-average performer on outcome in the aggregate, as are projects under the water supply, health, and environment sectors. Between 1999 and 2003, the outcome rating for CBD/CDD projects in post-conflict countries was better than the outcome rating for CBD/CDD projects in non-conflict countries.

The borrower government officials interviewed for this review were convinced that a participatory approach can contribute to poverty alleviation in their countries. However, they did not necessarily believe that allowing community control over investment decisions and resources in a Bank subproject is the best means of engaging communities. This appears to be partly because government officials have concerns about the capacity of communities to manage resources, but also partly because they feel threatened by devolution of complete control over decisions and resources to communities.

The Bank has not systematically and realistically assessed the costs and benefits of undertaking CBD/CDD projects to the institution, the borrower, or the communities.[5] CBD/CDD projects are more expensive than non-CBD/CDD projects for the Bank to prepare and supervise, and there are substantial costs in time spent by the borrower in putting a participatory approach in place. While CBD/CDD projects have helped lower the cost to governments for delivering service delivery infrastructure, the communities now bear an increased part of the cost of that infrastructure. The insufficient focus on costs and benefits in CBD/CDD projects, especially on measures of poverty impact, has prevented convincing comparisons with non-CBD/CDD investments and policy and institutional reform programs.

Much more success has been achieved in CBD/CDD projects on quantitative goals, such as the construction of infrastructure, than on qualitative goals, such as capacity enhancement or quality of training. However, without baseline data, and without appropriate indicators, it is often assumed that meeting the quantitative goals will automatically fulfill the qualitative goal—for example, holding a certain number of training courses is expected to enhance capacity. That said, since CBD/CDD projects have supported construction of infrastructure in scattered communities, they have also increased access to infrastructure for schools, health centers, and the like for the communities in which they intervene. Several of the CBD/CDD projects in conflict and post-conflict countries have met quantitative targets for infrastructure rehabilitation and have also provided substantial employment benefits to the local population. However, as with other Bank projects, increased access to infrastructure does not always translate into effective service delivery because of the inadequacy of complementary inputs such as teachers, doctors, and medicines.

Bank-supported CBD/CDD projects have had much more success with community capacity enhancement when they have supported indigenously matured participatory efforts or when they have provided sustained, long-term support to communities. The one year of a typical subproject cycle is generally too short a time to bring about the kind of enhancement of community capacity that is envisioned in Bank-supported CBD/CDD, particularly CDD projects; it is sufficient to allow successful subproject execution, but not to consistently enhance community capacity.

Sustainability

Sustainability ratings have improved over time for both CBD/CDD and non-CBD/CDD projects, although several concerns remain. Infrastructure and other activities supported by the Bank's CBD/CDD projects have been difficult to sustain beyond the Bank presence because of a lack of the needed resources from the government and communities to ensure their operation and maintenance. More broadly, Bank projects have often failed to provide consistent long-term support for an activity to become sustainable (for example, in a forestry project, support should be provided until the forest starts yielding adequate returns from timber and non-timber products).

Institutional Development Impact

Bank-supported CBD/CDD projects have enhanced the capacity of government institutions to implement participatory interventions, but so far few borrower governments appear to have adopted the approach more widely in their own development programs. At the country level the Bank's approach to promoting government decentralization under various CBD/CDD projects has not always been consistent. In other cases, the ad hoc parallel arrangements set up to implement Bank projects have hindered the long-run enhancement of local government capacity.

The Bank's Operational Policy Requirements and Processes

It is difficult to ensure fiduciary and safeguard compliance in CBD/CDD projects. It is easier for the Bank to monitor resource use and comply with safeguards in non-CBD/CDD investments, such as large bridges or a power plant, than where small subprojects are being implemented by hundreds of remote communities in scattered locations. Over time, adaptation of operational policies and decentralization of the Bank to field offices have enhanced the Bank's capacity to implement CBD/CDD projects, but additional changes are needed. Among the issues that need to be addressed are: weaknesses in monitoring and evaluation (particularly with regard to monitoring progress on community capacity enhancement), development of adequate guidelines for staff on safeguards for CDD projects, and the short time span of the Bank's subproject cycle.

In the end, the Bank should be aware that it is largely trying to use a single financial channel—project financing—to bring about changes in empowerment and social capital, which are affected by a long history of social, cultural, and political forces embedded in the societies in which the Bank is trying to support development. Sometimes, the Bank support works well, especially when it supports existing grass roots initiatives. But when the Bank tries to initiate empowerment and enhance social capital through CBD/CDD projects, it is often not enough—or can even be counterproductive if the better-off sections of the community gain more than the less-well-off. Where the Bank supports the creation of "temporary" arrangements for the implementation of CBD/CDD projects at the local level, they could further undermine long-term capacity building efforts and should be carefully considered, especially if financing is provided for only a few years.

Recommendations

Given the mixed and limited evidence on the impacts of CBD/CDD projects—particularly in terms of poverty reduction and empowerment—and questions about sustainability and safeguard and fiduciary compliance, the Bank should approach future CBD/CDD projects, particularly CDD, with greater care. In countries where the Bank is already supporting a CDD program, the institution needs to rigorously assess the poverty and institutional development impact of its projects before scaling them up. A cautious approach would be especially important in countries or areas where the Bank is just beginning to support CDD. In its future assistance to CBD/CDD, the Bank should:

At the corporate level, strengthen operational guidance and management oversight.

- The Bank should provide operational guidance for the application of Bank safeguard policies and fiduciary oversight of CBD/CDD projects and for the strengthening of cost-benefit analysis and M&E systems and should commission an audit of the fiduciary aspects of a representative sample of CDD projects for submission to the Board within a year.

At the country level, design the CBD/CDD program as an integral part of the overall assistance strategy and carry out periodic assessment of ongoing CBD/CDD projects to ensure relevance and effectiveness of the program to the country context.

- Future CASs should show how they have analyzed and addressed linkages, not only among various CBD/CDD projects to be undertaken in the country, but also among CBD/CDD and relevant non-CBD/CDD projects. In particular, the analysis should address whether arrangements for CBD/CDD project implementation come at the expense of local government capacity development.

At the project level, the Bank should give priority to helping countries build up existing indigenously matured initiatives; where there are no such existing initiatives, the Bank should tailor its project to the country and community context, while undertaking selective, rigorous impact assessments to ensure learning.

- For any new CBD/CDD project, the Bank should analyze (using existing processes, such as social assessments) whether it is building on indigenously matured initiatives or attempting to begin a CDD program in a country, and then tailor the intervention to local capacity; and the Bank should also selectively undertake rigorous impact assessments upon completion of its *ongoing* CBD/CDD projects to learn for the future.

ACRONYMS AND ABBREVIATIONS

AFR	Africa Region
AIDS	Acquired immunodeficiency syndrome
APL	Adaptable Program Lending
ASIP	Agriculture Sector Investment Project (Ghana)
CA	Community association
CAS	Country Assistance Strategy
CAE	Country Assistance Evaluation
CBD	Community-based development
CDD	Community-driven development
CBRIP	Community-Based Rural Infrastructure Project (Vietnam)
CFAA	Country Financial Accountability Assessment Report
CIDSS	Comprehensive and Integrated Delivery of Social Services (Philippines)
CPAR	Country Procurement Assessment Report
DFID	Department for International Development (U.K.)
DOLIDAR	Department of Local Infrastructure Development and Agricultural Roads (Nepal)
EA	Environmental assessment
EAP	East Asia and the Pacific Region
ECA	Europe and Central Asia Region
ERR	Economic rate of return
ESSD	Environmentally and Socially Sustainable Network (World Bank)
FI	Financial intermediary
FUMAC	Fundo Municipal de Apoio Comunitario (municipal-community scheme, Brazil)
FUMAC-P	Conselho Municipal de Apoio Comunitario – Piloto (Pilot Municipal Community Schemes, Brazil)
FY	Fiscal year
HIV	Human immunodeficiency virus
HNP	Health, Nutrition, and Population (sector)
IAD	Internal Auditing Department
ICR	Implementation Completion Report
ID	Institutional development
IDB	Inter-American Development Bank
IFAD	International Fund for Agricultural Development
JFM	Joint forest management
KDP	Kecamatan Development Project (Indonesia)
LAC	Latin America and the Caribbean Region
LIL	Learning and Innovation Loan
M&E	Monitoring & evaluation
MAP	Multi-Country HIV/AIDS Program
MDG	Millennium Development Goal

MIS	Monitoring and information system
MNA	Middle East and North Africa Region
NGO	Nongovernmental organization
NMPRP	Northern Mountains Poverty Reduction Project (Vietnam)
O&M	Operation and maintenance
OED	Operations Evaluation Department
OD	Operational Directive
OP	Operational Policy
OPCS	Operational Policy and Country Services
PAC	Programa de Apoio Comunitario (state-community schemes)
PAD	Project Appraisal Document
PPAR	Project Performance Assessment Report
PRSP	Poverty Reduction Strategy Paper
PSR	Project Status Report
QAG	Quality Assurance Group
QSA	Quality of Supervision Assessment
RPAP	Rural Poverty Alleviation Program (Brazil)
RPRP	Rural Poverty Reduction Project
SAR	South Asia Region
SEWA	Self-Employed Women's Association
VLPA	Village-Level Participatory Approach
ZAMSIF	Zambia Social Investment Fund

Origin, Scope, Design, and Methodology of the Evaluation

Participatory approaches that involve communities in their own development have gained substantial support among international donors over the past quarter-century and have become increasingly important in the work of the World Bank.[1] Community participation is an approach to development that can be used with any Bank lending instrument and across sectors. Projects can involve communities in different ways—by sharing information, consulting, collaborating, or empowering them.[2]

The World Bank's support for these participatory approaches has been largely manifested in the design and implementation of either community-based development (CBD) or community-driven development (CDD) projects. Although the literature makes no clear distinction between the CBD and CDD approaches, there is increasing consensus that CDD projects further the Bank's support for empowerment by, inter alia, giving communities control over resources and decisions in the context of a Bank project. These projects are distinguished from CBD, where the communities have less responsibility. Instead, the emphasis is on collaboration, consultation, and sharing information with the communities about the project. Since the late 1990s, the focus of Bank-supported CBD/CDD projects has shifted toward CDD, though many CDD projects also include CBD components.

Interest in community empowerment emerged in large part because donors, including the World Bank, were impressed by the poverty-reducing effects of local initiatives that developed independently in several countries. In these islands of success, local communities had taken control of their lives as a result of independent forms of social action. In its ongoing effort to reduce poverty, the Bank has emulated these local initiatives by attempting to enhance community capacity by building social capital and fostering empowerment in communities through its projects. Research into the multidimensional nature of poverty has further reinforced the importance of empowerment. Today, the Bank's Strategic Framework identifies empowering poor people to participate in development by investing in them as one of the two basic priorities in the fight against poverty (World Bank 2001b).

The Bank's Strategic Framework identifies empowering poor people to participate in development by investing in them as one of the two basic priorities in the fight against poverty.

Figure 1.1: The Universe of CBD/CDD Projects

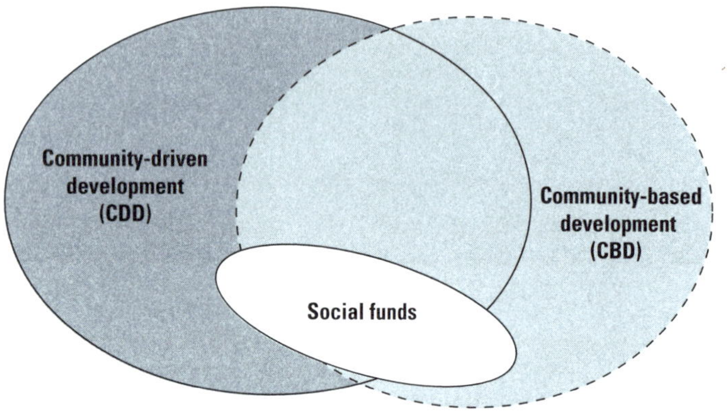

Source: Study research.

Interest in a community-based approach is also predicated on a feeling that not only would it lead to better allocation of resources to help communities, but also to reduced corruption and less misuse of resources, and thereby more development assistance would reach the poor. Community involvement would increase transparency and accountability by working directly with the ultimate beneficiaries, especially where state capacity is weak or has been weakened by conflict and other factors.

Bank lending for CBD and CDD approaches has increased significantly, but there is a lack of rigorous evaluative evidence on the development effectiveness of these approaches.

While Bank lending for CBD and CDD approaches has increased significantly over the years, recent reports by the Bank's research and social development departments (Mansuri and Rao 2004; Wassenich and Whiteside 2004) note the lack of rigorous evaluative evidence on the development effectiveness of these approaches.

Scope

As noted in the Approach Paper approved by the Bank's Committee on Development Effectiveness (CODE) in July 2003, the goal of this evaluation is to assess the development effectiveness of the Bank's CBD/CDD projects, not that of participatory development projects in general. Even though the Bank has been giving more emphasis to CDD in recent years, a large percentage of these projects continue to include both CBD and CDD components, which makes it impossible to carry out an evaluation of CDD projects only.[3] Social funds, in which funds are channeled through an autonomous agency, are also a subset of CBD/CDD approaches. Figure 1.1 illustrates the relationship between CBD, CDD, and social funds.

Because CBD/CDD projects can involve a community in different ways, depending on the nature of interaction required with that community, there is no typical CBD/CDD project, nor can a single causal chain—from inputs to outputs, outcomes, and impacts—be identified for all these interventions. However, a causal chain can be identified for CDD projects. (See figure B.1 in Annex B.) Support for a CDD project typically includes: (a) strengthening community groups with training support and providing them with an opportunity to control decisions and resources in a project context for building small infrastructure and (b) creating an enabling environment for these activities through appropriate policy and institutional reform. The underlying hypothesis in this approach is that such community control in the preparation and implementation of their donor-supported development plans will make interventions more suited to local needs and enhance community capacity for self-development. This will allow the community to hold accountable the institutions that affect their lives. More recently, emphasis is also being given to decentralization reform and promoting partnerships between local government institutions and communities. Strengthened local government institutions are also expected to build an enabling environment for CDD.

Design

The Bank has no explicit benchmark, such as a policy or strategy paper, against which the design and performance of CBD/CDD approaches in general, and CDD projects in particular, can be evaluated.[4] The CDD chapter of the *PRSP Sourcebook* (World Bank 2003b) and a Web site managed by the CDD Anchor are the principal sources of guidance for Bank staff on CDD (Annex C).

Box 1.1: Primary Data Collection for the Evaluation of CBD/CDD Projects

Two kinds of primary data provide perspectives from a range of stakeholders on the appropriateness of the CBD/CDD approaches to development: from the field and from Bank staff. Primary data were collected because (i) "projects lack careful evaluations with good treatment and control groups and baseline and follow up data" (Mansuri and Rao 2004); and (ii) though most Bank CBD/CDD projects are expected to contribute to community capacity enhancement, project monitoring and evaluation systems as designed are unable to systematically assess changes in that capacity because of the Bank intervention. Chapter 3 (box 3.1) explains how this evaluation assessed the capacity-building impact of Bank CBD/CDD interventions.

From the Field: Primary data were collected in the five case study countries and in India to assess project outcomes. All five country studies included interviews or surveys with central or state government officials and bilateral and multilateral donor representatives. Focus groups or interviews were also held with local and international nongovernmental organizations (NGOs) in each of the countries. Local government officials were interviewed in the State of Rio Grande do Norte in Brazil and the Borgou Region of Benin.[a] Extensive fieldwork was carried out in the respective areas of Benin and Brazil and in the context of two OED project assessments (Uttar Pradesh Sodic Land Reclamation Project and Madhya Pradesh Forestry Project) in India. These four project areas also involved focus group sessions and key informant interviews. In the absence of baseline data, OED's fieldwork adopted a non-experimental evaluation design that compared randomly selected CBD/CDD communities with comparator communities in the four projects (Annex M).

Comparators for the Fieldwork: The selected comparators varied according to project and country context. In two project areas (Benin and Brazil), the comparison group communities had benefited from similar subprojects as the CBD/CDD communities, but through a non-participatory approach adopted either by the government or by a religious organization. These two cases allowed the evaluation to assess whether a program that involves communities is more effective than one that does not. In another project area (Madhya Pradesh) the comparison-group communities benefited from a similar activity carried out through a participatory approach, but supported by the government. Here the evaluation assessed whether there is any difference in outcomes because of the participatory approach pursued by the Bank compared with the participatory approach pursued by the government. Finally, in the fourth project area (Uttar Pradesh), comparison communities did not benefit from a similar activity as project communities. Here the evaluation assessed the overall outcomes of the Bank CBD/CDD project, not only that of its participatory approach.

The Egypt, Nepal, and Vietnam studies also involved a limited number of focus group sessions with communities.

Within the Bank: An electronic survey was administered to 400 Bank staff and managers familiar with CBD/CDD issues. A response rate of 38 percent resulted in 152 completed surveys (Annex L).

	Benin	Brazil	Uttar Pradesh	Madhya Pradesh
Number of household surveys	1,376	1,097	1,197	1,147
Number of focus groups with community members	32	56	60	58
Number of local leader interviews	32	33	29	30
Number of interviews with committee/community association members	32	28	30	30
Number of interviews with municipal council members		32		

a. Henceforth, references to primary data collected in Benin and Brazil refer only to the areas studied.

In assessing the *relevance, efficacy, efficiency, institutional development impact, and sustainability* of the Bank's CBD/CDD projects, the evaluation addressed six questions:

1. Are Bank-supported CBD/CDD projects relevant to the achievement of the Bank's poverty reduction mission and borrower and community priorities? (*Relevance*)

2. To what extent have CBD/CDD projects met their objectives? (*Efficacy*)
3. How efficient have CBD/CDD projects been relative to alternatives? (*Efficiency*)
4. To what extent have these projects enhanced the capacity of the communities and of central/state and local government institutions? (*Institutional Enhancement*)
5. What are the challenges for ensuring sustainability of the benefits from a CBD/CDD project? (*Sustainability*)
6. Do internal policies and processes position the Bank to adequately support implementation of CBD/CDD approaches (and CDD projects in particular)? (*Bank Policy Requirements*)

Methodology

The greatest challenge this evaluation faced was in identifying the portfolio of CBD/CDD projects to be reviewed.[5] Though the Bank has been supporting CBD/CDD approaches for more than a quarter-century, the institution has no database that has tracked these projects since their inception. It is only very recently that the CDD Anchor in the Social Development Department has started maintaining a database. Records are being maintained on the basis of self-reporting from the Regions, but only for projects approved from fiscal year 2000 forward. Hence, OED had to develop a methodology for identifying the universe of projects approved during fiscal years 1989–2003 (see Chapter 2).

The Bank has no explicit benchmark against which the design and performance of CBD/CDD approaches in general, and CDD projects in particular, can be evaluated.

Both qualitative and quantitative evaluation tools were used to address the six evaluation questions (Annex D). The study drew on the following:

- A Portfolio Review included a desk review of project documents for a proportionate and representative random sample of 84 projects, stratified by time and sector board, drawn from the universe of 847 projects identified by OED. The Portfolio Review also reviewed relevant economic and sector work, as well as 73 Country Assistance Strategies (CASs), 29 Poverty Reduction Strategy Papers (PRSPs), and poverty sector work for a large number of countries covered by the sample.
- Five country case studies—Benin, Brazil, Egypt, Nepal, and Vietnam—involved desk reviews of the literature and project documents plus visits to the countries. Two of the country studies included extensive fieldwork (box 1.1).
- A Bank Staff Survey and interviews.
- Two thematic studies, one a review of portfolio projects for their compliance with safeguard policies, the other an assessment of how Bank capacity to undertake CBD/CDD, particularly CDD, projects in client countries has evolved over time.
- A Literature Review.
- Nineteen project assessments, with extensive fieldwork in the context of two (box 1.1).
- A desk review of documents for six (one in each Region) ongoing CDD projects.
- OED reviews of 33 Implementation Completion Reports.
- Past OED studies.

An external Advisory Panel of three experts provided guidance to the evaluation.

Since OED's rating methodology is objective-based, the Portfolio Review was able to compare the ratings for outcome, institutional development impact, and sustainability of CBD/CDD projects with those of non-CBD/CDD projects. For the projects covered by household surveys, country-specific comparators were selected as described in box 1.1 and Annex M. The compliance of the CBD/CDD portfolio with the Bank's fiduciary and safeguard policies was examined to assess whether internal policies and processes position the Bank to adequately support implementation of CBD/CDD projects, with particular attention paid to the cumulative impact of small subprojects and community control over resources in CDD. Results of this analysis were assessed against the Bank's benchmark of full compliance.

Some Limitations of the Study Design

Because few completed CBD/CDD projects had commissioned baseline surveys at the outset and project monitoring and evaluation systems are not systematically designed to assess changes in community capacity, OED had to adopt a pragmatic methodology based on a non-experimental evaluation design to assess the possible impact of CBD/CDD projects on changes in community capacity (boxes 1.1 and 3.1).[6] Such a methodology has its limitations, because there are several complexities in identifying comparators, as highlighted in Annex M, and the variables for measuring change in social capital and empowerment, as highlighted in Annex N. Nevertheless, the findings of the fieldwork are suggestive of the community capacity–enhancing impact of these projects and provide useful insights until sufficient baseline data are compiled under Bank projects to permit more comprehensive and rigorous (longitudinal) impact evaluations. The evidence from the fieldwork and the desk review of Bank-supported participatory development approaches was also corroborated with evidence from the literature (both Bank and non-Bank).

Both qualitative and quantitative evaluation tools were used to address the evaluation questions.

The CBD/CDD Portfolio

As noted in Chapter 1, the Bank has only recently developed a system for tracking its CBD/CDD projects.[1] Because the Anchor's database was incomplete and could not be directly used for the evaluation's purposes, OED developed a methodology to identify all CBD/CDD projects approved between 1989 and 2003.

A universe of 847 projects was identified (Annex E) this way, and a proportionate and representative random sample of 84 projects, stratified by time and sector board, was drawn for intensive review.[2] OED then categorized the sample of 84 projects into CBD, CDD, and mixed CDD/CBD interventions. Annex F explains how the largely CDD interventions were separated from the CBD/CDD ones.

Temporal, Regional, and Sectoral Distribution of the Portfolio

The total number of Bank projects that include a CBD/CDD component has increased substantially over time (figure 2.1a). The largest percentage of these projects is in the Sub-Saharan Africa Region (AFR), with the Latin America and Caribbean Region (LAC) in second place (figure 2.1b). Among sectors, the rural sector has the largest percentage of CBD/CDD projects (27 percent), with health, nutrition, and population in second place (16 percent) and social protection close behind (15 percent) (Annex E).

Analysis of the random sample of 84 projects (Annex F) found that over the period 1989–2003, overall CBD/CDD projects have grown at about 14 percent per year, whereas CDD projects have grown at about 19 percent per year. The analysis also found that "pure" CDD projects form about 23 percent of the CBD/CDD portfolio. The Latin America and Caribbean Region had the highest, and the Middle East and North Africa Region the lowest, number of CDD projects (Annex F). Further, more than 75 percent of the CBD/CDD portfolio consists of projects for which the majority of investment funding is for a large number of small and scattered subprojects.

Ways That CBD/CDD Projects Differ from Those in the Non-CBD/CDD Portfolio

A Greater Focus on Learning by Doing and Multisectorality

The literature on participatory development highlights the importance of a learning-by-doing, flexible approach,

The total number of Bank projects that include a CBD/CDD component has increased substantially. The largest percentage of these projects is in the Sub-Saharan Africa Region.

Figure 2.1a: Bank Commitments to Projects with CBD/CDD Approaches Have Grown

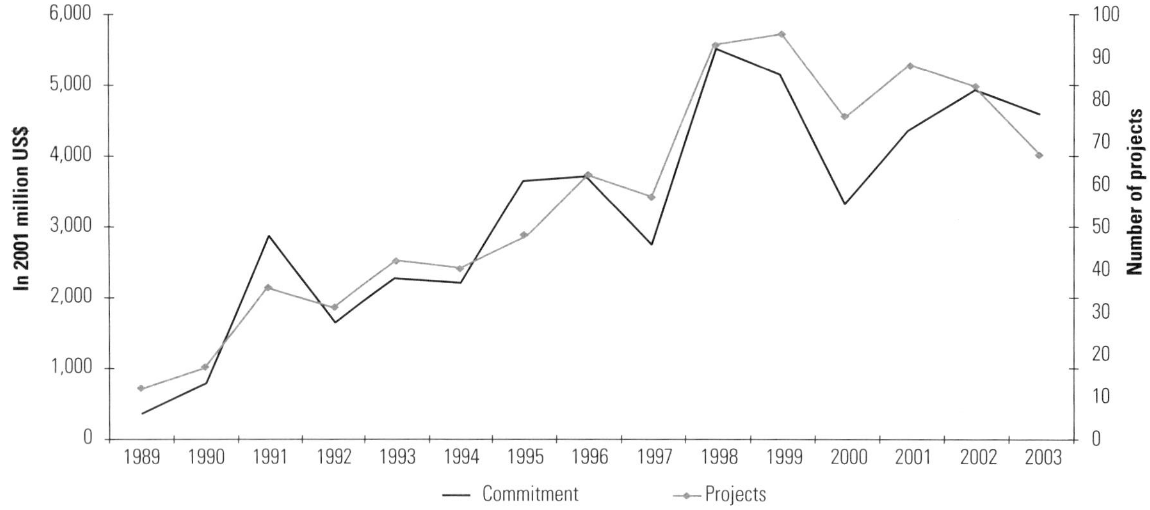

Source: World Bank database.

a concept developed from the learning process ideas of Korten (1980). Flexibility is being brought to Bank CBD/CDD projects through greater use of flexible lending instruments such as Adaptable Program Loans (APLs) and Learning and Innovation Loans (LILs); by allowing communities greater choice in the selection of activities, as in a multisectoral project; and by providing them the opportunity to control investment decisions and resources during project implementation in the case of CDD. Other issues that are relevant for flexibility are discussed in Chapter 5.

The percentage of APLs and LILs in the CBD/CDD universe is more than double that in the non-CBD/CDD universe (32 percent against 13 percent for the period 1999–2003). Over time, research into the multidimensional nature of poverty has led to an increase in multisectoral projects in the Bank's portfolio, and the percentage of these projects in the CBD/CDD universe is much higher than that in the non-CBD/CDD universe (51 percent versus 31 percent between fiscal years 1989 and 2003; see Annex E, table E.1). Analysis of the sample of 84 CBD/CDD projects also revealed that the CDD portfolio has a higher percentage of multisectoral projects (74 percent) than the overall CBD/CDD portfolio (48 percent). However, a large number of CDD projects continue to be sectoral interventions.

Figure 2.1b: Africa Has the Largest Share of Projects with CBD/CDD Approaches

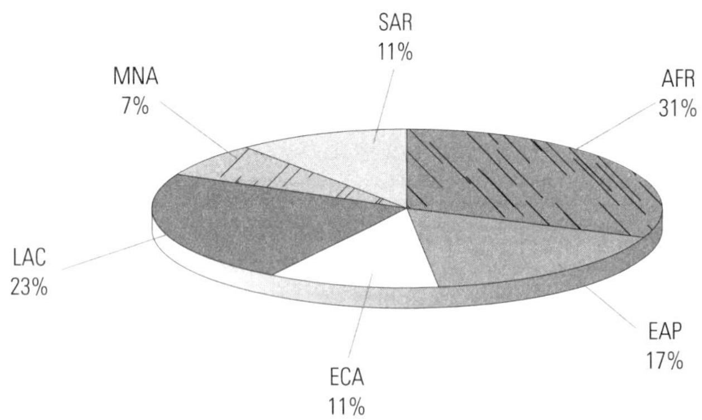

Source: World Bank database.
Note: MNA = Middle East & North Africa; SAR = South Asia; AFR = Africa; EAP = East Asia & the Pacific; ECA = Europe and Central Asia; LAC = Latin America & the Caribbean.

A Greater Focus on Giving More Responsibility to Communities

CBD/CDD projects, particularly CDD, emphasize process issues more than the non-CBD/CDD projects, because they attempt to enhance social capital and further the Bank's support for community empowerment. Within the CBD/CDD portfolio, the CDD projects differ from the others in that they are designed to put greater responsibility on communities for each phase of the subproject cycle (figure 2.2). Although there is little discussion in Bank documents (at appraisal, supervision, or completion) about the participatory process itself,[3] the importance given to empowerment in the Bank's Strategic Framework, the evidence from the Egypt and Nepal country studies, and the Portfolio Review indicate that the projects involving community participation have evolved toward allowing for a community role in decision making, rather than merely "informing" them of decisions. (See figure 3.3 and Annex H.)

CBD/CDD Projects Have Been Used to Promote a Variety of Objectives

Projects have sought to achieve their objectives through (i) material development and (ii) capacity-building support.

CBD/CDD projects have sought to achieve several kinds of objectives—poverty reduction, decentralization, employment generation, basic infrastructure development, access to health care and education, nutrition, natural resource management, private sector development, urban upgrading, mitigation of the socioeconomic impact of HIV/AIDS, and economic recovery. It is not uncommon to have several objectives combined in a single project, without a clear hierarchy. However, more recent projects generally have fewer objectives than those approved in the earlier part of the period.

The Portfolio Review found that most projects have sought to achieve their objectives through two broad kinds of activities: (i) *ma-*

Figure 2.2: Communities Have More Responsibility in CDD Projects

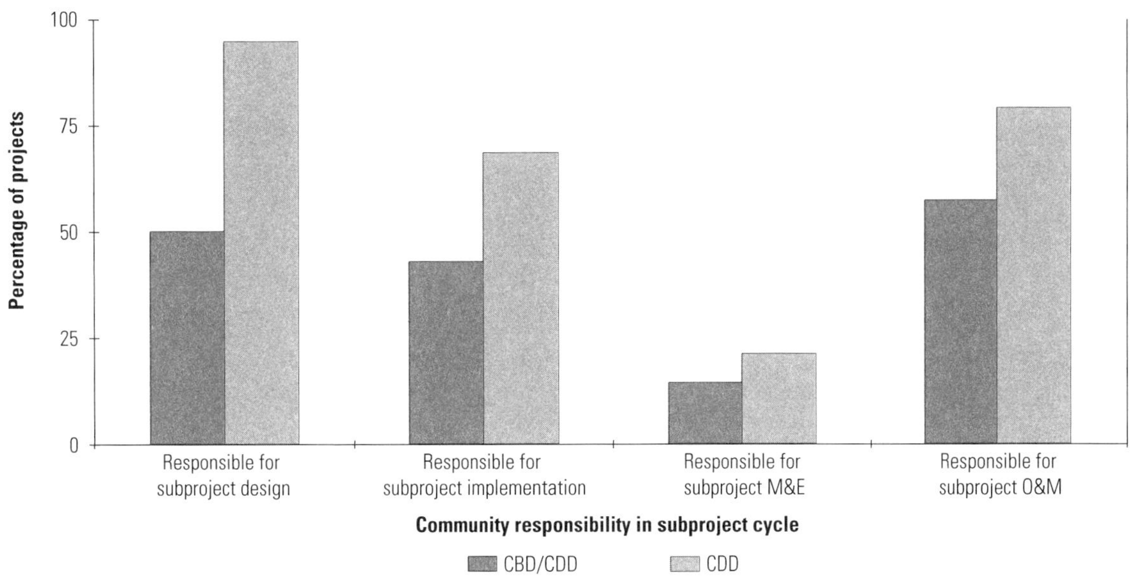

Source: Review of 84 project appraisal documents.

Note: M&E = monitoring and evaluation, O&M = operation and maintenance.

terial development, such as infrastructure construction and (ii) and *capacity-building* support for government (central, provincial, and local), communities, and other stakeholders, such as nongovernmental organizations (NGOs). Though the word "empower" is present in the stated objectives of only 2 of the 84 sample projects, other projects de facto seek to empower communities by building their capacity—for example, the Nepal Community School Support Project (2003) proposes to provide technical assistance and other financial support to build the capacity of communities to take over the management of government-funded schools.

CBD/CDD is Being Used in New Activities Such as AIDS and Post-Conflict Work

The recent Africa Multi-Country HIV/AIDS Projects, aimed primarily at assisting national governments in their strategies to cope with the disease, are also considered community-driven. These projects are the subject of another independent evaluation in OED. Community-driven reconstruction has also been used recently as an approach in the transition from war to peace. The portfolio of 847 projects includes 198 in conflict and post-conflict countries, several of which are designed to provide speedy delivery of reconstruction assistance and support for infrastructure rehabilitation.

Outcome of Bank-Supported CBD/CDD Projects

This chapter first reviews the overall outcome ratings of CBD/CDD projects before going on to examine their relevance, efficacy, and efficiency.

Outcome Ratings

Outcome Ratings of CBD/CDD Projects Have Been Better than Those of Non-CBD/CDD Projects

The outcome ratings (investment lending only) of closed CBD/CDD projects (when compared by number of projects), on average, have been better than those of non-CBD/CDD projects over the period covered by the evaluation, although the gap has narrowed over time (figure 3.1). Outcome ratings of CBD/CDD projects are also better when disbursement-weighted, with a few large projects—mostly concentrated in middle-income countries—doing much better than a large number of smaller projects.

The Latin America and Caribbean Region, with the second-largest portfolio (Chapter 2), has a significantly higher percentage of CBD/CDD projects rated satisfactory on outcome than all other Regions. Although the Africa, Middle East and North Africa, and Europe and Central Asia Regions have a lower percentage of CBD/CDD projects rated satisfactory on outcome, these Regions also show an increase in satisfactory outcome ratings in the period 1999–2003 over 1994–98 (figure 3.2a). The education sector has had the highest percentage of projects rated satisfactory on outcome, followed by projects in the transport, urban development, and social protection sectors. The rural development sector, with the largest CBD/CDD portfolio, is a below-average performer on outcome in the aggregate, as are projects under the water supply, health, and environment sectors (figure 3.2b).[1] OED's data also shows that between 1999 and 2003 the outcome rating for CBD/CDD projects in post-conflict countries was 4 percentage points higher than the outcome rating for CBD/CDD projects in non-conflict countries (Annex G, table G.2).

Relevance

Increasing Importance Is Being Given to CBD/CDD, Particularly CDD, in Recent CASs

A review of 62 CAS documents (two each from 31 countries covered by the sample of 84 projects) found that the CBD/CDD approach is considered an important

The CBD/CDD approach is considered an important element of the Bank's strategy in over 74 percent of countries.

Figure 3.1: Outcome Ratings of CBD/CDD Projects Have Been Better Than Those of Non-CBD/CDD Projects

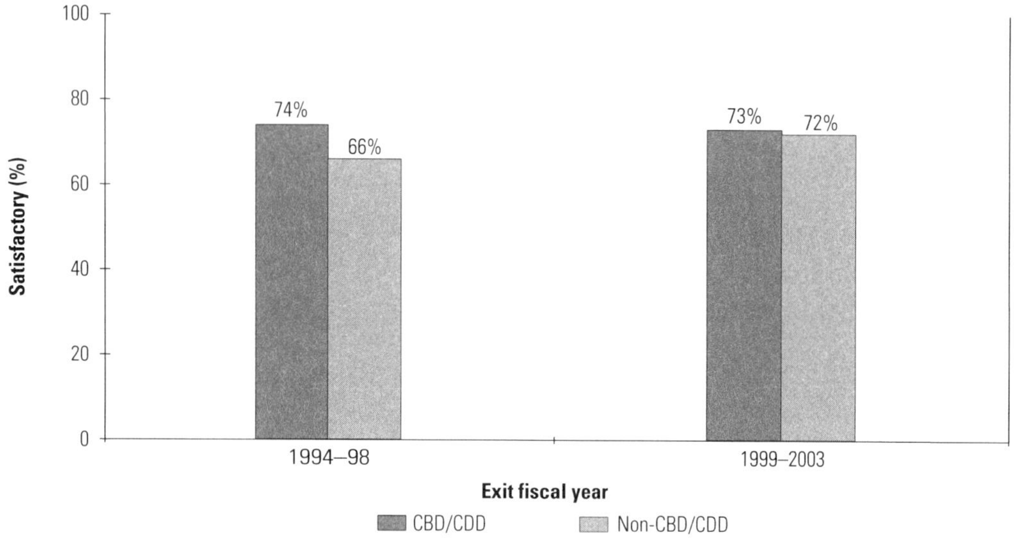

Source: World Bank database.

Note: OED ratings are based on OED reviews of Implementation Completion Reports (ICRs), 25 percent of which are subsequently revisited through OED field assessments. The outcome ratings of the closed investment projects reveal insignificant differences between CBD/CDD and non-CBD/CDD projects in the two time periods considered (1994–98 and 1999–2003). The differences between CBD/CDD and non-CBD/CDD projects were also insignificant for each exit year between fiscal years 1999 and 2003.

element of the Bank's strategy in over 74 percent of countries, and that the emphasis given to greater community participation in decision making and resource allocation in Bank interventions has increased over time (See Annex H and figure 3.3).

Borrower Government Officials Interviewed Were Convinced that a Participatory Approach Is Beneficial

Surveys of government officials in the 5 case study countries, past OED studies, and a review of 29 PRSPs (Annex H) indicate that borrower government officials are convinced that a participatory approach can contribute to poverty reduction in their countries. For example, in Vietnam, 86 percent of central government officials interviewed reported that projects with beneficiary participation can address poverty reduction better than those without (Annex I). One reason that governments in countries such as Nepal and Vietnam have accepted and adopted participatory approaches is because these countries have a relatively long history of community participation in their own development. Another reason why governments are convinced of the benefits of the approach is that in an age of shrinking budgets, it allows them to do more with less. For example, the OED India country study on forestry (Kumar and others 2000) reported that the forest department staff valued community participation in forest protection. Before Joint Forest Management (JFM), the forest department was fighting a losing battle, and one forest guard could not effectively patrol the large area under his control without the participation of the communities.

But They Didn't Necessarily Believe in Giving Communities Control over Decisions and Resources

Surveys of government officials in Benin, Nepal, and Vietnam also indicated that they did not necessarily believe that allowing communities control over investment decisions and resources

Figure 3.2a: CBD/CDD Projects in the Latin America and Caribbean Region Have Done Better than Projects in Other Regions

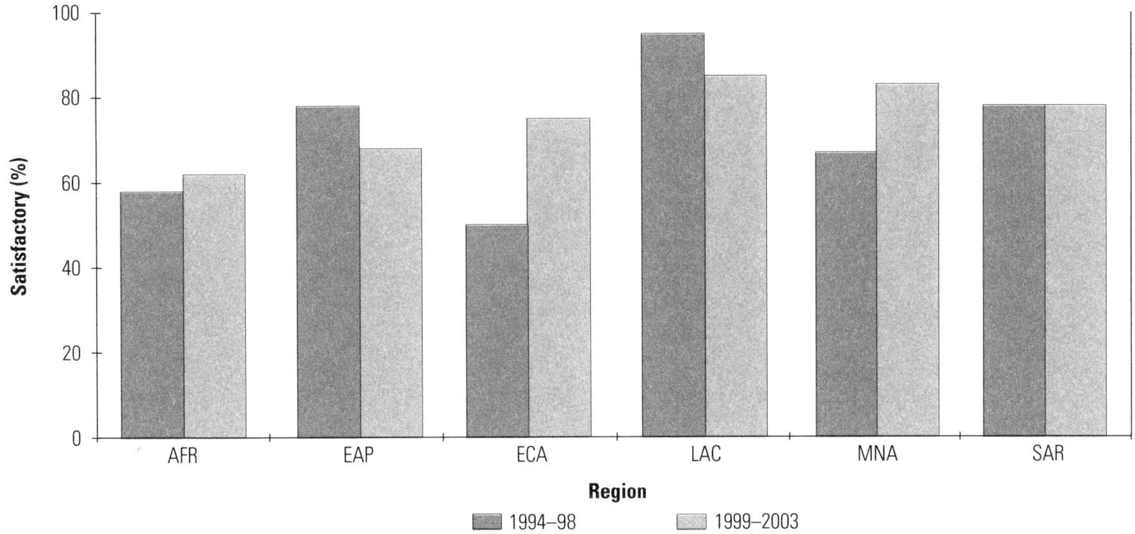

Source: World Bank database.

Note: OED ratings are based on OED reviews of ICRs, 25 percent of which are subsequently revisited through OED field assessments. AFR = Africa; EAP = East Asia and the Pacific; ECA = Europe and Central Asia; LAC = Latin America & the Caribbean; MNA = Middle East & North Africa; SAR = South Asia.

Figure 3.2b: CBD/CDD Projects in Education and Social Protection Do Better than Projects in Health and Rural Development

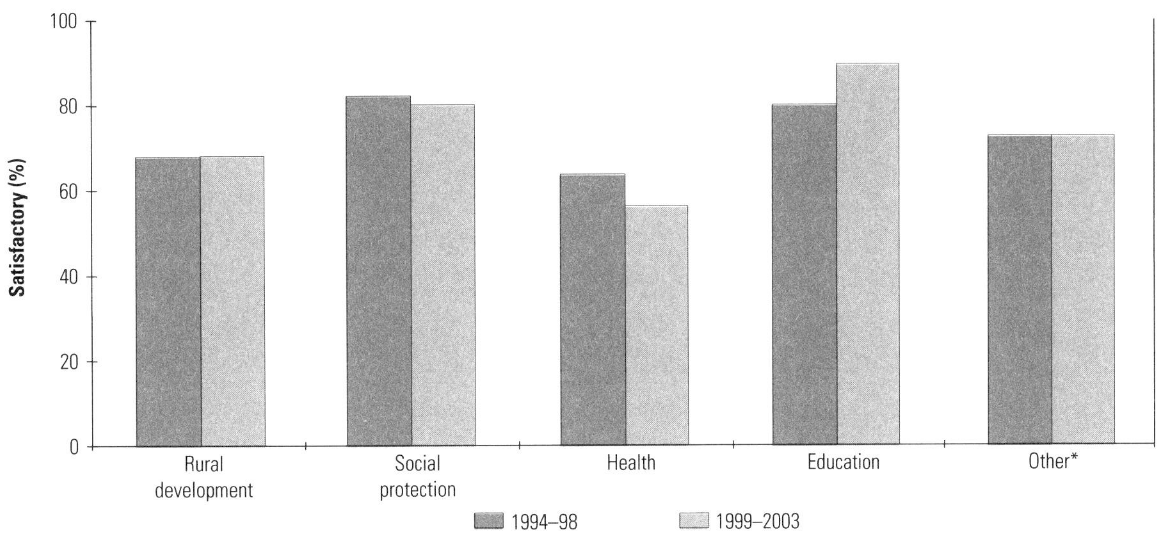

Source: World Bank database.

*Urban, Environment, Water Supply & Sanitation, Transport.

Note: OED ratings are based on OED reviews of ICRs, 25 percent of which are subsequently revisited through OED field assessments.

Figure 3.3: CBD/CDD Is Increasingly Important in Country Programs

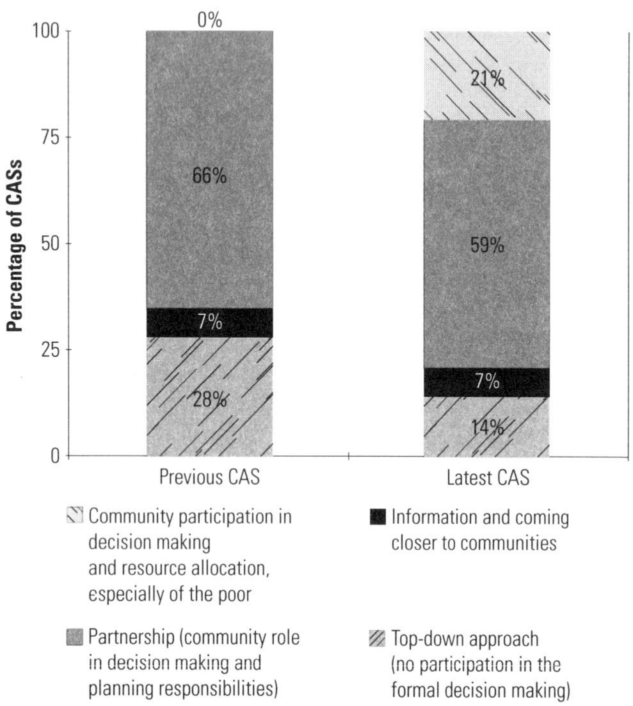

Source: Review of CASs (Annex H).

in a Bank project context was the best means of engaging them (Annex I). Over 90 percent of the PRSPs reviewed are also silent on such community control (Annex H). Central government officials in Benin were asked what form of participation is effective and efficient for development approaches; nearly 80 percent of the respondents said that it is where the community is informed and consulted on the government development plan for the area. The local government surveys in that country also suggest that local officials feel threatened by devolution of complete control over decisions and resources to communities (Annex I).

There appears to be a difference in understanding between the Bank and its clients on how to promote empowerment.

Central and local government officials surveyed in case study countries also appear to be unconvinced of the ability of communities to handle resources. For example, among the Vietnamese officials, only 21 percent said that more than 75 percent of the communities had the ability to identify their needs and prioritize them (Annex I). None of the local government officials in Benin said that the communities had the ability to manage and mobilize external or internal resources. Even in Brazil, a middle-income country that has had a CDD program for a decade, while over two-thirds of the municipal government officials interviewed in the state of Rio Grande do Norte said that most communities are capable of identifying and prioritizing their needs, the majority stated that most communities are not capable of preparing development plans, implementing and maintaining community projects, or mobilizing resources either within or from outside the community. Half of the municipal government officials interviewed also said that most communities are not capable of managing financial resources.[2]

Nor Did They Have the Same Understanding as the Bank about How Community Empowerment Is To Be Promoted

OED's field research, desk review of project documents, and interviews with Bank staff found that (i) within the Bank, there is a mismatch between the understanding of empowerment and the primary means of promoting it; and (ii) between the Bank and its clients, there is a consequent difference in the understanding of how to promote empowerment. The Bank's Web site defines empowerment as the process of increasing the capacity of individuals or groups to make choices and to transform those choices into desired actions and outcomes (box 3.1). However, the Bank's primary channel for promoting community empowerment is through design and implementation of CDD projects that have a definite yet narrower interpretation of how empowerment is to be brought about in a community—that is, through giving communities control over decisions and resources in a Bank project context. Interviews with borrower government officials in case study countries found that they see activities that help build the capacity of the communities to participate in the development process as empowering activities. In Uttar Pradesh, the implementing agency whose operational capacity was considerably enhanced with support from the

Sodic Land Reclamation Project did not see "empowering" communities as building toward a strategy of putting them in control. The OED assessment of the project notes:

> *From the implementing agency perspective, the most important aspect of community participation was ensuring farmer commitment to the reclamation process and sharing of reclamation costs. Hence, for them, even if they 'directed' and 'controlled' the discussion in the village-level implementing bodies, it was not a concern, as long as farmers participated and contributed and the reclamation was undertaken as per the technical standards.*

The way the government officials view empowerment is in harmony with the definition of empowerment displayed on the Bank's Web site, and not with the way it is interpreted in the implementation of the CDD projects. The need for clarity on how empowerment is to be promoted by the Bank becomes even more urgent when seen in the context of the discussion of the issue in the literature.[3]

Priority Needs Are More Likely to Be Addressed When Communities Are Given Multiple Options from which to Choose

Household survey data collected by OED in Benin and Brazil show that where communities were given a wide menu to choose from, Bank projects were more likely to meet one of the top-priority needs of the communities. The Madhya Pradesh Forestry and Uttar Pradesh Sodic Land Reclamation projects in India, by contrast, did not meet the priority needs of the communities (figure 3.4). These sectoral interventions were not designed to give communities a choice of activities.

Efficacy

So Far, More Success Has Been Achieved on Quantitative than on Qualitative Goals

Material development and capacity building activities (see p. 9) have both quantitative and qualitative dimensions. CBD/CDD interventions have generally been successful in achieving quantitative goals such as infrastructure built, employment generated, and number of training courses held. Since these interventions are sup-

Box 3.1: Change in Social Capital and Empowerment as a Means of Assessing the Community Capacity–Enhancing Impact of Bank CBD/CDD Interventions

This evaluation assessed changes in community capacity to undertake development through respondents' perception of changes in social capital and empowerment (as defined below) in CBD/CDD and comparator communities as captured through household surveys. The capacity assessed did not include changes in a community's technical capacity.

Social capital refers to the norms and networks that enable collective activity in a community. By drawing people in a community together to collectively decide and manage project activities and outputs, Bank CBD/CDD projects expect to expand the depth and range of communities' social networks. To assess the extent to which Bank-funded interventions have succeeded in enhancing social capital at the community level, the household surveys collected information on respondent perception of change in trust, associational life, participation in traditional events and in non-traditional/political events, and circle of friends.

The Bank's Web site defines **empowerment** as the process of increasing the capacity of individuals or groups to make choices and to transform those choices into desired actions and outcomes. The *Sourcebook on Empowerment and Poverty Reduction* (World Bank 2002b) identifies four key elements of successful empowerment approaches: access to information, inclusion/participation of poor people, accountability, and local organizational capacity. This understanding of empowerment has informed data collection for this study, which explores both the levels of empowerment at the time of fieldwork and respondents' perceptions of changes in empowerment before and after subproject implementation.

Source: See Annex N for details and results from household surveys on these variables.

Figure 3.4: Community Priorities Are Better Met When There Is Greater Choice

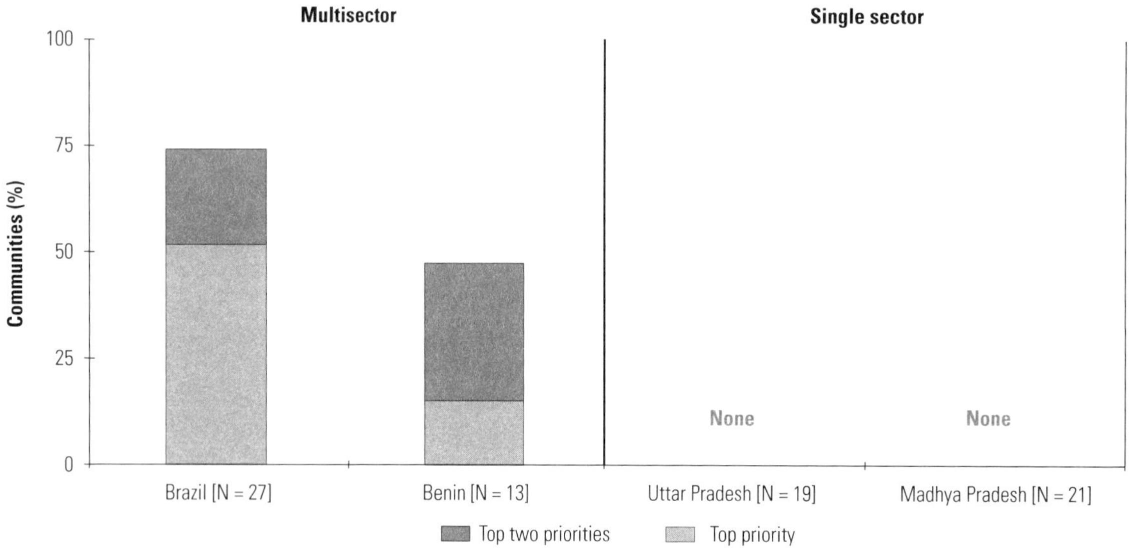

Source: Household survey data.
Note: Priorities are aggregated by community.

porting subprojects in scattered communities, they are also likely to help in increasing access to schools, health facilities, and the like for these communities. On the basis of evidence from a limited number of evaluations, a recent Bank review of CDD projects (Wassenich and Whiteside 2004) also presents a favorable picture of CDD impacts on access to infrastructure. Findings from 4 of the 5 case study countries and 13 of the 19 related OED project assessments support the conclusion that there has been relatively more success in achieving quantitative goals, such as infrastructure built and number of training courses held, than on qualitative goals, such as community capacity enhancement and training quality.[4]

Several of the CBD/CDD interventions in conflict and post-conflict areas have successfully met quantitative targets for infrastructure rehabilitation and reconstruction and have provided substantial employment benefits.

The Portfolio Review found that several of the CBD/CDD interventions in conflict and post-conflict areas have successfully met quantitative targets for infrastructure rehabilitation and reconstruction and have also provided substantial employment benefits to the local population (see box 3.2 for the Eritrea Community Development Fund). For example, 378,805 persons are reported to have benefited directly or indirectly from infrastructure activities under the Kosovo Community Development Fund Project (2000). In post-conflict situations, where a large part of the basic infrastructure has been destroyed by war or civil strife, this is a considerable achievement. The experience of the Nepal country study also found that well-planned participatory interventions can contribute to the mitigation of the social dissent that fuels conflict. However, in conflict and post-conflict situations, where the focus is on getting things done quickly, it is even more difficult to achieve the qualitative goals. While communities can play a major role in ensuring accountability and proper use of donor resources in these situations, what is often lacking in post-conflict communities is the ability to act together. As noted by an OED report on *The World Bank's Experience with Post-Conflict Recon-*

struction (OED 1998) "Inherent in violent civil conflict is the destruction of social capital, particularly institutions of governance and civil society and such basic attitudes and behaviors as trust and participation."

Inadequate tracking of progress on qualitative aspects has been a shortcoming in most Bank interventions. However, it becomes an even bigger issue with CBD/CDD projects, particularly in CDD projects, where enhancing the capacity of communities and local governments is a central objective. However, without baseline data, and without appropriate indicators, it is often assumed that meeting the quantitative goals will automatically fulfill the qualitative goal—for example, holding a certain number of training courses is expected to enhance capacity.

The Bank's CBD/CDD Projects Appear to Have Enhanced the Social Capital of Communities But Have Had Variable Success in Empowering Them

Wassenich and Whiteside (2004) found that only two Bank impact studies for CDD projects have findings on social capital that are reliably representative of all CDD projects, and those two studies showed mixed results regarding the contribution of CDD projects to the enhance-

Box 3.2: Highly Satisfactory Aspects of Design and Implementation in Selected CBD/CDD Projects

The **Peru Rural Roads Rehabilitation and Maintenance Project (1996)** achieved its key project objective of providing a well-integrated and reliable rural road system through rehabilitation and maintenance of rural roads and key links connecting to the primary road system. In this project **community participation was an important part of project preparation.** A logical framework designed by the participants in the first meetings was used to structure a community's involvement in the project. (PPAR July 2001)

The experience of the **Nepal Hill Community Forestry Project (1990)** shows that **clear policies, laws, and procedures are crucial to building trust** between the communities and the Forest Department. Even though the concept of User Group Management was adopted in 1988, implementation was slow in the early years as a supportive framework was missing. However, things changed with the passing of the Forest Act of 1993. The procedural clarifications on the implementation of the act followed with the Rules in 1995. As a result, identification of user groups and handing over of forests accelerated after 1995. (PPAR June 2001)

The **Uttar Pradesh Sodic Land Reclamation Project (1993)** exceeded expectations in carrying out large-scale reclamation of sodic soils. Over 68,400 hectares were reclaimed with farmer participation. The project also contributed to poverty reduction by helping increase returns to many small and marginal farmers. The project effort in **sequencing activities helped harness farmer commitment** for agricultural development on reclaimed lands. For example, the transparent land titling was done before undertaking of technical solutions to sodicity. (PPAR June 2004)

The **Turkey Eastern Anatolia Watershed Rehabilitation Project (1993)** largely delivered on its objective of restoring sustainable management of forest and farm activities in the upper watersheds of the three project provinces, reducing soil degradation, erosion, and sedimentation in reservoirs, as well as increasing productivity and incomes in this impoverished region of Turkey. With respect to processes, important experience was gained by the public sector with community-based participation. There was very good—unprecedented in Turkey—**coordination between ministries and departments** in this project. (PPAR March 2004)

The **Benin Borgou Pilot Project (1998)** interventions took place in 229 villages where the communities successfully completed a total of 296 infrastructure subprojects. A substantial number of literacy and training courses were held to improve technical capacity in the communities. The project **built on the Bank's experience in Benin** with the Village-Level Participatory Approach (VLPA) in the 1990s. Under the VLPA, extension staff and other government and private agencies encouraged village communities to analyze their situation, identify priority problems, prepare action plans to deal with them, and implement those action plans. (PPAR June 2003)

The **Eritrea Community Development Fund (1996)** financed the rehabilitation or creation of a significant amount of social and economic infrastructure in the rural and war-devastated areas of Eritrea. The Eritrea Community Development Fund made an **important contribution to population needs in a post-conflict situation.** The project adopted a short-term problem-solving approach and delivered outputs under extremely difficult conditions. (PPAR June 2002)

The Bank has had the most success in areas where it has either supported indigenously matured participatory initiatives or where it has provided consistent, long-term capacity building support to communities.

ment of social capital. Similar findings emerged from the fieldwork carried out for OED's Social Fund Evaluation (OED 2002b). OED's analysis of the household data from Benin, Brazil, and India found the association between CBD/CDD projects and respondents' perceptions of changes in social capital to be positive in Benin, Madhya Pradesh, and Uttar Pradesh; results in Brazil were mixed. Household data also show that the association between CBD/CDD projects and respondents' perceptions of changes in empowerment was variable across the four project areas. Four results patterns emerged from the information gathered for this evaluation that are suggestive of the differing impacts that Bank CBD/CDD projects can produce at the community level. This section also attempts to explain these results.

First, the Bank has had the most success in areas where it has either supported *indigenously matured* participatory initiatives, as it did with the India dairy program Operation Flood, or where it has provided consistent, long-term capacity building support to communities. Evidence from other Bank studies supports this finding.[5] The Bank provided support to India's Operation Flood through five projects during the period 1974–87. The program is dominated by farmer-controlled, village-level dairy cooperative societies; the Bank's financial support added value to this indigenously matured CBD/CDD effort, which had already experienced a critical amount of learning and institution building.[6] The OED impact study for the program noted that "Operation Flood is an Indian program....when the program was massively expanded under Operation Flood II, there was an already existing indigenous institution ready to implement the project. Bank institutional support thus involved genuine institution building, as distinguished from the institution creation characteristic of many Bank projects" (Candler and Kumar 1998). There are several other examples (such as the Self-Employed Women's Association [SEWA] in India, and the Orangi Pilot Project in Pakistan[7]) of well-known development initiatives where the initial idea and effort started indigenously, long before the Bank or another source of external support was provided. By similar logic, communities that have effective leadership and pre-existing ability to organize for

Box 3.3: Local Champions Can Effectively Use Bank CBD/CDD Funds: A Case from Ghana

Although the outcome of the Ghana Agriculture Sector Investment Project (ASIP, 1994) as a whole was rated unsatisfactory by OED, a few established groups were able to turn the financial opportunities offered by the ASIP to their advantage. The Nangbanyini Nyagsa Women's Group, Savelugu Nanton District, Northern Region, is an example. The group of 24 members (2 men and 22 women) had come into existence 10 years before the project and was then known as the Tiyum Taba Women's Group. It had started its activity with an agro-forestry unit for which the village chief had allotted the group five acres of land. The group is now considered a success story under the project, which provided the group with an agro-processing unit. However, the success of this subproject has less to do with the project than with the existing group capacity and the dynamic personality of the group leader, who is also helping other, less-effective groups in nearby villages. The agro-processing unit run by the group now consists of a grain mill, a shea nut crusher, and a rice huller. When the group heard that funds were being provided under the ASIP for income-generating activities, it contacted the local District Assemblies with a request for an agro-processing unit.

Source: OED Assessment of the Ghana Agriculture Sector Investment Project (OED 2001).

collective action have been able to turn the financial opportunities offered by a Bank-supported project to the advantage of the group, as in Ghana (box 3.3). Field visits for OED's project assessments of the Mali Natural Resource Management Project, the West Bengal Forestry Project, and the Pakistan Northern Resource Management Project support this finding.

Extending this logic further, when a Bank intervention has been built on past experience with a similar capacity-building approach and with a focus on the process of bringing communities together to organize for collective action, reasonable success has also been achieved. In these cases, the same communities have been the focus of the capacity- building effort for several years. As shown by OED's evaluation of the Aga Khan Rural Support Program in Pakistan (OED 2002c),[8] one of the basic reasons for success in this program has been the sustained support for processes in the same communities over 20 years. In Benin, the findings from OED's household survey indicate that the Bank's strategy for community participation had more success in enhancing social capital and empowering communities in the Borgou Pilot project than in the Social Fund or the Food Security projects. The Borgou Pilot built on the Bank's experience with the Village-Level Participatory Approach exercise in Benin, which included participatory rural appraisal and other partnership efforts that enabled communities and villages to coordinate and execute their own rural development, with assistance from extension agents and financial resources from a variety of programs. Bank staff are increasingly aware of the need for long-term support to build community capacity. One of the criteria for selection of communities under the Indonesia Kecamatan Development Fund Project (KDP) 3, which became effective in January 2005, is that they received support under KDP 1 or 2. About 52 percent of Bank staff surveyed said that community groups initially formed under a project need support for at least 6–10 years to reach a level of sustainability in community processes (Annex L).

Second, when the borrower has used the opportunity provided by Bank financing to *supplement its own efforts* to organize for collective action, and the com- munities believe in the long-term benefits of following the approach, interventions have met with reasonable success, as with forestry projects in India, where Bank lending helped the country bridge the financial resource gap it faced in implementing its forest strategy directed toward supporting joint forest management (Kumar and others 2000). The Government of Uttar Pradesh also placed a high priority on reclamation of sodic lands and looked to the Bank for financial support. In Madhya Pradesh, analysis of the household survey data indicated that the Bank's strategy of community involvement was positively associated with change in social capital, but much less so with empowerment. In Uttar Pradesh, the household data analysis indicates that the Bank's project was positively associated with change in social capital, and to a greater extent than in Madhya Pradesh with empowerment.[9] Indeed, had the Bank taken steps to ensure sustainability in both cases (see section on *Sustainability* in Chapter 4), even more positive results could have been achieved.

When the borrower has used the opportunity provided by Bank financing to supplement its own efforts to organize for collective action, and the communities believe in the long-term benefits of following the approach, interventions have met with reasonable success.

Third, when undertaken in circumstances *where political and social settings have not historically favored participation and collective action*, as in the state of Rio Grande do Norte in Brazil, the Bank's strategy of community participation may have little influence on community social capital and empowerment.[10] Analysis of the household survey data from that state indicate that, at best, there is no difference in respondents' perceptions of change in empowerment, while results for social capital have been minimal (Annex N). The literature (Costa and others 1997; Tendler 1997) reveals that the states of Northeast Brazil are known for their clientelistic ways of governing. The patron-client relationships that pervade the Northeast create a

Figure 3.5: Focus Groups Report Significant Decision Making by Local Leaders

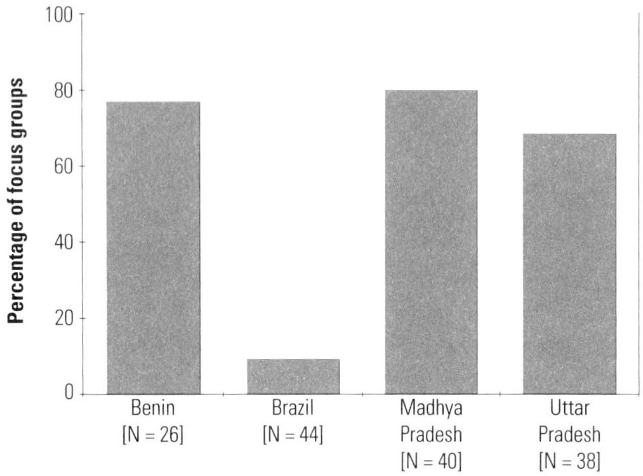

Source: Focus group interviews.

social system in which vertical ties of mutual dependence hinder development of strong horizontal links of solidarity within communities.[11] Although the Brazilian government's decentralization policies appear to have weakened these traditional forces, they continue to exercise a strong influence. An issue raised in some focus group sessions with communities in Rio Grande do Norte is that communities that receive subproject funds do so through political relationships, and not because of need. It is thus not always a case of a community needing a motivated individual, but a "connected" one.

Fourth, *when a Bank-supported intervention attempts to build social capital and empower communities*, the capacity-building benefits may be cornered by the "better-off" community members. Various studies in the literature on participatory development point out that the better-educated members of the community and the relatively better-off are often the ones who represent the community in participatory interventions (Desai 1996; Gibson and Marks 1995; van der Linden 1997; Ribot 1998). The 2004 World Development Report, *Making Services Work for Poor People,* also notes that "elites can mobilize more quickly, master the rules of submitting applications (if they can read and the majority of the community cannot), and present themselves to the community as an effective conduit for receiving funds" (World Bank 2004d, p. 73). Therefore, the report cautions that "Rushing to create social capital where it does not exist can do more harm than good." OED's focus groups in Brazil found that many communities indicated dependence on an individual or a small group of community leaders to bring donor-funded projects to the community. In Benin also, focus group sessions revealed that decision-making procedures surrounding the selection of subprojects lacked the active participation of community members. Village leaders, whether traditional, administrative, or the *Groupement Villageois* (which in the Borgou region are mainly structured around the cotton sector), took the lead in identifying subproject activities, and only later brought them to the communities for approval. In Madhya Pradesh and Uttar Pradesh also, a majority of villages in OED's focus groups indicated that most decisions taken by the *Panchayat* were largely devoid of any broad community participation. OED's household data shows that in Madhya Pradesh, Uttar Pradesh, and Brazil, respondents who were members of community organizations set up by the Bank projects had a higher socioeconomic profile, including greater mobilization skills and a more extensive social network, than non-members before the Bank intervention. Further, in Madhya Pradesh and Uttar Pradesh, these members of project organizations also reported a greater increase in social capital than did the non-members. In Madhya Pradesh, Uttar Pradesh, and Brazil they also reported a greater increase in empowerment (Annex N, endnote 7).[12]

When a Bank-supported intervention attempts to build social capital and empower communities, the capacity-building benefits may be cornered by the "better-off" community members.

These results are not difficult to explain. Three factors appear to be responsible.

Projects generally do not tailor capacity building to community capacity: The literature shows that communities are at different stages in the evo-

Figure 3.6: Subproject Cycle Is Too Short for Meaningful Enhancement of Community Capacity

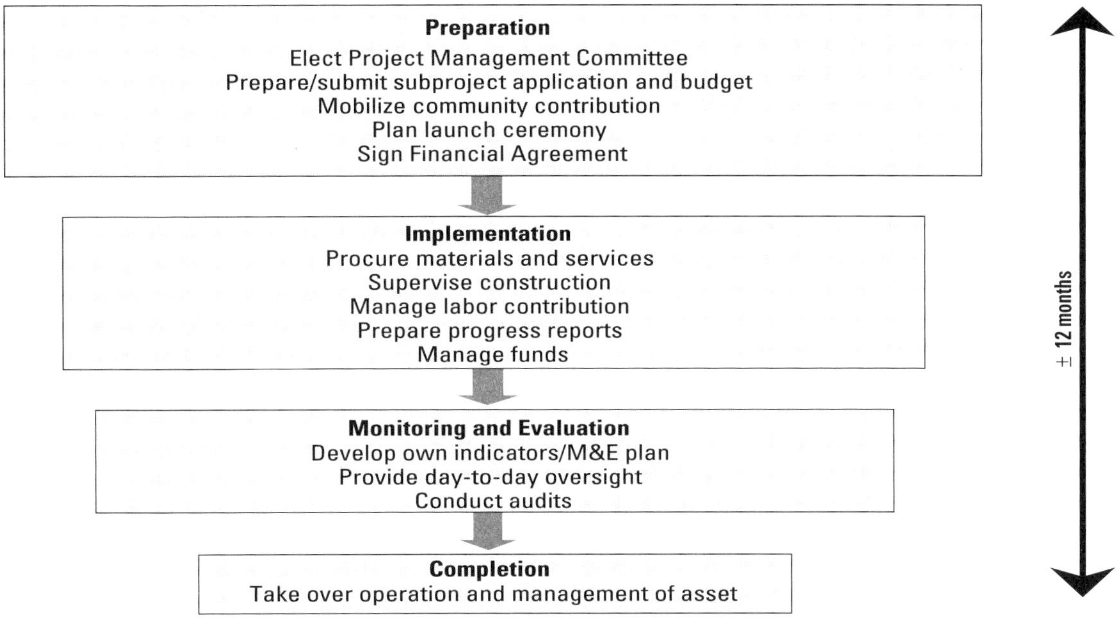

lution of social capital and empowerment, and hence have different capacities (Greiner 1972; Handy 1985; Pretty and Ward 2001). Communities in Brazil, Benin, and India (and within these countries) likely have different capacity levels; therefore, the change that can be expected as a result of exposure to a Bank-supported project is also likely to be different. Yet project documents indicate that Bank-supported projects do not diagnose community capacity or tailor capacity building to existing community capacity.

The Bank subproject cycle is too short: The literature also shows that building capacity is a time-consuming process (Ostrom 1999; Pretty and Ward 2001).[13] However, Bank interventions have not been designed to provide long-term support. Village societies traditionally have been hierarchical, with the local leaders making the decisions. It is difficult for a Bank intervention to change this with the limited money and short period of support in a subproject (figure 3.5).[14] The flexibility that many of the CBD/CDD projects appear to have because of the use of an APL or LIL instrument (Chapter 2) has not changed the subproject cycle at the community level. The one year of a typical subproject cycle (figure 3.6) is enough time to implement a subproject and, in several cases, to start a process of change in a group, or move a group further along the evolutionary process if it is at a higher level of development, but in most cases is insufficient to take it far enough for sustainability to be ensured. OED's Social Fund Evaluation also found that the nature and extent of information sharing and participation by community members in social fund projects was sufficient to allow successful subproject execution, but not to consistently have a significant positive impact on community capacity.[15] Further, a group with little capacity may even regress at the end of the subproject cycle.[16] If a group's capacity is at a higher level, as was the one in Ghana (box 3.3), then it is able to use the

The one year of a typical subproject cycle is enough time to implement a subproject and to start a process of change in a group, but in most cases is insufficient to take it far enough for sustainability to be ensured.

CBD/CDD projects can enhance social capital and foster empowerment at the community level, but the link between CBD/CDD and social capital and community empowerment is weak.

Bank financing to its advantage.

Also, Bank projects typically have not gone back to the same community with the same approach to enhancing capacity to follow up where the initial subprojects left off. Even if another Bank project does go back to the same community, in most cases it does not build on the capacity-building effort of the earlier interventions. Where it does, as in the Borgou Pilot in Benin, positive results can be expected. The change a year of effort can bring about in social capital and empowerment in a given community cannot be expected to be very dramatic.

Communities have a different understanding of the role they are expected to play in CDD projects than does the Bank: Focus group data in all three countries indicate that the communities' understanding of participation in a subproject cycle is different from that of the Bank.[17] This does not appear surprising given that there is also a difference in the understanding of participation between the Bank and the borrowing government, which is technically "in charge" of implementation and sees it primarily as an opportunity to do more with less (see p. 12). The Bank CDD projects visualize communities taking the lead in the choice and implementation of the subproject. However, analysis of qualitative data from Benin and Uttar Pradesh found that villagers see participation in a Bank project primarily as a requirement for them to meet part of the subproject cost, and they see the advantage of meeting the 10 to 15 percent community contribution requirement, if that amount can leverage a much larger sum of money.

Even strong NGO interventions have found it difficult to reach the poorest.

With this understanding of participation, and given that a large number of communities are trying to "attract" the limited amount of donor resources, the existing social capital and the energy of the communities and their leaders is marshaled toward ensuring the maximum resource inflow to their village. Hence, as noted by OED's Social Fund Evaluation, it appears that the participatory interventions are "users" of existing social capital rather than "producers" of it. "Using" social capital may ultimately contribute to its increase, but this increase does not seem to be of the kind envisioned in a Bank intervention. The social capital that appears to be strengthened is that which can ensure that each community has the best opportunity to attract the maximum external resources. While the literature confirms that social capital represents a potential—a propensity for collective action (Narayan 1995; Narayan and Pritchett 1997)—and provides examples where investing in it has led to desirable returns through increased benefit flows (Uphoff and Wijayaratna 2000), it also notes that whether or not its potential is activated and for what purpose depends on several factors (Krishna 2001).[18]

In conclusion, this study finds that CBD/CDD projects can enhance social capital and foster empowerment at the community level, but the link between CBD/CDD and social capital and community empowerment is weak. It also finds that the extent to which a Bank project is able to enhance the capacity of *whole* communities is determined by various local social, cultural, and political factors and by the very approach of the Bank's capacity building effort. The short time that the Bank allows for implementation of a subproject can lead to the benefits of the capacity-building efforts being cornered by the better-off in the community.

Targeting the Poor Is Not Enough to Reach the Poor

Even strong NGO interventions, such as the Pakistan Aga Khan Rural Support Program, most recently evaluated in 2001 and operating for nearly 20 years, have found it difficult to reach the poorest. The reason it is so difficult is that it involves not just economic change, but also social and cultural changes. Effecting such fundamental changes requires considerable time and sustained effort of a sort that is unusual in a Bank-supported project of any kind.[19]

CBD/CDD Projects Have Yet to Overcome Major Obstacles to Reaching the Poor

The Bank-financed CBD/CDD projects have tried to reach the poor through targeting, but there is limited evidence to show that they have done this more successfully than any other Bank investment. It is not surprising, therefore, that a recent literature review (Mansuri and Rao 2004) found that projects that rely on community participation have not been particularly effective at targeting the poor. A recent study on community-driven rural development projects carried out by the Inter-American Development Bank notes that the poorest and the most vulnerable generally are not reached (Dahl-Ostergaard and others 2003). OED's evaluation of the Aga Khan Rural Support Program in Pakistan came to a similar conclusion (OED 2002c).

OED project assessments have found instances of improved living standards, but the improvement was greater for the better-off among the communities than for the poor.[20] This suggests that the project may have had little effect on socioeconomic factors. Specifically, the OED assessment for the Egypt Matrouh Resource Management Project (approved in 1993) noted that although genuine attempts to reach the poorer farmers were made, the gains to the large and medium-size farmers were more than those to small farmers, since many benefits were based on land ownership. The literature also supports this finding.[21]

The thoroughness of the Bank's effort also fell short in some cases. OED project assessments and studies found that even when supporting an activity such as forestry, which can benefit the poor, issues critical to their livelihood have not received adequate attention. For example, in Bank-supported community forestry interventions in Nepal and India, marketing of non-timber forest products has been neglected (Kumar and others 2000; Kumar 2002). One reason for this is found in the literature, which notes that the poor remain largely excluded from participatory "spaces" created by donor-supported CBD/CDD interventions (Kumar and Corbridge 2002; Turton and Farrington 1998).[22, 23] Even where they are "formally" included in a participatory "space" because projects may require that there be representatives from the poorest in meetings, their views, as well as their priorities, are likely to remain excluded from collective decision-making processes.[24]

OED project assessments have found instances of improved living standards, but the improvement was greater for the better-off among the communities than for the poor.

There are even cases where the position of the poor has actually worsened in the context of a Bank project. For example, in the Eastern Anatolia Watershed Rehabilitation Project (1993) in Turkey, OED's assessment found "that there had been some short-term losers, in particular landless livestock owners." While the assessment does acknowledge that village leaders generally have attempted to allocate compensatory benefits to losers, there have been challenges in doing this effectively. In India, the OED assessment of the Andhra Pradesh Forestry Project found that livestock herders, fuelwood headloaders, shifting cultivators, and a disproportionate number of women, all within the poorest groups, may have been losers. In Nepal, the OED Review of Community Forestry (Kumar 2002) noted several reasons why the poorest may be the losers. The OED assessment of the Borgou Pilot Project in Benin noted that the community contribution typically required in Bank interventions created hardships for the poor. It is very difficult for the poorest to make their cash contribution, so they usually have to contribute time and labor, which takes them away from income-earning activities. In situations where the rich contribute on behalf of the community, the position of the elite is strengthened relative to that of the poor.[25]

Sophisticated Targeting Strategies May Help, but They Are Too New to Assess

Some more recent CDD projects incorporate quite sophisticated poverty targeting strategies (box 3.4), and their ability to achieve greater success in reaching the poor will need to be carefully assessed upon com-

The poorest are likely to remain excluded from the collective decision-making processes.

Box 3.4: Example of Sophisticated Poverty Targeting in Two Recent Vietnam CDD Projects

The two CDD projects in Vietnam—the Northern Mountains Poverty Reduction Project (NMPRP; fiscal 2002) and the Community Based Rural Infrastructure Project (CBRIP; fiscal 2001)—include sophisticated targeting mechanisms to reach the poor.

The NMPRP targets 368 of the poorest communes in 44 districts in the 6 provinces of the Northern Mountains Region using established government criteria (geographic targeting). Using participatory planning processes, the project attempts to involve the poor within the targeted communes. Subproject selection criteria favor small-scale subprojects implemented in or giving access to the poorest and most remote villages within each project commune (self-targeting). The commune development budget component, which puts small budgets under the control of the communes, will target the needs of the very poor households and groups (social targeting).

The CBRIP targets 3,600 poor people in the 540 poorest communes in 13 provinces (geographic targeting). Poor communes were selected based on the criteria established by the government for its own Program 135. The project will support small-scale public infrastructure works intended to increase household incomes, improve living standards, and reduce poverty and vulnerability (self-targeting).

(See Annex O for definitions for different targeting mechanisms.)

Source: Vietnam Country Study.

pletion. But findings from project assessments, ICR Reviews, country studies, and a desk review of project documents for six ongoing CDD projects indicate several reasons why it may be difficult to realistically implement these strategies.

First, political pressures in the country may make things difficult. For example, in Indonesia, fieldwork done for the OED assessment of the Kecamatan Development Fund Project found that while poverty-related survey data were used for ranking communities, provinces with lower percentages of poor still had to be included for political reasons. The early findings of the OED assessment for the Pakistan North West Frontier Community Infrastructure Project also reported political interference in the selection of communities.

CBD/CDD projects have contributed to greater "formal" inclusion of women in participatory "spaces" than was possible in the past. However, they have had limited success in promoting women's "substantive" inclusion.

Second, projects could find it difficult to reach the poor communities because of data limitations. For example, in Vietnam, government data are being used to identify poor communes in the latest CDD projects (box 3.4), but there is skepticism about the reliability of the methodology used by the government to identify poor people (Minot and Baulch 2004; Yukio 2001). In India, the lack of reliable information on who the poor are has been a major constraint in the Andhra Pradesh District Poverty Initiatives Project (2000).[26]

Third, in some countries, Bank efforts to reach poorer communities have been constrained by their lack of easy accessibility. For example, the household data for the forestry project in Madhya Pradesh indicate that, on average, community members in dispersed villages are less wealthy than those adjacent to towns that are less dispersed. However, it appears that a relatively larger part of the project resources were directed toward villages of the latter type.

Substantive Participation of Women in the Development Process Has Remained Elusive

The Bank considers promoting gender inclusion a key design principle for CBD/CDD interventions because women in most parts of the world experience significant socio-cultural constraints on their participation in development. There are two aspects to assessing progress on gender inclusion for CBD/CDD interventions: how much have women benefited from the participation process, and has the infrastructure or activity that was supported specifically benefited them?

The literature, OED assessments, and country studies show that because of specific gender-targeting strategies and the support these projects have given to laws that promote gender inclusion, CBD/CDD projects have contributed to greater "formal" inclusion of women in participatory "spaces" than was possible in the past.[27] However, they have had limited success in promoting women's "substantive" inclusion, which, according to the literature, can be largely attributed to social norms that define gender roles (Agarwal 2000a, b, 2001; Cornwall 2003). OED's thematic review of the community forestry program in Nepal noted that "the extent of women's participation and involvement in user group activities is a reflection of their position in Nepalese society. Community forestry, in so far as it empowers women, can help improve their social status, but it is unreasonable to expect that it would radically transform gender relations" (Kumar 2002). OED's assessment of the Benin Borgou Pilot Project noted the need to give careful attention to local social and cultural factors in framing realistic gender-related project objectives. In the Matrouh Project in Egypt, where there had been a substantial focus on women, focus group meetings with communities revealed that the percentage of women who believed that they had benefited from the project was highly variable. The seven focus groups conducted found that there were no elected women leaders or women's associations, and there were substantial concerns about marketing of products produced by women.

Efficiency

Efficiency Has Not Been a Primary Consideration in the Bank's Support for CBD/CDD Projects

Ideally, efficiency should be addressed at two levels in CBD/CDD projects: first, absolute efficiency at the level of the individual project, as is normally expected in all Bank projects, through rate of return or other measures; and, second, comparative efficiency as an alternative approach to development, comparing the costs and benefits of attempting to undertake development through a CBD/CDD approach versus achieving the same results through a non-CBD/CDD approach (Annex J).

Less than a Fifth of Closed CBD/CDD Projects Have Calculated an Economic Rate of Return

At the individual project level, an economic rate of return (ERR) has not been calculated either ex-ante or ex-post for the majority of CBD/CDD interventions. Of the closed projects in the population of 847, only 24 percent attempted an ERR at appraisal and 17 percent reported an ERR at completion. This is significantly different from 39 percent of the non-CBD/CDD projects at appraisal and 34 percent at completion. While it may be reasonable to argue that an ERR cannot be calculated in CBD/CDD projects ex-ante because the subproject investments are not identified at appraisal, what reasonably can be calculated is expected ERRs for typical subprojects that the intervention is proposing to support. Calculation of ERRs at completion for at least a sample of subprojects should be a requirement for all projects, because by then all costs and many benefits are known or can be estimated. In many ICRs that do not calculate an ERR at completion, the only reason given for not doing so is that it was not done at appraisal.

In recent years, much more attention also has been given to impact studies. In several interventions, impact studies have been attempted at midterm and completion. This study reviewed some of these impact studies for their quality and found them lacking in methodological soundness.[28] A major reason for this seems to be the poor data and lack of a reliable baseline for making comparisons. In the absence of baseline data, the "with-without" approach is attempted, but often with limited success.

Bank Costs for CBD/CDD Have Been Significantly Higher than for Non-CBD/CDD Projects

Other than limited attempts as a part of cost-effectiveness analysis, there has been no systematic analysis of costs and benefits of CBD/CDD projects in

OED found the operational costs to the Bank to be higher for CBD/CDD than for non-CBD/CDD projects.

Figure 3.7: CBD/CDD Projects Cost the Bank More Than Non-CBD/CDD Projects

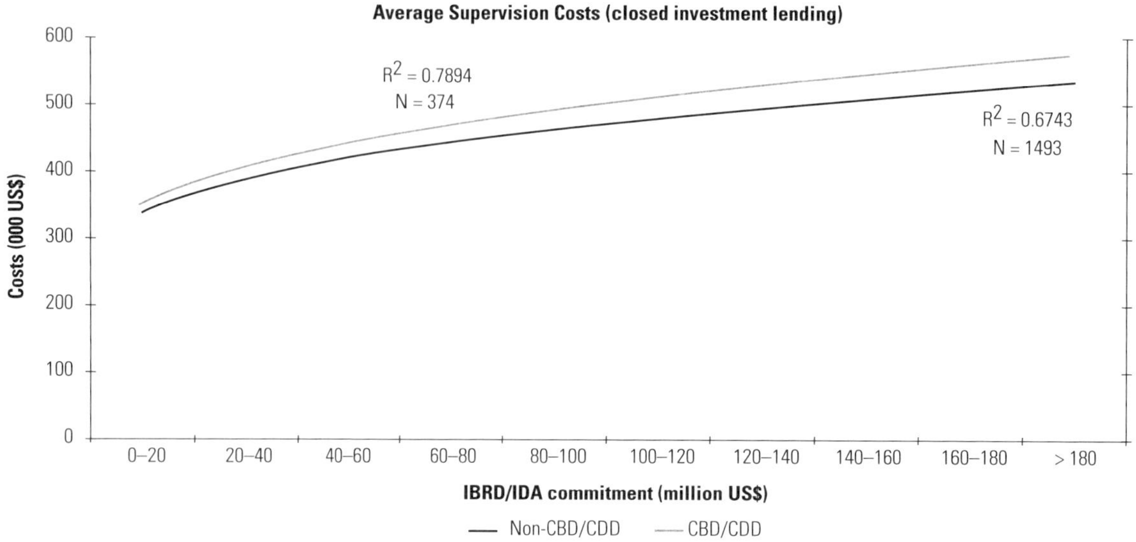

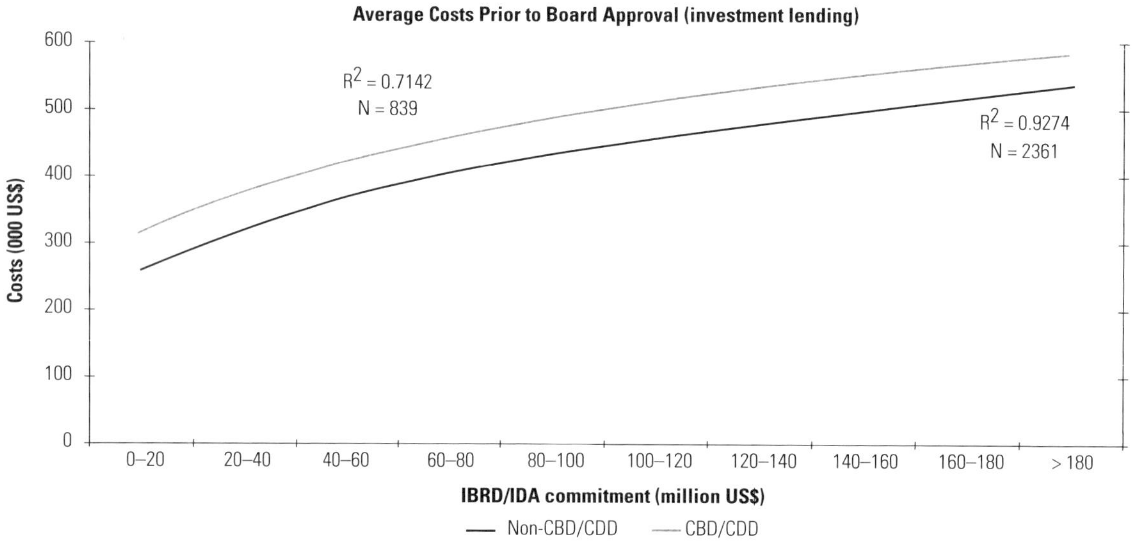

Source: World Bank data.

Note: *Significant difference is noted between CBD/CDD and non-CBD/CDD projects for investment lending of less than $60 million for costs prior to Board approval. The mean investment lending for CBD/CDD projects is $54 million. Results on costs were aggregated across projects and represent an average. Hence, individual project and country experience could vary. CBD/CDD costs are higher than non-CBD/CDD, even when costs are normalized by loan size.

comparison with non-CBD/CDD projects from the Bank's perspective. The only relevant source that OED could locate is a working paper (Hentschel 1994) that undertook a comparative study of costs for preparation of Bank participatory versus non- participatory projects. It found those for the former to be higher. For this study, OED compared operational costs to the Bank of CBD/CDD versus non-CBD/CDD projects and found them to be higher for CBD/CDD by about 10 percent (figure 3.7 and Annex J). Bank staff perceptions (Annex L), revealed through a staff survey, are in line with these findings. No study has yet taken this issue further to explore what this higher cost to the Bank means in comparison with benefits from a CBD/CDD approach.

For the Bank, these higher costs could be justified under two conditions: first, if the higher costs are fixed, and ultimately—as the Bank does more CBD/CDD—its average costs for undertaking these interventions would potentially fall; and, second, if the benefits to the client countries are going to be so large from the new approach that the Bank is willing to bear the additional costs in the interest of achieving poverty reduction. There is no evidence that the first condition is going to hold. If Bank projects adhere to a true learning process approach (Korten 1980), each community intervention must be made specific to the needs of the particular community involved. Under these circumstances, the likelihood of a decline in costs resulting from scaling up is low.

The Cost to the Government of Introducing a CBD/CDD Approach Has Been Substantial...

In dealing with the second condition, the surveys of government officials in case study countries (Annex I) revealed that there is a substantial cost in time spent by government officials in putting a participatory approach in place, though it is reasonable to expect that these costs will decline over time. About 75 percent of central government officials in Benin, Nepal, and Vietnam and 75 percent of local government officials in Benin and 80 percent in Brazil recognized the increased time and, hence, cost implications for the government in initially putting a participatory process in place.

Though the Actual Costs to the Government for Infrastructure Have Been Lower...

The cost to the government for infrastructure through CBD/CDD projects was found to be lower than that for non-CBD/CDD projects. Studies carried out in Nepal (SAPROS & IFAD 2002; SAPROS and World Bank 2000) and work done for the Egypt and Brazil case studies and an OED assessment in Indonesia confirm this finding.

There is a substantial cost in time spent by government officials in putting a participatory approach in place.

...Communities Bear a Part of the Cost of Service Delivery Infrastructure in CBD/CDD Interventions

Lower infrastructure unit costs to the government are often the result of communities' sharing in the cost of construction and contributing (or providing) for operation and maintenance. The Bank's recent self-evaluation of social funds in six countries (World Bank 2003d) also noted that community management of investments provides a significant opportunity for cost savings of as much as 25–50 percent.[29] However, the merit (or its lack) of shifting part of these costs to the communities has not been a factor in the decision to increase support for CBD/CDD projects. As the literature shows, the cost of community participation (in cash, kind, or labor) can be substantial, particularly under the more intensive participatory approaches.[30] If the opportunity cost of the time that community members spend in meetings with donor and government officials is also considered, the costs are higher still. The lack of discussion of the issue of beneficiary time in any appraisal reports suggests that the opportunity cost of time is assumed to be low for households in poor communities. However, farm management studies over the years have generally shown this not to be so, and have shown high costs at peak agricultural labor periods (Schultz 1964; Collinson 1982; Renata and Houston 2002).[31]

Further, considering costs only in terms of infrastructure construction and flow of services is not enough (even if it takes into account community costs) because CBD/CDD projects, and particularly CDD projects, are also trying to enhance the capacity of the communities. It is thus necessary to consider the cost for the capacity-enhancing exercises, both in resources and in time spent by government officials and by communities. By estimating community time for both subproject implementation and capacity enhancement, it may be possible to approximate overall costs for a CBD/CDD intervention. (See Annex J, box J.1, for an example.)

Undertaking a Comparative Assessment of All Benefits Constitutes an Equally Challenging Exercise

Benefits from capacity-enhancing activities are particularly difficult to assess—for instance, what should be done if the gains from the capacity-enhancing exercise are concentrated in a small section of the population? Is that a positive or a negative? The only sure way to assess benefits appears to be in terms of the poverty impact. If CBD/CDD projects are delivering poverty-reduction benefits, and non-CBD/CDD projects are failing to do so, or doing so inadequately, then spending more to get the desired results may be worthwhile. However, if poverty-reduction impact is not noticeably better for CBD/CDD projects, then the extra costs of the CBD/CDD approach may not be worthwhile. Even though poverty reduction is the major objective of many of these projects, a full-fledged comparative assessment of the poverty impact of different approaches would require further research. The limited evidence available is in the form of the beliefs of the government officials in the case study countries and some limited references in the literature.[32] Government officials in four case study countries reported that projects with participation have better outcomes than those without participation (Annex I). It is also commonly argued that if communities are willing to contribute for subprojects, they must perceive the benefits of the CBD/CDD interventions to be at least equal to the costs.

Institutional Enhancement and Sustainability

This chapter draws on country studies, project assessments, and the literature to discuss the extent to which CBD/CDD interventions have enhanced the borrowers' capacity at the central, state, and local government levels to allow them to make effective use of their human, financial, and natural resources.

Recent CBD/CDD projects have given greater emphasis to building partnerships between community groups and local government organizations, and decentralization reform. While it is beyond the scope of this evaluation to delve into the merits and demerits of decentralization, it does attempt to assess whether the design and implementation of Bank-supported CBD/CDD projects has helped enhance the capacity of local governments in client countries. Capacity at the community level, a critical issue for CBD/CDD projects, is covered in Chapter 3.

This chapter also assesses the sustainability of CBD/CDD projects. Interviews with Bank staff revealed that in the context of CBD/CDD interventions, the understanding of sustainability itself varies among Bank staff. For some it implies predominantly sustainability of community processes, for others CBD/CDD is simply a *means* to an *end*, and sustainability is related to infrastructure investments. For still others, it is related to overall resource allocation, including support for decentralization.

Institutional Enhancement

Institutional Development Impact Has Improved over Time

Projects Have Not Brought about the Radical Reorientation in Institutions Required to Undertake CBD/CDD, but They Have Helped Enhance Government Institutions

The literature shows that the institutionalization of a CBD/CDD approach requires a radical reorientation of the way governments and bureaucracies operate (Shepard 1998; Thompson 1995). This requires changes in management and organizational procedures, as well as in the attitudes and behaviors of personnel, that take time to consolidate (Pimbert and others 2000). This study found that such a radical reorientation has not yet come about in most of the Bank's client countries, as seen by the experience in OED case study and project assessment countries, although CBD/CDD interventions have helped change the attitude of government officials and enabled supportive policy and legal reform.[1]

Projects Have Supported Changes in the Attitude of Government Officials toward Working with Communities

Surveys of government officials in all five case study countries and findings of project assessments indicate greater acceptance at all levels of government of the value of involving communities in service delivery/activities and greater understanding and ability to implement a participatory approach to development. For example, the OED assessment of the Eastern Anatolia Watershed Rehabilitation Project in Turkey notes that at the central, provincial, and community levels it was widely acknowledged that the Bank had introduced new ideas related to community participation processes. The OED assessment for the Community Development Fund Project in Eritrea also notes that the project's emphasis on community contribution was perceived as a useful lesson by line agencies in the country.

Projects Have Supported Policy and Legal Reforms

The presence of the Bank has often provided the incentive and opportunity for the government to "push" for legal and policy changes on politically sensitive issues. OED studies indicate and project assessments confirm that the Bank's presence in sectors such as forestry encouraged the governments of India and Nepal to take action on several critical policy issues that helped generate momentum for change in the sector. However, important overarching policy issues have occasionally been shortchanged, as in Egypt, probably because of the burden of trying to get the community participation in place.[2]

The presence of the Bank has often provided the incentive and opportunity for the government to "push" for legal and policy changes on politically sensitive issues.

It appears that most countries today subscribe to an approach to participation that is somewhere between a fully "bottom-up" and a fully "top-down" way of doing development. As noted in Chapter 3, surveys and interviews of government officials in case study countries suggest that officials at the central and local levels interpret community participation a little differently than does the Bank—more as a means of doing more with less, rather than actually putting communities in control. As also noted, however, attitudes are changing.

But neither the policy and legal reforms nor the change in attitude guarantee that the CBD/CDD approach will be implemented effectively. Several factors could challenge the translation of reform initiatives into effective working arrangements. The following sections explore some of the issues around policy reform, including the connection with decentralization.

CBD/CDD Projects are Hampered by Weak Coordination across Government Departments and Government Levels

Although the majority of central government staff in case study countries report an increase in the number of interministry meetings held (Annex I), progress in actual coordination has been limited, at least in the case study countries. Interdepartmental coordination problems arise primarily because government ministries continue to be organized sectorally, and the sectoral culture is so firmly ingrained that it is difficult for departments to work together in the context of a Bank intervention. While weak coordination between government departments negatively affects the implementation of both CBD/CDD and non-CBD/CDD interventions, the negative implications are greater for CBD/CDD interventions, which also require interdepartmental coordination at the local level. For example, in Egypt, most government staff interviewed believed that interdepartmental coordination at the higher levels across sectors had improved somewhat over the past few years, but coordination problems among government staff at the community level persist. Each CBD/CDD project is implemented by a different department and has its own unique mechanism for community consultation and subproject phasing.

Further, despite progress on decentralization, the Benin, Nepal, and Vietnam country studies found that relations between different layers of government remain difficult. Capacity at the lower levels of government in all three countries continues to be weak, and the roles of officials at various levels are not clearly defined. As in the case of coordination among government departments, weak capacity at the local government level is more problematic in the context of CBD/CDD interventions, where local officials are often directly involved in project implementation. Only about 20 percent of Bank staff surveyed reported being satisfied or very satisfied with coordination within the government of countries borrowing for CBD/CDD interventions (Annex L).

There Is No Evidence to Indicate That the Participatory Approach Has Been Widely Adopted beyond Bank CBD/CDD Projects

The evidence from country studies and project assessments also indicates that while a Bank project may succeed in getting a country to experiment with (or adopt) a demand-driven approach in a project context in a particular sector, other government departments do not necessarily support the approach. For example, in Vietnam, evidence from an internal Bank review indicates that while the Coastal Wetlands Protection and Development Project (2000) is undertaking mangrove plantations with beneficiary participation, the government has its own separate programmatic approach to replanting mangrove coastlines. The report notes that it is unclear how government ownership will be achieved for the Bank project when there is a rival government project under way, or why the Bank is not financing the government program, with whatever cost-effective improvements could have been devised and negotiated. In Indonesia, while the field mission for the OED assessment found quite strong evidence that the processes introduced by the Kecamatan Development Fund Project had been accepted by the government at the district government level and below as the right approach for development, sustainability remained difficult to predict and depended to a large extent on the attitude of the new government toward decentralization.

Finally, the Bank itself has not had a consistent policy across projects in the same country, a point that is evident in its approach to decentralization reform.

CBD/CDD Projects Have Increasingly Supported Government Decentralization Reform

Support for decentralization reform and enhancing local government capacity under CBD/CDD projects has increased significantly in recent years. Of the 84 sample projects, 57 supported some form of government decentralization, and the largest percentage of these was in the later years. Analysis carried out for this study as a part of the Portfolio Review and country studies revealed two fundamental factors that could constrain progress in decentralization, no matter how well-designed the CBD/CDD project. First, success in promoting decentralization in a country depends on borrower commitment to the reform process. For example, in Egypt, the country study found that progress on decentralization has been limited primarily because of lack of government ownership. In this context, the CBD/CDD projects reviewed in that country could not accelerate decentralization and responsiveness at the local level. Second, success can also be constrained if there is lack of harmonization between the legal framework for decentralization and the level at which the Bank's CBD/CDD project is implemented. For example, in Benin, the OED assessment of the Borgou Pilot Project found that the project supported activities at the village level, while decentralization stopped at the commune level.[3, 4]

Individual CBD/CDD Projects Adopt Varying Strategies

The evidence from four of the five country studies indicates that the Bank has not followed a consistent decentralization strategy under its CBD/CDD projects within each country. For example, in Nepal, recognition of weak capacity at the local level has led Bank-supported CBD/CDD projects to provide technical assistance to strengthen local government institutions. Yet the Bank has also supported creation of "temporary" arrangements for the implementation of CBD/CDD projects at the local

Support for decentralization reform and enhancing local government capacity under CBD/CDD projects has increased significantly in recent years.

Box 4.1: Inconsistent Strategies: The Road Sector Experience in Nepal

To assist with the limited capacity of District Development Committees, the government established the Department of Local Infrastructure Development and Agricultural Roads (DOLIDAR) under the Ministry of Local Development, with branches in the districts. DOLIDAR's mandate, which is to provide guidance and technical support to district committees in development activities, has often stretched to interference with the committees' autonomy. While the ICR for the Rural Infrastructure Project claims that a balance between the roles of DOLIDAR and the district committees in implementing the project was achieved, the very presence of a temporary solution and a branch of a central government organization at the district level has two implications. First, a significant amount of resources get spent on strengthening the temporary structures. A part of the resources from the Rural Infrastructure Project also went toward strengthening DOLIDAR. These resources could have been spent on strengthening the district-level bodies. The proposed Rural Access Improvement Project, which is still under preparation, is expected to continue to provide capacity-building support to DOLIDAR. Second, the presence of the parallel structures sends a confusing message about the authority of the district-level bodies to take charge of development activities.[a]

Source: Nepal Country Study.

a. Management notes that most CDD operations in Nepal have performed well.

level. These arrangements have had a negative effect on the progress of decentralization. The implications are particularly worrying when formal training and other capacity-enhancing activities for district-level organizations fall short of plans, as in the Rural Infrastructure Project in Nepal. This perpetuates the need to continue the "temporary" arrangements for a longer period, impeding further decentralization progress (box 4.1). Perhaps it is this inconsistency in Bank strategy that is picked up in the Central Government Survey in Nepal, where only 19 percent of officials interviewed said that the Bank has the capacity to enhance local government capacity to support participatory interventions (Annex I). Similarly, in Vietnam, while projects such as Community-Based Rural Infrastructure (2001) have provided technical support to local governments, their implementation has proceeded through establishment of temporary parallel structures that manage implementation at the local level under central ministries.

Brazil, where the Bank has been supporting CDD projects in the Northeast for more than a decade, is another case where the Bank has provided support for parallel structures. The CDD projects in the Northeast are essentially building a structure that is parallel to the planning process of the municipal government (box 4.2). By instituting ad hoc municipal councils for implementation, the project has contributed to the proliferation of municipal councils, with little coordination between them. In Rio Grande do Norte, OED found that municipal councils had weak capacity, in part because they had received little training.[5] Although the project Technical Unit provides assistance to the councils, it is not enough. Most of the councilors interviewed said they needed more assistance, as they often need clarifications on issues, without which they cannot make progress. However, it is important to put the low level of institutional development of the projects' municipal councils into context. Many of the other municipal councils share similar weakness, and some are less effective than the Bank-supported councils. Indeed, it is worth asking whether it is even beneficial for both the municipality and project or program to have so many councils. Were the disparate efforts for capacity building to be focused on a single integrated municipal council, the result would likely be a stronger, more effective, and efficient council.[6]

The Bank may not have supported a consistent decentralization strategy.

This lack of consistency in Bank support to decentralization under CBD/CDD projects within the same country is particularly visible in countries where the Bank has been supporting projects under different institutional arrangements. This has the potential to send a conflicting message to the borrower and district officials, especially when both projects are expected to result in similar poverty outcomes. For example, in the Philippines, the Bank is supporting more than two competing institutional arrangements.[7] Piloting with different institutional arrangements makes sense if the purpose is to study which would work best before scaling up. But supporting different arrangements side by side over large areas on a long-term basis does not send the right signals to the borrower and does not augur well for long-term institutional development.

Recent Social Funds Have Given Much More Attention to Decentralization Issues

On the positive side, the question of whether, how, and in what circumstances social funds can support decentralization is receiving increasing attention (OED 2002b). This is a notable improvement, since older social funds frequently resulted in structures outside local government that have had limited (perhaps even negative) impact on enhancing local government capacity. Some projects, such as the Zambia Social Investment Fund (ZAMSIF), approved in fiscal year 2000, are designed to integrate into the larger decentralization effort in the country. District authorities are to be devolved increasing responsibility in the project cycle for community-level subprojects. But while supervision documents report on the considerable amount of capacity enhancement of district officials being undertaken, they also note that the actual transfer of social fund responsibilities to the districts is taking much longer and is a much more difficult exercise than was visualized.

The question of whether, how, and in what circumstances social funds can support decentralization is receiving increasing attention.

NGOs Have Been Development Partners in CBD/CDD

According to Bank data, 36 percent of the CBD/CDD portfolio, versus 8 percent of the non-

Box 4.2: Bank CDD Projects Have Added to the Proliferation of Municipal Councils in Rio Grande do Norte (Brazil)

Brazilian municipalities have large numbers of municipal councils (IBGE 2003). Many federal programs require the creation of an ad-hoc council to implement them at the municipal level. These councils typically have representatives from both government and civil society organizations. Field research in Rio Grande do Norte found that many of these councils are weak in capacity and that there is a substantial overlap in their membership. In rural agricultural development, the issue of council proliferation is particularly evident. Municipalities receive funds from two main sources, the World Bank (through the Rural Poverty Alleviation Program, RPAP, and RPRP [Rural Poverty Reduction Project]) and the Ministry of Agriculture (through its PRONAF [Brazilian Federal Program to Support Family Agriculture] program). Both funding bodies require that municipal councils be set up to implement their programs.[a] These two types of councils differ in two main respects: membership structure and funding modality. While the Bank requires civil society to hold the majority of the seats in FUMAC (Municipal Community Scheme) councils, in PRONAF councils, representation of civil society and the government is equal. Under PRONAF, funds are transferred to the municipal government, which is responsible for allocation. Communities do not manage funds directly, but receive equipment and infrastructure from the municipal government. Under the Bank's program, the municipal government never manages project funds, which are transferred directly, or through the FUMAC-P (Pilot Municipal Community Scheme) council, to the communities. These differences (especially the second) render it difficult for municipalities to argue for the fusion of the two councils, even if the overlap in membership is often significant. Only one of the 13 municipalities surveyed in Rio Grande do Norte was able to persuade the 2 funding bodies that a single council for rural development constitutes a better institutional arrangement, and that having two parallel municipal councils that work in an uncoordinated fashion on rural development is likely lead to a suboptimal allocation of resources.

Source: Brazil Country Study.

a. Follow-on Bank projects use the municipal councils established under earlier projects.

Middle-income countries have a limited number of NGOs, and consequently less participation of NGOs in CBD/CDD projects compared with low-income countries.

CBD/CDD portfolio, had some form of NGO involvement. NGOs have traditionally provided community development support, including participatory diagnosis and the preparation of local development plans. In some projects, such as the Uttar Pradesh Rural Water Supply and Environmental Sanitation Project (1996), however, NGOs have also provided engineering support to communities. NGOs have also played a role in design and implementation of community subprojects, as in the HIV/AIDS projects in Africa.

CBD/CDD Projects Have Contributed to the Development of NGO Capacity

The evidence from several project assessments and all five country studies shows that local NGO capacity varies widely across—and even within—countries, and it is difficult to generalize. However, several Bank CDD projects, such as the Uttar Pradesh Sodic Land Reclamation Project, have also provided support for development of NGO capacity.

Evidence from the Bank's database (figure 4.1) and the case study countries shows that middle-income countries (Brazil, Egypt, and Turkey among the cases) have a limited number of NGOs, and consequently less participation of NGOs in CBD/CDD projects compared with low-income countries. Among other reasons, this is because of the presence of other private and public technical assistance providers in the middle-income countries. Among the low-income countries, Vietnam has active international NGOs but few active local NGOs. In contrast, Benin and Nepal have numerous active local NGOs. In Benin, particularly, the country study found that momentum created by CBD/CDD interventions was largely responsible for the recent multiplication of local NGOs. Elites in the country that traditionally were a part of the government began forming NGOs and increasingly shifted their focus toward donors, where resources, and hence opportunities, were available.[8, 9] What this means for the future is still unclear. However, surveys show that a largely

Figure 4.1: Low-Income Countries Work with More Partners

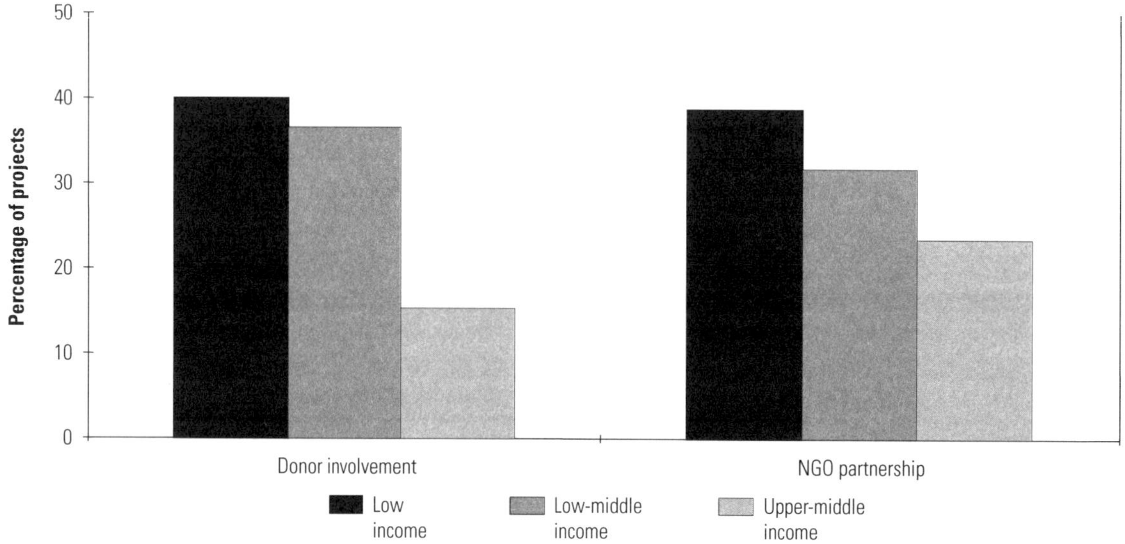

Source: World Bank data.

shared opinion among both donor agency representatives and government officials in the country is that these intermediaries have little accountability toward either the communities or the government.

Partly as a result of the difference in capacity among NGOs, the degree of success of the partnership between the Bank and NGOs has also varied. This was also the finding of an OED study of NGO involvement in all Bank projects (OED 1999a). Bank staff, when asked in the staff survey whether NGO-supported interventions generally achieve a better outcome than Bank interventions, were fairly evenly divided: 31 percent disagreed or strongly disagreed, 26 percent agreed or strongly agreed, and 24 percent fell in between. Such responses may not be particularly revealing because this is a complicated question, and the answer is likely to depend on the respondent's experience. NGO focus groups in country studies, however, revealed dissatisfaction among NGOs with the unequal relationship that they have with the Bank in a CDD intervention and with Bank procedures.

NGO Partnership Can Be Important in Reaching the Poor

The Portfolio Review, project assessment findings, and country studies found that local NGOs, because of their familiarity with local conditions, have been important in helping some CBD/CDD projects to reach the poor and disadvantaged populations and as catalysts in mobilizing communities. For example, NGOs helped mobilize farmers and disseminate technology, and assisted village-level institutions in developing links with government agencies in the Uttar Pradesh Sodic Land Reclamation Project. OED's project assessments also found that NGOs played an important role in enabling the Peru Rural Roads Rehabilitation and Maintenance Project to exceed its target number of villages benefited and in implementing the Andhra Pradesh Forestry Project. That said, the Benin country study found that NGOs with poor qualifications handicapped project implementation in that country. In both the Social Fund and the Food Security Projects in Benin, a large number of NGOs had to be suspended for unacceptable performance. Many stakeholders, including Bank staff and other donor agency representatives, expressed concern about the potential role of NGOs in a number of CBD/CDD projects in Benin, noting that when they are paid a fixed proportion of the total cost of the project, NGOs tend to push the choice of the subprojects that are the most costly but have the minimum operating cost. When NGOs behave this way, they may compromise the participatory process. The OED assessment of the Northern Resource Management Project in Pakistan found that there are both pros and cons to handing over all or most community mobilization to NGOs. The assessment notes, "In favor of such an approach is the generally acknowledged skills of NGOs. Against it, however, is that public technology transfer will continue to be needed and, in order to play a key role, public services can benefit from the first-hand experience of participatory approaches. The aim should be to work out effective and efficient service delivery arrangements involving all actors: central government, NGOs, private sector, local governments, and local communities."

Most Donors Support Community Participation as a Strategy, but There Is Lack of Agreement on Implementation Procedures

Bank data show that 40 percent of both CBD/CDD and non-CBD/CDD projects have multidonor involvement. Several evaluations of Bank projects (CBD/CDD and non-CBD/CDD) have highlighted problems that arise when donor efforts are not well coordinated. However, the case study and project assessment evidence shows that the challenge of donor coordination is greater in a CBD/CDD project than in a non-CBD/CDD project. The country studies in Benin, Nepal, and Vietnam and fieldwork for project assessments in Benin, Ghana, and Mali confirm that several donors are often present in the same community, with different CBD/CDD strategies, providing infrastructure or activity support in a seemingly uncoordinated

Local NGOs have been important in helping some CBD/CDD projects to reach the poor and disadvantaged populations and as catalysts in mobilizing communities.

The challenge of donor coordination is greater in a CBD/CDD project than in a non-CBD/CDD project.

manner. Each donor intervention at the community level may require a separate committee to meet the implementation requirements. The substantial confusion that this creates at the community level is a much more serious issue than the strain on institutional capacity at the government level. Thirty-nine percent of the Bank staff surveyed agreed or strongly agreed with the observation that inadequate donor coordination in a cofinanced project is likely to have a greater negative impact on outcomes in a CBD/CDD project than in a non-CBD/CDD project.

Interviews with Bank and other donor staff for three of the five country studies found that although most donors endorse community participation as a strategy, there is less agreement on implementation plans and procedures. For example, in Nepal, the coordination efforts of individual donor representatives are hindered by a feeling of competition among donors. Most donor officials interviewed in Benin said that the coordination issue could be resolved by allocating different sectors among donors based on their comparative advantage, with regular meetings among them to keep the group informed. In Vietnam, in contrast, nearly all donor representatives said that stronger coordination by the government could resolve the issue.

Figure 4.2: Sustainability Has Been Consistently Lower for CBD/CDD Projects but Is Improving

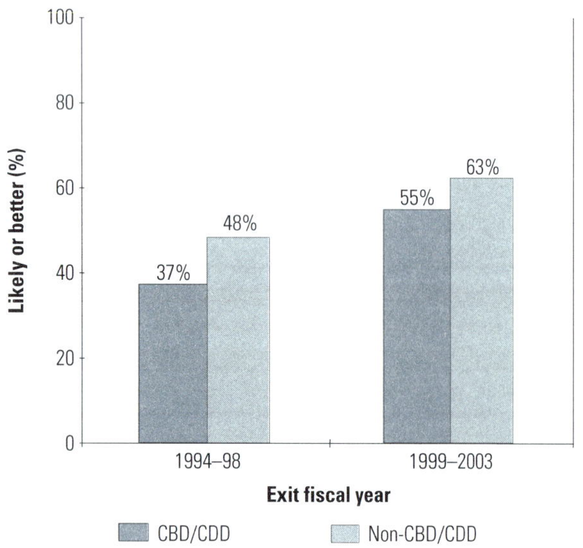

Source: World Bank database.

Coordination among Donors Is More Difficult for Small, Low-Income Countries Than for Middle-Income Countries

The experience of Benin, Nepal, and Vietnam also indicates that the presence of numerous bilateral and multilateral donors, each implementing CBD/CDD projects, but with different institutional arrangements and procedures, has put a tremendous coordination burden on these governments and stretched their limited institutional capacity. This finding is supported by evidence from the literature.[10]

In middle-income countries, however, the Bank's data reveal (see figure 4.1), and the experience of the Brazil and Egypt country studies confirms, that fewer donors are involved in CBD/CDD projects in those countries. In Brazil, in the state of Rio Grande do Norte, for example, no other donor is supporting CBD/CDD projects. In addition, countries such as Egypt have better administrative and institutional capacity to handle coordination.

Few of the Poverty Reduction Strategy Papers (PRSPs) reviewed—but most Country Assistance Strategies (CASs)—note donor coordination as an issue (Annex H). Since PRSPs are meant to be the outcome of a country-driven process of discussion on priorities and challenges, this finding indicates that for the large majority of the borrowers, this issue may not be high on their agenda.

Sustainability

Infrastructure and Activities Have Been Difficult to Sustain beyond the Projects

The sustainability of the CBD/CDD portfolio has been improving, but shows considerable scope for further improvement (figure 4.2). The sustainability ratings have varied by Region, with the highest rating in the Middle East and North Africa, followed closely by Latin America and the

Caribbean[11] (Annex G, table G.3). As with the outcome ratings, some of the larger CBD/CDD projects show higher sustainability compared with a large number of smaller ones.

About 37 percent of the OED project assessments that inform this study rate sustainability as unlikely, and more than 30 percent rate it either nonevaluable or uncertain. Even those that rate sustainability likely raise concerns either about maintenance of supported infrastructure or activities, as in the OED assessment for the Egypt Matrouh Development Project, or lack of adequate analysis of the capacity of the government with respect to government contribution during the project and post-project phase, as in the OED assessment of the Pakistan Northern Resource Management Project.[12]

Scarcity of Resources for Operations and Maintenance Has Been a Constraint

CBD/CDD projects have supported a large amount of social infrastructure—such as schools and heath centers—at the community level in many countries. These have been difficult to sustain beyond the Bank intervention. Mansuri and Rao (2004, p. 32), quoting studies on water projects in Sub-Saharan Africa and South Asia, found that even if communities are initially successful in creating the project, they may lack the material resources to sustain their efforts. OED project assessments also show that poor communities find it difficult to raise resources internally to provide for continuous operation and maintenance (O&M).[13] Governments, too, are fiscally constrained.

A previous OED study (Kumar 2003) notes that Bank projects typically do not plan for simultaneous investment in social and productive sectors. Doing so could ensure long-term sustainability, because village-level capacity to provide for O&M of social investments ultimately depends on increased capacity to generate revenue at the local level. Field research in Brazil found that most of the communities in the state of Rio Grande do Norte had only one subproject approved, largely because project municipal councils could not justify a second investment in any community before all communities had been covered with at least a single investment.[14]

While the Portfolio Review shows that CDD projects provide for a greater role for communities in O&M of subprojects than CBD/CDD projects (figure 2.2), the resource constraint remains an issue even in these projects.[15]

Social infrastructure has been difficult to sustain beyond the Bank intervention.

Several Bank projects require the setting up of maintenance funds.[16] The Benin country study found that commitment to maintenance funds is significantly reduced if communities know that they can go to another donor or to the government when earlier investments cease to be functional.[17, 18] The uncoordinated presence of several donors and NGOs in the same villages in support of different activities can foster dependence and soften the commitment of communities toward maintenance activities.[19] Fieldwork carried out for the OED assessment of the Indonesia Kecamatan Development Project found that the community approach is generally to postpone maintenance until it is unavoidable—for example, the road is about to become impassable, or the bridge is about to collapse, and then to do the minimum that will get it back into usable shape. OED's project assessment of the Mali Natural Resource Management Project also found that a large amount of infrastructure was constructed at the village level, but there were few arrangements made at the community level for its maintenance. Hence, although community members were aware of the importance of maintenance and a significant number of them had been trained, the lack of available resources on a continuous basis to allow for O&M was a significant constraint.

Maintaining a Quality Flow of Services or Income Has Proven Even More Difficult

The World Development Report *Making Services Work for Poor People* (World Bank 2004d) acknowledges the challenge of ensuring service delivery.[20] While it is argued that services can be improved by changing

Bank projects typically do not plan for simultaneous investment in social and productive sectors. Doing so could ensure long-term sustainability.

the relationships of accountability as with CDD, there is little evidence yet. A recent Bank review (Wassenich and Whiteside 2004) found that there is little evidence regarding CDD impacts on quality of service delivery. OED project assessments and a review of ICRs show that most CBD/CDD projects, including CDD projects, give little thought at the design stage to the issue of maintaining a quality flow of services or income.[21] Hence, even though infrastructure may be standing in a village or community, it is often underused or not being used for the purpose that was originally intended. Further, the flow of services or income from an infrastructure requires consideration of issues related to coordination with different government departments. It also implies increased financial responsibility for the government in the form of supplemental resources, such as to pay the salaries of teachers and doctors. Annex P draws on the experience of the projects in Benin to illustrate this point in the case of school subprojects.

And Some Types of Services Have Been Much More Difficult to Maintain Than Others

OED project assessments and country study findings show that sustaining a quality service flow from some types of infrastructure depends on the scale and complexity of the service. For example, quality flow of education services from a school will require coordination with the education department to ensure the availability of certified teachers and books, as well as adherence to a centrally planned curriculum, among other things. Key informant interviews in Benin revealed that 50 percent of the teachers in schools supported under the Borgou Pilot Project and 80 percent of teachers in schools supported under the Social Fund were not state certified; in the comparator schools, fewer than a third were not certified (Annex P). In Eritrea, the OED assessment of the Community Development Fund Project found that health centers supported under the project have been negatively affected by the severe overall shortage of doctors in the country. In contrast, flow of services from a village water supply scheme can be maintained with minimum technical support from outside the village. Ironically, in several of the poorest countries where the institutional environment is the weakest, and coordination among various government departments the biggest problem, Bank projects are supporting social infrastructure such as schools and health centers. In contrast, in Brazil, Indonesia, and the Philippines, where the level of institutional development is higher, Bank CBD/CDD projects have provided support for activities that often do not require the same kind of coordination and support from higher levels of government, such as water supply schemes and roads.[22] Since the focus is on the number of schools and health centers built, the actual issue of how the flow of services from these facilities will be maintained receives less attention.

Since the focus is on the number of schools and health centers built, the actual issue of how the flow of services from these facilities will be maintained receives less attention.

Villagers May Also Not Have the Necessary Information or Technical Knowledge

Project assessment findings show that communities often may not have the information and technical expertise they need to allow for maintenance. The OED assessment of the Community Development Fund Project in Eritrea notes that in addition to ownership and willingness of different actors to sustain investments, sustainability requires that the relevant actors have the financial, managerial, and technical capacity to operate and maintain the infrastructure. Focus group sessions with villagers in Benin found that several communities had not received adequate training to be able to maintain their subprojects. In Uttar Pradesh, where the Bank supported sodic land reclamation, villagers are interested in keeping the reclaimed land from reverting to its former state, but the OED fieldwork found that they may not have the technical knowledge or capacity to do so.[23] Maintenance of main drains critical to the sustainability of reclaimed lands could only be done by the Irrigation Department. The implementing agency staff believed that the political pressure from the farmers would be sufficient to ensure that the government provided adequate resources to the Irrigation Department to maintain the main drains. However, household survey data analysis found that 96 percent of the farmers in the CDD communities were unaware that the Irrigation Department had the responsibility for maintaining the main drains. Further, the household survey analysis also indicated that most villagers were not even aware of the critical importance of drainage for containing sodicity (Annex P).

Lack of Clear Communication about the Role of Communities in a Bank Project Has Added to the Problem

As already indicated, villagers mainly see participation in a Bank project as a requirement for them to meet part of the subproject cost. The project assessment of the Uttar Pradesh Sodic Land Reclamation Project also found that the community members' understanding of their contribution to the participation process has led them to expect support from the government for maintenance of drains that were critical to sustainability. In a situation where the implementing agency expects communities to take the lead and the communities are not clear about this, sustainability issues are generally neglected. The assessment noted, "The farmers continued to think of the reclamation activity as an 'outside' effort brought to them by UPBSN [implementing agency] rather than something that they had to carry out on their own. It is understandable then that they would think that the drainage problem too would be 'taken care' of by UPBSN and the Gram Pradhan."

And Sometimes Bank Interventions Have Failed to Provide Consistent Support Long Enough for a Sustained Income Flow To Be Established

Project assessments and OED country studies found that where the issue is a sustained flow of income from a particular activity, such as forestry, project support is often unavailable until the returns from the forest could allow for a sustained flow of income from non-timber forest products and timber (Annex P). For example, in India's forestry projects, popular support for joint forestry management (JFM) was contingent on forging a link in villagers' minds between protection of the forest and improvements in livelihoods. Hence, the projects provided for complementary investments in communal infrastructure to give villagers an incentive to cooperate. The OED study on forestry in India notes: "The regenerated forest area can be kept under tree cover only if the FPC [forest protection committee] members get enough returns to compensate for the income forgone. This would mean that JFM and the Economic Development Program have to be part of one strategy of ensuring returns in the future. Currently this is not the case" (Kumar and others 2000). Although in several states, the projects, when appraised, were presented as the first phase of a long-term operation to consolidate the JFM strategy, in several states (including Madhya Pradesh) the Bank did not commit to funding a follow-on operation, which considerably jeopardized sustainability of the effort already made.

The recent emphasis on empowerment and social capital has focused much more attention on the importance of understanding the rules and regulations that govern behavior in village society.

Formal and Informal Organizations Are Both Important in Determining Collective Activity at the Community Level

The literature shows that, at the community level, both formal and informal organizational systems influence collective activities. Community Associations set up in Brazil under the Rural Poverty Alleviation Program (RPAP) are a good example of formal organizations, because these groups need to be legally constituted before they can participate in the Bank-supported project. Village societies also typically have informal arrangements that determine how groups collectively manage resources such as water. These informal arrangements are not explicit rules or regulations, but are based on customs and conventions or what people consider "the generally accepted way of

But customs and conventions that could be specific to a particular community and are important in determining collective activities have received inadequate attention.

doing things" (Cleaver 1997, 1998; Tripp 2001) (see Annex K).

Yet Bank Projects Have Primarily Focused on Formal Organizations

A review of project documents and evidence from country studies shows that in Bank projects, the focus is primarily on formal organizations and manifestations of collective action, such as the creation of a user group or committees and the holding of their meetings. The recent emphasis on empowerment and social capital has focused much more attention on the importance of understanding the rules and regulations that govern behavior in village society, but customs and conventions that could be specific to a particular community and are important in determining collective activities have received inadequate attention. As a result, little thought appears to have been given to how the formal structures that are created under a Bank intervention will affect the informal organizations, customs, and conventions of a village society and how the interaction of the formal and informal rules could influence empowerment.

Since the formal and informal systems influence each other, it could be argued that the formal arrangements created under a Bank intervention will influence and bring about adequate changes in the informal arrangements that are in keeping with the formal systems. However, as will be seen in Chapter 5, Bank support is rarely provided long enough to allow the new structures to become an effective part of the way the village operates. Project assessments and evidence from focus groups (box 4.3) show that new structures established to implement Bank projects tend to fade away once the project implementation period is over.

Box 4.3: Why Formal Groups Do Not Last Long

"Only 7 out of 12 [committee] members participated in meetings. Today, this number has been reduced to three. The other members of the committee said that there is no profit in their being on the committee and for this reason they prefer to go deal with their own affairs [fieldwork]." Benin Borgou Region (AgeFIB)

"No committee was set in the village to monitor or manage the project. Only the [village committee] secretary had played some role. There has been no discussion as to community contribution and participation. Financial contribution was paid on [committee] revenue while households were requested to contribute with free labor, especially for fetching water for the building." Benin Borgou Region (PAMR)

"People do not even mention collective work anymore. Not even meetings are any longer held. There is only a meeting when money is concerned." Rio Grande do Norte, Brazil

"[Maintenance of the infrastructure] is the job of the district government and the project people. No one has come to repair the field drains and connecting drains. On being asked why they don't repair the connecting drains the reply is, that we were paid to make them, no one has paid us to repair them." Uttar Pradesh, India

"Why has our community association become inactive? ...our main target was to get the water system; we got it and the people stopped mobilizing so we were benefited with no other projects. Our target was to have water and then people stopped mobilizing." Rio Grande do Norte, Brazil

"When the Samiti was formed, it had promised to start 7 village-based organizations. They could remember just 4...Once these Samitis were started, they operated for 4 to 5 years but later they were dissolved... None of them exist today....One man said that there had been no meetings for the last 2 years." Madhya Pradesh, India

Source: Focus groups.

Bank Operational Policy Requirements, Processes, and CBD/CDD Interventions

This chapter assesses the extent to which internal policy requirements and processes position the Bank to support implementation of CBD/CDD, in particular CDD, interventions. Although the Bank's mission is to fight poverty and improve the living standards of people in the developing world, it is also a lending institution, and its shareholders want assurance that funds provided by their taxpayers achieve expected results and that operations are economically, socially, and environmentally sound.

Consequently, in addition to meeting efficiency conditions (Chapter 3), all Bank projects need to meet two basic policy requirements—fiduciary, which govern the use of project-related funds, and safeguards, to prevent unintended adverse effects on third parties and the environment.

The Bank Has Attempted to Adapt Its Policies to Design and Implement CBD/CDD Projects

Both fiduciary and safeguard policies were originally developed for non-CBD/CDD projects that generally involved large-scale "lumpy" investments at specific locations, typically implemented by a central government department or agency that monitored and reported on resource use. Bank missions supervised the investment site periodically and reported on resource use systematically. A typical CBD/CDD project is very different. Each project includes numerous small subprojects that are heterogeneous and scattered, sometimes in remote locations with poor communication. They involve multiple actors, and many communities with varying socioeconomic, cultural, and political backgrounds. Unlike the more traditional investments, the subprojects under CBD/CDD are often not even known in advance. Moreover, in the case of CDD, communities are also expected to control resources and decisions and be in charge of contracting for their implementation. These significant differences have made it difficult to ensure the compliance of CBD/CDD projects with fiduciary and safeguard policies that were developed for non-CBD/CDD investments.

As a result, the Bank attempted to adapt its policies to be able to design and implement CBD/CDD interventions, while meeting the institution's fiduciary and safeguard obligations.[1] This chapter examines three issues that are pertinent to assessing Bank capacity to implement CBD/CDD projects: first, whether CBD/CDD projects can

While the environmental and social impact of individual subprojects may be insignificant, their cumulative impact can be substantial.

pose a challenge for safeguard and fiduciary compliance; second, whether adequate changes have been made in Bank policies to effectively support implementation of CBD/CDD projects; third, whether the Bank has the capacity to ensure effective implementation of CBD/CDD projects.

CBD/CDD Projects and the Challenge for Safeguard and Fiduciary Compliance

Compliance with Safeguard at Entry Has Improved over the Years

A thematic study that reviewed the sample of 84 projects for their compliance with safeguards (Annex Q) found that such compliance at entry has improved over the years. In terms of Regions, all projects in Europe and Central Asia were found to be satisfactory. The Middle East and North Africa recorded the next strongest record, followed by Africa, and East Asia and the Pacific. The study also found that despite format changes in the Project Status Reports that encourage detailed reporting on the implementation of safeguard measures, such reporting remains sparse and inadequate. Further, the study found that the overall quality of implementation was rated satisfactory for fewer than 40 percent of the cases. In terms of Regions, South Asia and East Asia and the Pacific score highest for quality of implementation of safeguard issues. These findings at entry and implementation are disturbing given the Bank's current emphasis on full compliance with safeguard requirements. The thematic study also found that 6 of the 11 projects rated unsatisfactory on overall quality were in the Bank's largest borrower countries.

However, Cumulative Impact of Subprojects Has Been an Issue for Safeguard Compliance

Some have argued that individual subprojects in CBD/CDD interventions are so small that they cannot have a substantial negative social or economic impact. However, the thematic study found that while the environmental and social impact of individual subprojects may be insignificant, their cumulative impact can be substantial. The study also notes that too little attention is being paid in CBD/CDD projects to the environmental and social consequences of changes in land use, especially for livestock, irrigation, and reforestation projects. Moreover, subprojects are often not small and may include investments—such as wastewater treatment plants in Poland or dams in China and Brazil—with the potential for major negative environmental and social impacts.[2] Further, as decision making is decentralized, there is some danger that potential impacts, particularly in resettlement cases, may not be recognized and suitably mitigated. For example, it was only when OED carried out an assessment of the Andhra Pradesh Forestry Project (1994) that cases of uncompensated land were discovered.

Wrong Environmental Category Assignment Can Have Serious Implications

Typically, projects in areas such as health, education, nutrition, institutional development, technical assistance, and human resources are placed in environmental Category C (see box 5.1) because they are considered to be unlikely to have adverse environmental impacts, or that any such impact would be minimal. However, health projects supporting immunization programs, basic packages of drugs and syringes, and laboratory services for infectious diseases (including AIDS) raise concerns about the safe collection, storage, and disposal of medical waste. The thematic review found that 9 percent of the projects classified as Category B and 38 percent classified as Category C had been misclassified—that is, projects had been classified as C or B when they should have been B or A. Assignment of Category B induces a B mindset, which implies concentrating attention on documentation to be produced before Board approval, rather than on appraising the capacity of the project agencies to screen subprojects, analyze their potential impacts, and design and implement mitigation measures, and on specifying the needed institutional strengthening and monitoring systems. Assignment of Category C generally means that no further work is done to identify and mitigate impacts and there is no further review by safe-

Box 5.1: The Meaning of the Environmental Categories

The Bank classifies proposed projects into one of four categories, depending on the type, location, sensitivity, and scale of the project and the nature and magnitude of its potential environmental impacts.

Category A: A project is classified as Category A if it is likely to have significant adverse environmental impacts that are sensitive (a potential impact is considered sensitive if it may be irreversible), diverse, or unprecedented. These impacts may affect an area broader than the sites or facilities subject to physical works.

Category B: A project is classified as Category B if its potential adverse environmental impacts on human populations or environmentally important areas—including wetlands, forests, grasslands, and other natural habitats—are less adverse than those of Category A projects. These impacts are site-specific; few if any of them are irreversible; and in most cases mitigatory measures can be designed more readily than for Category A projects.

Category C: A project is classified as Category C if it is likely to have minimal or no adverse environmental impacts.

Category FI: A proposed project is classified as Category FI if it involves investment of Bank funds through a financial intermediary, in subprojects that may result in adverse environmental impacts.

Source: Bank Operational Policy 4.01—Environmental Assessment.

guard specialists. For example, OED's project assessment of the Mali Natural Resource Management Project also found that since the project was wrongly categorized as a C, important environmental issues were not given attention.

Attention to Safeguards during Implementation Has Also Been Inadequate

While quality at entry needs improvement, safeguards compliance during implementation warrants much greater attention by the Bank and borrowers, and may indicate the need for greater allocation of supervision resources. The low percentage of moderately satisfactory or better Category A projects appears to conflict with the expectation that A's would receive much more intensive scrutiny during supervision. The inadequacy of funding to address safeguard issues is strongly endorsed by Bank staff in the staff survey. If resources for safeguard supervision were increased, it would add to the already higher costs of supervision for CBD/CDD projects in comparison with non-CBD/CDD projects, with efficiency implications. Some of the more recent projects (such as Nigeria Community-Based Poverty Reduction) have had special assessments of safeguards implementation, usually by specialist consultants, a practice that would be valuable to adopt more widely, especially where there are several CBD/CDD projects in the same country. The Bank is also currently exploring ways to streamline the application of safeguard policies by delegation, both within the institution and to national authorities.

Although Fiduciary Compliance Is More an Issue for CDD Projects

Where the handling of resources in scattered subprojects remains in the hands of a central implementing unit, the fiduciary challenge is not very different from that for a non-CBD/CDD project—that is, the need to set in place within the implementing unit a system that can adequately monitor and report on resource use. The challenge occurs when control over resources, and often procurement responsibility as well, is transferred to communities (often remote ones), as happens in CDD projects. The country studies show that this fiduciary challenge is likely to be greater in countries where institutional capacity is weaker, such as Benin, Nepal, and

Safeguards compliance during implementation warrants much greater attention by the Bank and borrowers.

Box 5.2: The Fiduciary Challenge: The Case of Vietnam

The Country Financial Accountability Assessment for Vietnam notes the challenge for financial management at the subnational government levels created by weak capacity, especially in budgeting, accounting, and financial reporting.[a] With deficiencies and irregularities in procurement as well (Vietnam CPAR 2002), it is unclear how the Bank will be able to manage the fiduciary risk in its ongoing portfolio of CDD interventions. An internal Bank review of the Quality of Supervision for a CBD/CDD project, the Coastal Wetlands Protection and Development project (2000), identified the serious challenge that the Bank team faces.[b] It reports that the Bank's procurement procedures were almost completely rejected by the client in favor of directing works under the International Development Association (IDA) credit to monopoly state-owned enterprises. In the view of the reviewers, this represented a possible failure of the Bank's entire project implementation system in Vietnam. The report acknowledges that Bank staff must be attentive to situations where the Bank's policies may not apply or where there may be more economical, efficient, or transparent ways of doing things, but, in the end, Bank management is responsible for the environment in which projects are conceived, prepared, negotiated, and implemented. This should be an environment in which both parties are focused on getting results they value.

a. Concerns are already being noted by Bank staff on financial management in the supervision reports for the Community-Based Rural Infrastructure Project (2001) that started disbursement to communes in fiscal 2003.

b. Management notes that the operational issues highlighted are not related to the CDD aspects of the project.

Vietnam (box 5.2), than in middle-income countries such as Brazil, Egypt, and Indonesia, where capacity to monitor resource use at the local level may be greater. The country studies also show that the understanding and interpretation of fiduciary responsibility and accountability can be very different in local communities in several countries. In Benin's rural communities, for example, property rights are poorly defined and enforced. Commercial exchanges are based on trust rather than on enforceable contracts, and fiduciary rules are typically informal. In this kind of environment, applying fiduciary management and accountability through the Bank's rules may be more difficult and costly than is envisaged in CDD projects.

Most Bank Documents Have Not Reported on Community Capacity to Undertake Fiduciary Management Responsibility

This fiduciary challenge is likely to be greater in countries where institutional capacity is weaker than in middle-income countries.

Fiduciary sector work, internal audit reports, and project documents for 12 CDD projects were reviewed to assess fiduciary compliance. The review found that the majority of appraisal and supervision documents still do not report on community capacity to undertake fiduciary responsibility, even though the project envisages communities being responsible for managing resources. It is thus unclear how extensively capacity at the community level is actually assessed before a Bank CDD project is introduced in a particular setting. The majority of Country Financial Accountability Assessments (CFAAs) and Country Procurement Assessment Reports (CPARs) reviewed also do not report on community capacity.

The Readiness of Country Financial Procedures and Internal Control Systems to Support CDD Is Not Given Adequate Attention

While CFAA and CPAR documents can indicate whether the existing processes in the country at the central and regional levels are strong enough to monitor resource use, this information does not seem to be used to assess country readiness for CDD. For example, the documents on Nepal, Nigeria, Pakistan, and Senegal have raised concerns about the extent of capacity in these countries to monitor resource use and to report on poor compliance with financial procedures and internal control systems.[3] However, all these countries have several CDD projects either ongoing or in the planning stages. While some have argued that it is much more likely that resources provided through CBD/CDD interventions will reach the poor than those provided through non-CBD/CDD work, the concern is that, given the level of transparency and accountability in several poor countries, unless adequate processes are put in place, it is quite possible that despite the best intentions, these resources may not actually benefit the poor.[4] In addition to fiduciary sector work, the weakness in these aspects of public sector governance has also been noted in other Bank-IMF documents.[5] The importance of adequate follow up to such diagnostic sector work in the design and implementation of CDD projects cannot be emphasized enough.[6] It is worrying that several internal audit reports have picked up lack of fiduciary compliance as an issue in several CDD projects. It is worth mentioning that some project supervision reports have also raised concerns about fiduciary issues.[7]

Changes in Bank Policies to Effectively Support CBD/CDD Projects

More Progress Has Been Made on Refining Fiduciary than Safeguard Policies

While it is to the credit of the institution that the need to adapt its policies has been recognized, policies have not yet been completely refined, although CBD/CDD lending is growing rapidly. More progress seems to have been made on refining the fiduciary policies (as a fiduciary reference guide at least exists and was issued in May 2002) than on safeguard policies. But it is important to recognize that the procedure for developing adequate guidance on safeguards is complicated. The Andhra Pradesh forestry experience, and more recently that of the Indonesia Kecamatan Development project, shows the difficulty of applying the Bank's safeguard policies, particularly resettlement policies, to situations where it is not easy to determine what is a "loss" for which a displaced person needs to be compensated.[8] The challenge for the Bank today is to ensure that safeguard violations are minimized while the new guidelines are being developed.

Although the thematic study found that guidance to staff on safeguard issues is still being developed, with fiduciary issues, application of the guidelines is a challenge. The guidance note states that the Bank rules and guidelines apply to CDD projects in the same way that they do for any other Bank project, but that their application needs to be adapted to the capacity of the project and the community. Since there are capacity differences among communities, fiduciary requirements need to be adapted to each project—if not to each community's capacity. The Bank's policy on fiduciary management for CDD projects leaves the decision about what communities are required to do for each CDD project's appraisal team. As a result, whether and how this policy translates into simpler procedures at local level is less clear, and the simplification, if any, may be quite variable across projects.

Policies have still not been completely refined, although CBD/CDD lending is growing rapidly.

In response to the questionnaire on the subject in the staff survey—that task managers of CBD/CDD projects can monitor fiscal accountability as satisfactorily as can managers of more traditional non-CBD/CDD projects—36 percent agreed or strongly agreed, 28 percent were in the middle, and 23 percent disagreed or strongly disagreed (Annex L). While on other questions this might be considered a reasonably positive response, on matters related to accountability, calling for some necessary minimum standard, having approximately one-quarter of staff expressing concern about the ability of task managers to monitor suggests a significant problem.

Bank Capacity to Ensure Effective Implementation of CBD/CDD Interventions

Two issues are central to assessing Bank capacity to ensure effective implementation of CBD/CDD interventions. These are: the Bank's mode of operation and institutional organization and the Bank's capacity to undertake adequate monitoring and evaluation of its operations. The following sections deal with them in turn.

With fiduciary issues, application of the guidelines is a challenge.

Mode of Operation and Institutional Organization

The Information Access Chain is Much Longer and Has Greater Gaps in CBD/CDD Interventions than in Non-CBD/CDD Interventions

Borrowers almost universally said that supervision by field offices has helped them.

Regular "supervision" missions were largely adequate to ensure that implementation was proceeding as planned in non-CBD/CDD operations. In CBD/CDD interventions, and particularly CDD, where the implementation is being undertaken by communities, the information access chain for the Bank is much longer and has larger gaps:

- **First**, while the Bank relies on the borrower to provide reports, several layers of government are involved. The extent to which the borrower is able to maintain accurate records depends on its ability to coordinate among different layers and get information from the community level.
- **Second**, the reliability and accuracy of the information from the community level depends on the capacity of the communities to maintain the records and of the local government agencies or facilitators to monitor community record keeping.
- **Third**, it is almost impossible to expect the borrower to "supervise" and cross-check for accuracy and consistency the information that is coming from thousands of remote communities. The government has to rely for this accuracy on facilitators that may have a vested interest in reporting that implementation is going well, since the facilitator's survival often depends on the availability of donor resources.
- **Fourth**, given that there is no systematic way of checking for cumulative impact, and that baseline data are often not available, it is almost impossible to tell how, say, the simultaneous digging of 500 wells will affect the water table in a given area.

The Bank itself is compartmentalized, so integrated approaches across several sectors have remained limited.

- **Fifth**, the Bank's own supervision resources allow missions to "inspect" only a very limited number of subprojects, and internal audit reports show that these are mostly in sites that can be easily visited.

Bank Decentralization Has Increased the Capacity of the Institution to Track CBD/CDD Interventions

Nearly 3,000 of the 10,000 Bank staff now live and work in client countries.[9] With this decentralization to the field, the Bank is today better connected with its borrowers than it in the past. During OED project assessment field missions, borrowers almost universally said that supervision by field offices has helped them. Sixty-five percent of Bank staff were somewhat satisfied or better with the impact of Bank decentralization to field offices on the efficacy of Bank support for participatory projects. Only 13 percent were not satisfied, suggesting fairly widespread satisfaction with Bank decentralization. While decentralization has undoubtedly brought the Bank closer to the borrower, it can do little about the government and community side of the information chain and about the Bank's own ability to monitor what is happening in thousands of remote communities. The staff survey raised concerns about the availability of adequate supervision resources to be able to monitor compliance with safeguards. As Chapter 3 indicates, the Bank's preparation and supervision costs for CBD/CDD projects are already higher than for non-CBD/CDD project, and there are no additional incentives for country directors to provide the additional resources required to prepare and supervise these operations.

But the Sectoral Organization of the Bank Continues to Handicap the Design and Implementation of CBD/CDD Interventions

Further, despite the attempt by Regions to create multisectoral teams to coordinate CBD/CDD, the Bank itself is compartmentalized, so integrated approaches across several sectors have remained limited.10 Only 9 percent of Bank staff surveyed reported being satisfied or very satisfied with coordination within the Bank across sectors in CBD/CDD interventions. It is striking that this concern about Bank coordination was actually greater than staff concern about borrower coordination. Only about 14 percent reported being fully satisfied with the support from the current matrix-management organizational structure for CBD/CDD projects and about 27 percent were not satisfied (Annex L). A key finding of a recent Regional review of Bank supervision of CDD projects in the East Asia Region was that there was little collaboration between the Region's sector units in supervising CDD projects despite the multisectoral scope of these operations (World Bank 2003c).

Monitoring and Evaluation

Monitoring and Evaluation Have Improved Over the Years

Since an Operational Memo in January 1996 from the Operations Policy and Country Services (OPCS) unit provided guidance to staff on preparing indicators, most projects, including CBD/CDD, have given more attention to M&E capacity and indicators, though there is variation in quality across projects. A review of the sample of 84 projects found that M&E was very weak in most of the early projects (pre-1994), and most of the indicators were output-related rather than outcome-related. Some projects had very little monitoring of any kind. For example, the OED assessment for the Turkey Eastern Anatolia Project, a 1993 intervention, notes the weakness of M&E and the fact that the first baseline was not done until 1998. In Egypt, the OED assessment of the Matrouh Resource Management Project (1993) also noted that M&E started too late and analysis focused largely on number of adoptions rather than quantified impacts, so not much could be said about gains in productivity.

But Little Has Been Done about Monitoring Capacity Enhancement

There has been progressive improvement, and more projects approved in later years (after fiscal 1995) have outcome and impact indicators. The Portfolio Review found that 95 percent of these projects have indicators to monitor progress and impact, compared with 50 percent in the earlier period. However, most indicators continue to focus on quantity rather than quality. For example, the OED assessment of the Borgou Pilot Project, a fiscal 1998 intervention, shows that monitoring indicators still track quantitative input and output achievements (such as days of training provided, number of villages covered, and the like) rather than qualitative progress toward achieving the primary project objective of improving the capacity of village communities to better manage their socioeconomic environment. Similarly, the Yemen Third Social Fund and the recently approved Cameroon Community Development Program APL have large capacity building components and progress toward the objectives should thus be measured by qualitative and process-oriented indicators. Yet most of the outcome and impact indicators noted in the report continue to be quantitative and will be able to say little about the quality and impact of the capacity-building effort. However, on the positive side, there are examples of some projects, such as the India Andhra Pradesh District Poverty Initiatives Project (2000), which make some provision for process monitoring in design and may be able to indicate improvement in capacity assuming adequate follow up.

Most projects, including CBD/CDD, have given more attention to M&E capacity and indicators, but most indicators continue to focus on quantity rather than quality.

Several projects, such as the CWPII in Albania, Kalahi CIDSS in the Philippines, Kecamatan Development Project in Indonesia, and the Third Social Fund for Development in Yemen, are emphasizing participatory M&E to involve communities in tracking progress on activities. This is not only likely to support the Bank capacity-enhancing effort at the community level, but is also likely to help build greater ownership of Bank activities in communities, with positive implications for sustainability (Estrella and Gaventa 1998). Some projects have attempted to combine participatory M&E with other measures in a pluralistic approach that could prove invaluable in tracking progress (box 5.3). But, given the difference in the understanding of participation between the Bank and the borrower/community noted earlier, it remains to be seen how effective participatory M&E will be in tracking progress on process issues.

Box 5.3: Some Monitoring and Evaluation Features to Emulate: The Case of the Indonesia Kecamatan Development Project (KDP)

The KDP project illustrates some features that an M&E system for CDD should emulate:

- Involvement of beneficiaries in monitoring performance (for example, measuring quantities of materials delivered by contractors).
- Public display of financial data at the village level on notice boards so that all beneficiaries could see, monitor, and question.
- The establishment of relatively strong record-keeping systems and bookkeeping skills at the village level (although skills in the wrong hands can make corruption easier to hide also).
- A quite strong central government monitoring system.
- Baseline studies, impact studies, and other studies on particular issues that were contracted out (though not all these reports have been assessed for their quality).
- Qualitative and quantitative indicators measure physical achievement, corruption, and conflict.
- Contracted, but independent, journalists to be another eye in monitoring, which enabled the publicizing of corruption cases.
- Contracted NGOs to monitor performance at the community and local government levels (in most CDD projects NGOs are the facilitators, in KDP they were only monitors).
- A project-run public grievance system that generally responded quite quickly.
- A series of related studies, such as an innovative quantitative assessment of corruption in infrastructure (for example, through core sampling of roads), a study of microfinance performance, and studies of conflict problems.
- A general readiness to respond with new, quick studies as new performance issues arose.

This said, the KDP system also has some weaknesses (for example, related to community process measurement, insufficient measurement of poverty and gender impact, and methodological problems with measuring impacts), which are planned to be addressed under KDP3, which became effective in January 2005.

Source: Portfolio Review.

Further, the preparation for most Bank projects does not include establishing a baseline. The Portfolio Review found that fewer than 10 percent of the projects involve establishing a baseline against which to assess the impact of Bank intervention, instead relying largely on with-without comparison with weak counterfactuals. Hence, even if studies are carried out, it is very difficult to tell whether there are any achievements.

Furthermore, well-designed M&E is pointless if it is not effectively used. For example, the OED assessment of the Uttar Pradesh Sodic Land Reclamation Project notes that the latest monitoring technology is available to the Remote Sensing Application Center in Uttar Pradesh, but the large amount of data being generated is not being used effectively. This is also because project-related M&E procedures contribute little to systematically building evaluation capacity in the country. Most project-related M&E effort comes to an end when projects close. There appears to be little, if any, systematic relationship between evaluation capacity development activities and individual project-level M&E.

The preparation for most Bank projects does not include establishing a baseline.

An ideal M&E system for CBD/CDD should be able to do at least five things:

- Tell whether adequate qualitative and quantitative progress is being made toward meeting the project objectives.
- Tell whether the Bank resources are being used effectively and efficiently.
- Give some indication of whether progress is being made in reaching the poor and the poorest.
- Provide information on safeguard and fiduciary compliance.
- Give an indication of whether sustainability can be ensured.
- If the first five are not happening, it should provide flags for mid-course corrections.

Existing M&E systems in Bank CBD/CDD interventions are a long way from meeting these criteria.

Conclusions

This evaluation of the Bank's support for CBD/CDD interventions in client countries supports four broad findings.

The Bank has not, until recently, systematically identified and tracked its portfolio of CBD/CDD projects, and therefore has lacked a comprehensive understanding of the evolution and scope of its work in community development. It also has not been sufficiently clear about the objectives of using CBD/CDD approaches, criteria for choosing among different community development approaches, or about how to measure the results.

Although the Bank has been involved in CBD/CDD for a long time, a database of projects using community development approaches was only established for projects approved from 2000 onward. Overall development effectiveness can be assessed only on a clearly defined portfolio. Furthermore, effectiveness can only be assessed against clear objectives, preferably with clear indicators against which to judge success. Different community development approaches have varying community capacity requirements, so it is important to ensure that Bank staff, as well as the Bank's clients and the ultimate beneficiaries, understand the expectations under the project. For example, the concept of empowerment, a major justification for the most recent generation of CDD projects, is not uniformly understood within the Bank or, even more important, between the Bank and its clients. Regarding community participation, the surveyed beneficiaries appear to have a very limited, pragmatic understanding of the concept that differs significantly from the Bank's intent.

The Bank's structure and mode of operation limit its ability to ensure sustainable outcomes from CBD/CDD projects. This limitation has become much more apparent since the institution began emphasizing CDD in the late 1990s.

It is easier for the Bank to monitor resource use and be in compliance with safeguards in non-CBD/CDD investments such as bridges or a power plant than where small subprojects are being implemented by hundreds of remote communities in scattered locations. In CBD/CDD projects, and more so in CDD ones, the critical challenge that the Bank faces is that the process must be managed "close to the ground," but normally without direct Bank involvement at the local level. As a result, with its mode of operation, distance from implementation, and its current monitoring and evaluation system, the

Bank has found it difficult to ensure safeguard compliance and sustainability of development outcomes from its CBD/CDD projects.

The Bank's support for CBD/CDD has produced different, though systematic, result patterns depending on local political and social conditions, government commitment, and community capacity.

Bank-supported CBD/CDD projects have had much more success, particularly regarding capacity enhancement, in supporting indigenously matured participatory efforts or where it has provided consistent long-term capacity-building support to communities over time. However, most projects make little effort to tailor capacity building to community capacity or to go back to the same communities with a consistent capacity-building strategy; the one year of a typical subproject cycle is sufficient to allow successful subproject execution, but not to consistently have a significant positive impact on community capacity; and communities do not appear to have understood that their participation is meant to drive the development process, and see participation in a Bank project primarily as a requirement for them to meet part of the subproject cost.

To effectively support CBD/CDD projects, and especially CDD ones, the Bank will not only need to carefully consider its own capacity but also to assess borrower commitment, community capacity, and the costs and benefits of the alternatives available. Four issues need special attention when future CBD/CDD projects are considered:

- Clear articulation of expected achievements of CBD/CDD interventions. While the design of CBD/CDD projects has emphasized both material development and capacity building activities, during project implementation relatively greater importance has tended to be given to achievement of material development goals. This raises concerns about whether the Bank is using CBD/CDD as a means for facilitating an investment program rather than for sustainably improving community decision processes.
- Calculation of the costs and benefits, including the long-term poverty impact, of undertaking the CBD/CDD approach as a basis for comparison with alternatives. The Bank has not systematically and realistically assessed the distribution of costs and benefits of undertaking CBD/CDD projects to the institution, the borrower, and the communities. The insufficient focus on costs and benefits, especially measures of poverty impact, in CBD/CDD projects has prevented convincing comparisons with more traditional investments and policy and institutional reform programs.
- Focus on sustainability and long-term development. Project experience indicates that in a number of cases there has been a lack of adequate follow through of activities supported by Bank projects in order to address and minimize risks to long-term outcomes. In other cases, the ad hoc parallel arrangements made to implement Bank projects have hindered the long-run enhancement of local government capacity.
- Addressing constraints related to the Bank's mode of operation, its operational policies, and its monitoring and evaluation systems. For individual communities, the Bank's subproject cycle is generally too short to bring about the kind of enhancement of community capacity that is visualized in Bank-supported CBD/CDD, particularly CDD projects. Further, Bank processes and systems have not been geared toward supporting long-term processes such as empowerment and social capital enhancement.

Recommendations

Given the mixed and limited evidence on the impacts of CBD/CDD projects—particularly in poverty reduction and empowerment—and questions about sustainability and safeguard and fiduciary compliance, the Bank should approach future CBD/CDD projects, particularly CDD initiatives, with greater care. In countries where the Bank is already supporting a CDD program, the institution needs to rigorously assess the poverty and institutional development impact of its projects before scaling them up. A cautious approach would be especially important in countries or areas where the Bank is just beginning to support CDD. In its future assistance to CBD/CDD, the Bank should:

At the corporate level, strengthen operational guidance and management oversight.

- The Bank should provide operational guidance for the application of Bank safeguard policies and fiduciary oversight of CBD/CDD projects and for the strengthening of cost-benefit analysis and M&E systems; and should commission an audit of the fiduciary aspects of a representative sample of CDD projects for submission to the Board within a year.

At the country level, design the CBD/CDD program as an integral part of the overall assistance strategy and carry out periodic assessment of its ongoing CBD/CDD projects to ensure relevance and effectiveness of the program to the country context.

- Future CASs should show how they have analyzed and addressed linkages not only between various CBD/CDD projects to be undertaken in the country but also between CBD/CDD and relevant non-CBD/CDD projects. In particular, the analysis should address whether arrangements for CBD/CDD project implementation come at the expense of local government capacity development.

At the project level, the Bank should give priority to helping countries build up existing indigenously matured initiatives; where there are no such existing initiatives, the Bank should tailor its project to the country and community context, while undertaking selective rigorous impact assessments to ensure learning.

- For any new CBD/CDD project, the Bank should analyze (using existing processes, such as social assessments) whether it is building on indigenously matured initiatives or attempting to begin a CDD program in a country and then tailor the intervention to local capacity; and the Bank should also selectively undertake rigorous impact assessments upon completion of its ongoing CBD/CDD projects to learn for the future.

ANNEXES

ANNEX A: DEFINITION OF "COMMUNITY"

The Community

All Bank participatory projects exhibit three basic assumptions about communities (from OED 2003):

- They comprise a group of people who share broad development goals.
- Their social behavior and relationships are governed by social norms that are expected to provide solidarity.
- By extension, those who do not belong to that community are "excluded."

The "community" in this approach is often considered a "unified, organic whole" (Agrawal and Gibson 1999). Since the group of people in a "community" live in a particular area, share a common interest (water users associations, herders, and the like), and are governed by a set of norms, its members are assumed to be in the best position to identify their most pressing needs and problems.

The latter idea suggests that there are common problems that can be solved through community consensus. While this may be true, it neglects community members' differences and power relationships, the conflicts, and the diversity of interests that determine day-to-day behavior and that have an impact on the effectiveness of participatory approaches. The poor themselves are rarely a homogenous group; they live in different geographic areas and face different kinds of deprivations, and each seeks a personalized way of reducing poverty (Schneider 1999).

The shared norms that are expected to unify the community can themselves hinder community action (Western and Wright in Agarwal and Gibson 1999). Such norms may dictate patterns of behavior, such as deference to the elite, which do not allow the poorest and the marginal to effectively demonstrate their choice. Moreover, participation may lead to significant psychological and even physical duress for the most socially and economically disadvantaged, typically the prime potential beneficiaries of CDD projects, since genuine participation may require them to take positions that are contrary to the interests of more powerful groups (Mansuri and Rao 2004).

Participation starts a process of institutional change in communities. A distinction between formal and informal "rules of the game" and organizations is essential to understanding this change process. Many crucial decisions in a village community are made not through formal committees and groups, but through informal organizations that vary from community to community.

ANNEX B: RESULTS CHAIN FOR WORLD BANK CDD PROJECTS[1]

How are CDD interventions ***expected*** *to work in a Bank project?* Since the 1992 Wapenhans report, the World Bank has tried to increase the results focus of its operations to track the progress of Bank interventions, including CDD. The relationship among Bank inputs, outputs, expected outcomes, and impacts of CDD operations are shown in figure B.1. The arrows indicate the direction of the results-based chain that links inputs to impacts through outputs and outcomes.

Within this framework, the principal *impact* of a CDD approach is expected to be sustained development and positive impact on the lives of the poor. Underlying this is a hypothesis that empowered communities (outcome) can participate in decision making, create and implement their own development plans, and hold ac-

Figure B.1: The Results Chain in a Bank-Supported CDD Intervention

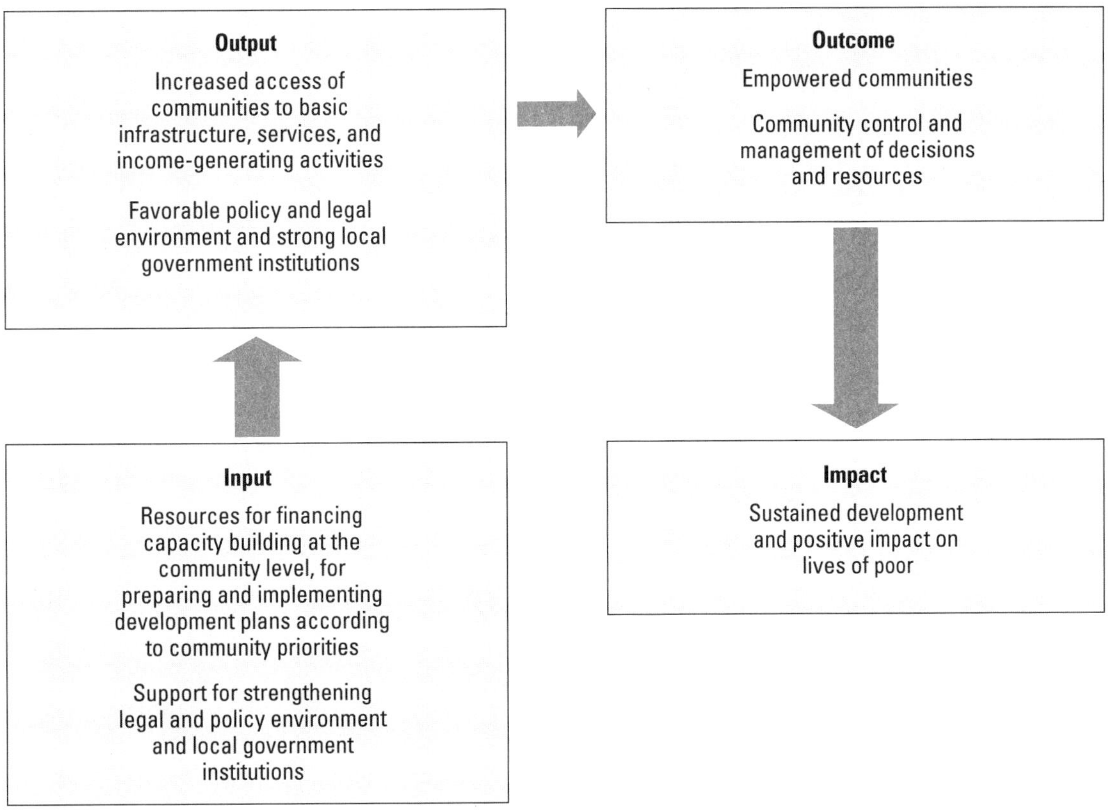

countable the institutions that affect their lives. This is expected to allow for improved effectiveness and targeting of development interventions, which in turn is expected to promote sustainable development. However, this can happen only if benefits are not captured by the elite and donor support is available over a defined period to allow elements of sustainability to be built. The major *outputs* would be increased access of communities to basic infrastructure and services and income-generating activities, a favorable policy and legal environment, and stronger local government institutions. Bank interventions—through resources for financing capacity-enhancing efforts at the community level, resources for preparation and implementation of development plans, support to the country for improving the legal and policy environment and for strengthening local government institutions are the *inputs*.

ANNEX C: WORLD BANK GUIDANCE ON KEY DESIGN PRINCIPLES FOR CDD

The CDD Anchor has identified 10 principles to guide policy formulation and program design to enhance the effectiveness and sustainability of support to CDD.[1]

1. Establish an enabling environment through relevant institutional and policy reform. CDD involves more than strengthening community-based organizations (CBOs) and funding their projects—it also requires active measures to establish an appropriate enabling environment. Large programs of support to CDD will not be sustainable without the policies, laws, systems, and governance processes that encourage effective collaboration among local governments, central governments, civil society, service providers, and CBOs. Specifically, such an environment should include: (a) elected local governments that are responsive to constituents and are empowered to serve them; (b) intergovernmental arrangements for fiscal flows to local governments and CBOs; (c) a conducive legal and regulatory framework that supports community action; and (d) clear sector policies with well-defined financing rules and defined roles and responsibilities of key players in each sector.

2. Make investments responsive to informed demand. Enabling communities to be involved in decision making is not sufficient to achieve sustainable outcomes. Decisions need to be based on accurate information about the costs and benefits of various options, and communities need to have some of their own resources invested.

- Informed, meaningful choice. Communities and stakeholders should have access to sufficient information to weigh tradeoffs and make realistic choices from a range of options that meet their needs and fit local conditions, culture, values, and available operation and maintenance capacity.
- Community contributions to investment and recurrent costs. Community co-financing has been shown to be an important factor in building ownership and in helping to ensure that appropriate choices are made and that investments are sustainable. People seem to make better choices when they have their own resources at stake and when opting for a more expensive option implies a proportionally higher cost.

3. Build participatory mechanisms for community control and stakeholder involvement. Communities that have ownership of a project or program are more likely to sustain outcomes. This implies providing inclusive community groups with knowledge, control, and authority over decisions and resources throughout all phases from program inception. Programs should be designed to engage relevant stakeholders (government, local leaders, NGOs, civil society, the community) at the earliest opportunity and dynamically over time. Political will—garnered through broad-based support and/or "political champions" to drive necessary reforms—have played critical roles in the scaling up of many existing CDD programs. Broad stakeholder participation helps tap into local technical and financial resources in support of community initiatives. It also ensures that local knowledge and preferences are incorporated into the project design.

4. Ensure social and gender inclusion. Community-driven development has the potential to increase the power of poor communities to negotiate with government, the private sector, and civil society. But to fulfill this potential, CDD needs to be responsive to the priorities of all poor groups. Communities are not homogeneous; thus CDD needs to be designed to be socially inclusive, giving voice and decision-making responsibility to women, the elderly, youth, religious and cultural minorities, indigenous and other ethnic groups, those with HIV/AIDS, and the disabled. When community-driven development does not pay attention to issues of social inclusion, groups of poor people may be excluded, investment choices may not reflect the true needs of the poor, and impacts may be significantly compromised.

5. Invest in capacity-building of CBOs. The lasting impact of CDD programs depends on the capacity of CBOs to provide services and goods on a sustainable basis, often in partnership with responsive formal institutions. Capacity building of CBOs, and strengthening linkages with formal institutions, is a critical area for investment. The impact of CDD programs is directly related to the strength of the CBOs driving the process. Experience and studies have shown that those CBOs with clear lines of responsibility, open decision-making processes, and direct accountability to the community improve service provision, make more effective use of resources, and are more sustainable.

6. Facilitate community access to information. Support to CDD is as much about facilitating flows of information among all groups in a community as it is about facilitating flows of funds. The lack of information is often the most significant limitation on CBOs' capacity to play a part in the development enterprise—community organizations need information on market opportunities, on what support resources are available, and on how to use these resources productively and efficiently. A variety of media may be used to facilitate access to and stimulate flows of information. Information technology and the internet, adapted to community needs, are playing a growing role in this process and can dramatically accelerate local learning and connections with a wide range of opportunities.

7. Develop simple rules and strong incentives, supported by monitoring and evaluation. Experience indicates that sustainability and effectiveness of CDD is enhanced when processes are simple and transparent and when actors have strong and consistent incentives for performance. Regular monitoring and evaluation then provides the necessary information to ensure that the integrity of the system is maintained.

- **Simple rules.** Community access to resources needs to be governed by simple rules that are easy for participating communities to interpret and apply. To maintain the credibility of the system, these rules should be monitored and transparently enforced.
- **Strong performance incentives.** Key actors at all levels should be rewarded for performance through objective evaluation based on clear criteria.
- **Regular monitoring and evaluation.** Systematic monitoring and evaluation of program processes and outcomes is critical for ensuring that programs continue to grow and adapt to changing conditions.

8. Maintain flexibility in design of arrangements. Flexibility in design, often through piloting, is essential to allow systems to evolve and better adapt to local demand and capabilities. Flexible program planning and decentralized decision-making mechanisms, situated as close to the community as possible, facilitate quick response to change. For example, in Zambia, the Social Recovery Program is experimenting with more direct capacity building and integration of local governments into the project cycle. In both the Moldova and Albania Social Investment Funds, the initial pilot phase was extremely important to work out operational procedures before the program was offered nationwide. As part of this learning process, direct feedback from the community on program performance is essential.

9. Design for scaling-up. Despite the many islands of success in community-driven development, most countries still have significant opportunities for scaling up CDD. To have a material impact on macro indicators of poverty, CDD needs to take place in many communities simultaneously. It is no longer acceptable to design CDD as small, non-replicable, isolated interventions. However, the challenge of scaling up is not about bigger projects or bigger organizations, but rather about achieving sustainable results in a large number of communities. The section entitled "Scaling Up" provides more detail and links to documents and sites with more information.

10. Invest in an exit strategy. An exit strategy for external support is a critical component of all CDD interventions. A clear distinction must be made between support services that are recurrent or permanent in nature and those that are temporary. For recurrent services, sustainability requires putting in place permanent institutional and financing arrangements at a cost that can be supported over the medium- and long-term. Temporary services, such as initial intensive capacity-building support to community-based organizations, may, however, not require sustainable financing or permanent institutional structures. For such temporary services, explicit exit strategies need to be designed and implemented.

ANNEX D: STUDY FRAMEWORK, METHODS, AND INSTRUMENTS

Study Methods and Instruments

The study had four components: a Portfolio Review, country case studies, a Literature Review, and thematic studies.

Portfolio Review

The Portfolio Review was a desk study of CBD/CDD projects (and project components) supported by the Bank between fiscal 1989 and fiscal 2004. The study:

- Identified all International Bank for Reconstruction and Development (IBRD), IDA, and Special Financing CBD/CDD and non-CBD/CDD lending approved Bankwide between fiscal 1989 and fiscal 2003 using the Bank Business Warehouse database. (Annex E notes the methodology used to identify the 847 CBD/CDD projects.)
- Examined CBD/CDD-related nonlending activities—economic and sector work in each case study country, relevant participatory poverty assessments, beneficiary assessments, local-level studies of institutions, and other formal and informal sector work.
- Reviewed project documents—appraisal documents (PAD, SAR), Project Status Reports (PSRs), Aide Memoires, Implementation Completion Reports (ICRs), and Operational Manuals—for a sample of 84 CBD/CDD projects.
- Reviewed 73 CASs and 29 PRSPs and poverty sector work for a number of countries covered by the sample of 84 projects. (See Annex H for details.)
- Reviewed six recent CDD projects (one in each Bank Region) to better assess the attributes of the most current CDD projects under implementation in the Bank.[1]
- Reviewed 33 OED ICR Reviews.[2]
- Reviewed 19 OED Assessments.

Country Case Studies

The country case studies were undertaken to complement the portfolio review. The five country studies include two middle-income countries, Brazil and Egypt, and three low-income countries, Benin, Nepal, and Vietnam. The selection of case study countries was done to provide an opportunity for pairing of middle- and low-income countries. This provided a basis for comparing the performance of CBD/CDD interventions in countries where institutions are relatively more developed, where literacy levels are relatively higher, and where the policy and legal environment is stronger with countries that have less developed institutions, lower levels of literacy, and a weaker enabling environment for CBD/CDD interventions. These country case studies also provided an opportunity to gain in-depth understanding of participatory approaches supported by the Bank in client countries and to provide national perspectives from a range of stakeholders on the appropriateness of the approach to development. All five case studies—Benin, Brazil, Egypt, Nepal, and Vietnam—involved desk reviews plus visits to the country, interviews and surveys of central government officials and other international donors, and focus group sessions with NGOs. The Egypt, Nepal, and Vietnam case studies involved limited visits to relevant project sites to meet with communities and hold focus group sessions. In Benin and Brazil, extensive household-level fieldwork was undertaken in approximately 30 communities involving 1,200 household surveys, 60 focus group sessions,

Figure D.1: Study Framework

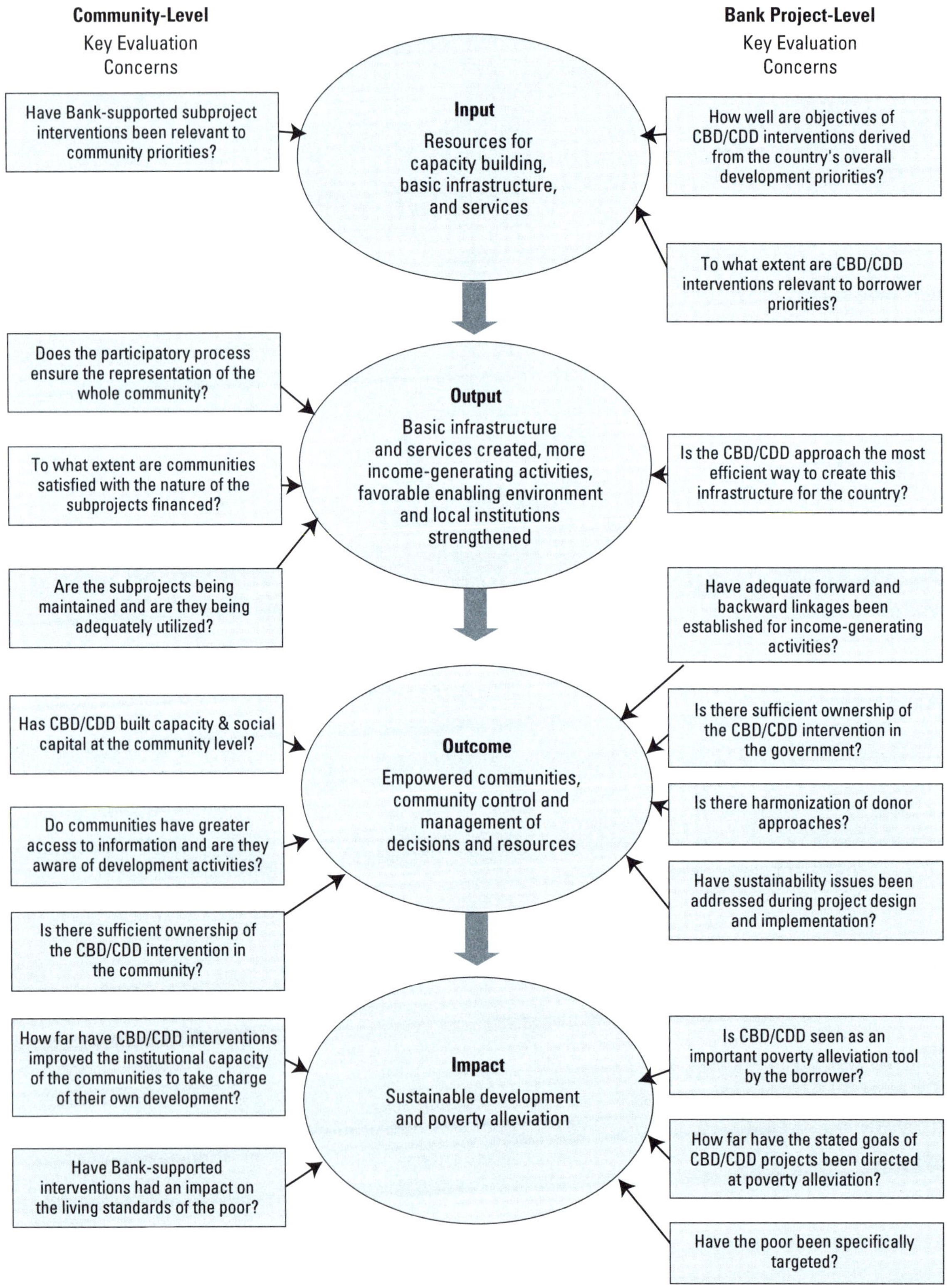

Source: From the "CDD Evaluation Design Paper": http://www.worldbank.org/oed/cbdcdd/documents/discussion_paper.pdf.

and 60 key informant interviews with local government officials. (See box 1.1 of the main report and Annex M for details.)

Similar household-level fieldwork was undertaken in two states in India—Uttar Pradesh and Madhya Pradesh. (See box 1.1 in the main report and Annex M for details.) The two projects covered were Uttar Pradesh Sodic Land Reclamation project and Madhya Pradesh Forestry.

Thematic Studies

Two thematic studies were undertaken to investigate issues that could not be adequately addressed in either the Portfolio Review or the case studies:

- The **Bank Capacity** study reviewed Bank documents and interviewed and surveyed Bank staff (152 completed surveys analyzed of 400 mailed to the relevant group of staff). Annex L presents the main results of the survey.
- The **Safeguards** study reviewed project appraisal documents, ICRs, and a limited number of supervision reports for the 84 sample projects to gather information related to safeguard compliance. Relevant safeguard literature was also reviewed, as were a limited number of OED assessments. (Annex Q).

In addition, a small number of projects from the portfolio were reviewed specifically for their fiduciary compliance. A limited number of Country Financial Accountability Assessments (CFAAs), Country Procurement Assessments (CPARs), and Internal Audit Department reports were also reviewed.

Literature Review and Associated Events on CBD/CDD around the Bank

The Literature Review had four objectives: (i) to gather qualitative, quantitative, and anecdotal evidence on participatory approaches to local development; (ii) to draw on the evidence in the literature to understand the different kinds of "participatory spaces" that the Bank's CBD/CDD interventions have fostered at the local level;[3] (iii) to explore the evidence on factors that have a bearing on the development effectiveness of CBD/CDD–type interventions; (iv) to provide a means for "testing" the validity of findings emerging from other study components, particularly case study countries and the Portfolio Review.

OED also participated in or attended brown bags, seminars, and other training events around the Bank on issues relevant to CBD/CDD and drew on relevant information disseminated at these events.

Project Assessments of Participatory Assessments

Nineteen project assessments informed the study: Uttar Pradesh Sodic Lands Reclamation Project (India); Borgou Pilot Project (Benin); Household Energy Project (Mali); Natural Resource Management Project (Mali); Eastern Anatolia Watershed Rehabilitation Project (Turkey); Matrouh Resource Management Project (Egypt); Nepal Hill Community Forestry Project; Nepal Second Forestry Project; West Bengal Forestry Project (India); Kerala Social Forestry Project (India); Ghana Agricultural Sector Investment Project; Second Village Infrastructure Project (Indonesia); Kecamatan Development Project (Indonesia), Andhra Pradesh Forestry (India), Northwest Frontier Province Community Infrastructure Project (Pakistan), Community Development Fund (Eriteria), and Rural Roads Rehabilitation and Maintenance Project (Peru), Northern Resource Management Project (Pakistan).

Review of All Relevant OED Work

All relevant Country Assistance Evaluations, Impact Evaluations, and studies were reviewed, including: *The Next Ascent: An Evaluation of the Aga Khan Rural Support Program, Pakistan; Social Funds: A Review of World Bank Experience; India's Dairy Revolution; An OED Review of Social Development in Bank Activities; Nongovernmental Organizations in Bank-Supported Projects: An OED Review;* a participation process review; *Books, Buildings, and Learning Out-*

comes: An Impact Evaluation of World Bank Support to Basic Education in Ghana, World Bank Forestry Strategy, Striking the Right Balance, and associated country studies.

Interviews with Bank Staff

Supplemental interviews were conducted with Bank staff working on CBD/CDD and related issues to get their views on various aspects of the Bank's work.

ANNEX E: THE UNIVERSE OF CBD/CDD PROJECTS AND ITS DISTRIBUTION

Universe

The universe of CBD/CDD projects was identified using a key word search on a textbase of appraisal documents (Project Appraisal Documents, or PADs, and Staff Appraisal Reports, or SARs) for all Bank projects approved between fiscal 1989 and fiscal 2003.[1] A total sampling frame of 847 projects was identified. The population of 847 (as of September 2004) includes projects that are largely CBD/CDD and others with CBD/CDD components (a complete list of the CBD/CDD portfolio as identified is available upon request). Since the portfolio was identified using a word search, it is likely that some projects with very small CBD/CDD component were missed.[2]

The total number (and commitment) of Bank projects that include a CBD/CDD component has increased substantially overtime (figure E.1).

Distribution of the CBD/CDD Portfolio

Regional. Africa had the largest number of CBD/CDD projects approved between fiscal 1989 and fiscal 2003 (266 projects, 31 percent), followed by Latin America and the Caribbean (193 projects, 23 percent). South Asia, East Asia

Figure E.1: Commitment and Number of CBD/CDD Projects Have Increased from Less than 5 Percent to 25 Percent of Bank Totals

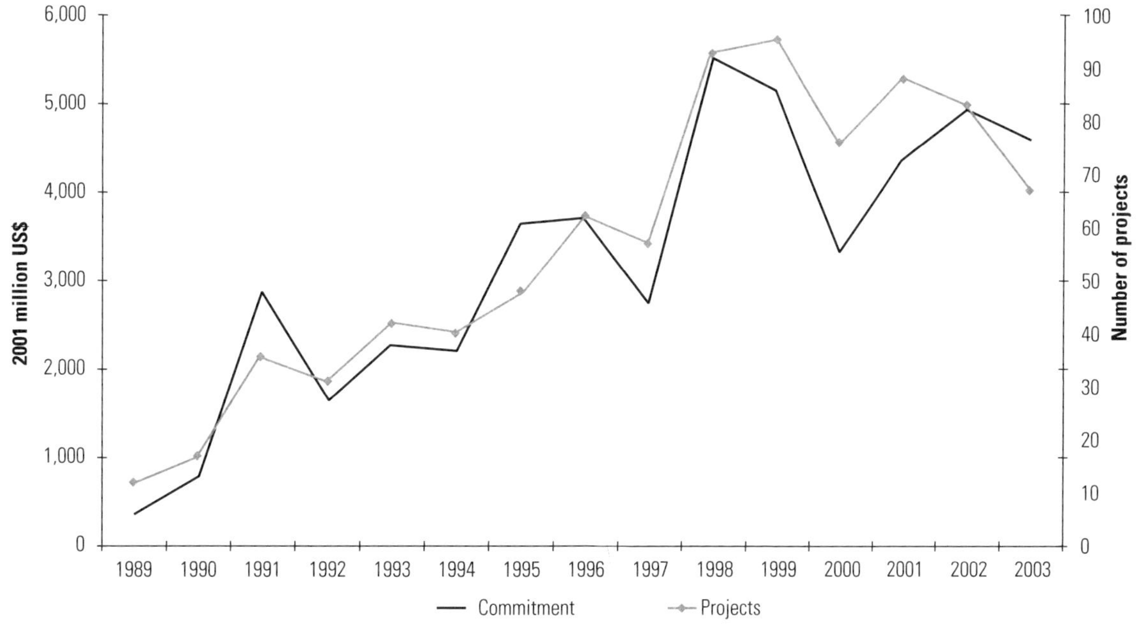

Source: World Bank data.

and the Pacific, and Europe and Central Asia had 110 projects (13 percent), 118 projects (14 percent), and 94 projects (11 percent), respectively. The Middle East and North Africa Region had the smallest portfolio with 66 projects (8 percent).

Sector Board. The Rural Development (RDV) Sector Board had the largest number of CBD/CDD projects approved between fiscal 1989 and fiscal 2003 (226 projects, 27 percent). The Health Sector Board (HE) followed with 135 projects (16 percent) over the same period. Social Protection (SP) was a close third with 131 projects (15 percent). The other important sector boards for CBD/CDD projects were Education (111 projects, 13 percent), Urban Development (61 projects, 7 percent), Water Supply And Sanitation (53 projects, 6 percent), and Environment (43 projects, 5 percent).

Table E.1: A Majority of CBD/CDD Projects Are Multisectoral (percent)

	Fiscal years			
	1989–93	1994–98	1999–2003	1989–2003
CBD/CDD	43	51	53	51
Non-CBD/CDD	28	31	33	31

Source: World Bank data and calculations.

Sector. While the sector board under which a project is categorized manages the project, each project is also assigned, at most, five subsectors. The number of projects assigned two or more sectors (multisectoral operations) has been increasing over time (table E.1). The percentage of multisectoral projects has been rising for the non-CBD/CDD portfolio as well. However, the percentage of multisectoral projects is much

Figure E.2: Distribution by Lending Instrument

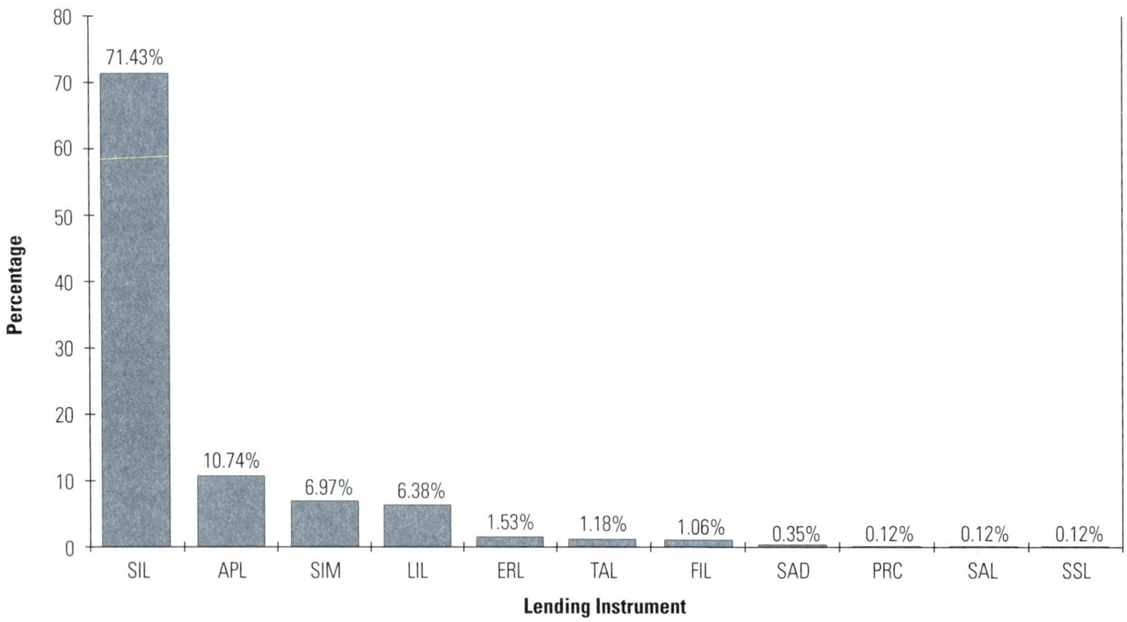

Source: World Bank data and calculations.

Note: APL=Adaptable Program Loan; ERL=Emergency Recovery Loan; FIL=Financial Intermediary Loan; LIL=Learning and Innovation Loan; PRC=Poverty Reduction Support Credit; SAD=Sector Adjustment Loan; SAL=Structural Adjustment Loan; SIM=Sector Investment and Maintenance Loan; SIL=Specific Investment Loan; SSL=Special Structural Adjustment Loan; TAL=Technical Assistance Loan.

higher for the CBD/CDD portfolio compared to the non-CBD/CDD portfolio for the period (fiscal 1989–2003).

Lending Instrument (figure E.2). Of the 847 CBD/CDD projects, 841 are investment lending. The instrument chosen for 605 Bank CBD/CDD projects was the Specific Investment Loan (SIL).

Lending instruments deemed to allow for greater flexibility, APLs and LILs, were adopted in 91 projects and 54 projects, respectively. The percentage of lending channeled through the two instruments has increased over time (the instruments were introduced in 1997). Since fiscal 1999, 32 percent of CBD/CDD projects approved have used either an APL or a LIL, compared to 13 percent of the non-CBD/CDD projects.

Income Category. The portfolio of 847 projects was distributed among 119 countries: 60 in the lower-income category, 38 in the middle-income category, and 18 in the upper-middle-income category (figure E.3A). Three countries/territories in the portfolio, Barbados, Kosovo, and West Bank, had unspecified poverty categories. Of the 847 projects, 503 were in low-income countries, 230 were in middle-income countries, 101 were in upper-middle-income countries, and 13 were in the unspecified category (figure E.3B).

Figure E.3: Distribution of the Portfolio Countries/Projects by World Development Indicator (WDI) Poverty Category

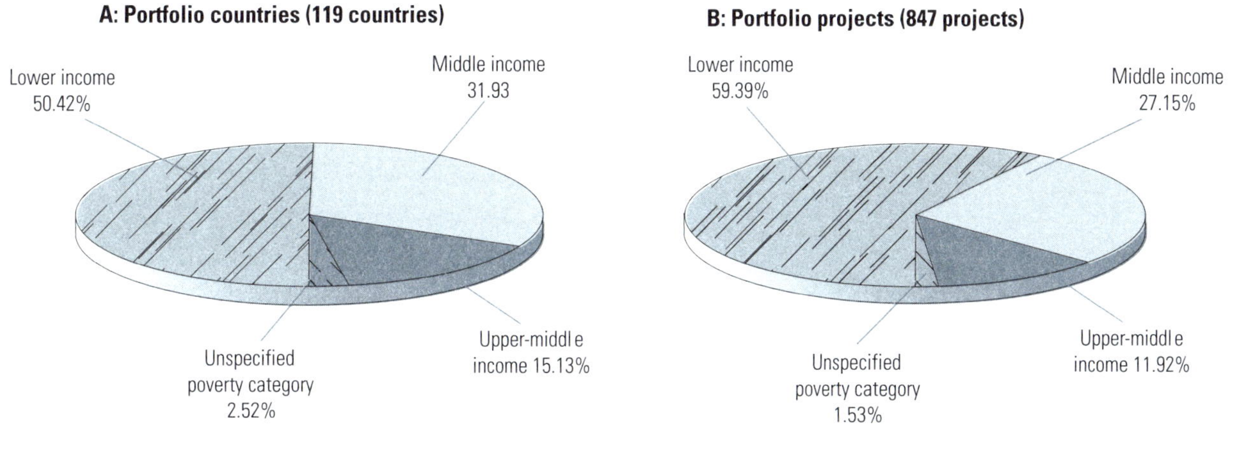

Source: World Bank data, SIMA, and calculations.

ANNEX F: SAMPLE OF CBD/CDD AND CDD PROJECTS

According to accepted sampling methodology, a 10 percent proportionate random sample of 84 projects, stratified by time and sector board, was drawn from the universe of 847 projects for intensive review. The stratification was done to ensure that important characteristics in the universe of 847 projects were adequately represented in the sample. (See table F.3 for the list of CBD/CDD sample projects.)[1]

The CDD Anchor classifies CDD projects in fiscal year 2000 and beyond into four categories that are not mutually exclusive. It was difficult to apply this classification to projects approved in the early 1990s, when the four kinds of CDD had not been identified. Hence, OED developed a simple methodology to categorize the projects into two broad groups: CBD/CDD and CDD based on percentage of project cost (box F.1).

In the sample of 84 projects, 19 (23 percent) were identified as CDD. Extrapolating this proportion to the entire universe (since the sample was randomly selected) implies that the World Bank has approved close to 192 CDD projects in the fiscal years 1989–2003 period (table F.1).

Table F.1: CBD/CDD Projects Approved by the Bank

	Sample	Universe
CBD/CDD projects	84	847
CDD projects	19	192 [= 19/84*847]

Some characteristics of the sample of CBD/CDD and CDD projects are presented in table F.2. CDD projects have grown at an annual rate of 19.6 compared with 11.7 for the CBD/CDD projects (excluding CDD). Nearly three-quarters of the CDD are multisectoral, compared to 40 percent of the CBD/CDD projects (excluding CDD). Over 80 percent of the CDD projects are under two sector boards—Social Protection and Rural Development.

Box F.1: Methodology for Identifying CDD Projects

Step 1: For each project in the sample of 84, project cost was divided among different aspects of community participation, starting from information sharing and ranging to community control over decisions and resources based on information in the World Bank appraisal documents (PAD/SARs).[a]

Step 2: All costs devoted to (i) community control over decisions and/or resources, (ii) creating an enabling environment, and (iii) capacity enhancing for the community were combined and this cost was divided by total project cost.

Step 3: A project was classified as CDD if the percentage calculated in step 2 was 85 percent or more (85 percent being an arbitrary cutoff).

a. The level of information contained in appraisal documents varies widely, so some value judgments were required. For example, if the project was participatory, but only in a consultative sense, it was designated CBD, but if it involved communities in a more holistic sense it was designated CDD. Within the latter, it was a matter of determining whether or not communities would be in charge of the funds allocated to them or if an outside group would manage their funds. Consequently, the amount of CDD in a project as classified by OED may be different from the amount reported by the CDD Anchor. However, an attempt was made to follow a clearly defined strategy.

Table F.2: Composition of the Sample

		CDD	CBD/CDD
Number of projects		19	84
Annual growth rate (%)		19.6	14.2
Percentage of projects	Multisectoral	74	48
	Sectoral (single sector)	26	44
	Sectoral (single subsector)	0	8
	Sector Board		
	Social Protection	47	18
	Rural Development	37	29
	Education	5	13
	Urban Development	5	6
	Water Supply and Sanitation	5	2
	Health, Nutrition and Population	0	18
	Transportation	0	7
	Region		
	Africa	26	32
	East Asia and the Pacific	21	17
	Europe and Central Asia	5	11
	Latin America and Caribbean	32	23
	Middle East and North Africa	0	7
	South Asia	16	11

Source: World Bank data and calculations.

The CDD operations are designed to provide communities with greater responsibility for each aspect of the subproject cycle. Based on information from the appraisal documents, the community's role in different aspects of the subproject cycle was categorized (figure 2.2 in Chapter 2). The analysis revealed that communities were responsible for subproject design in nearly all CDD projects (compared with a third in other CBD/CDD projects, excluding the CDD projects). Communities were also responsible for subproject operation and maintenance for over 75 percent of the CDD projects, and for subproject implementation, for nearly two-thirds of the CDD projects.

While the community's role in subproject M&E for CDD projects was higher than that of other CBD/CDD projects, the absolute number of projects identifying community responsibilities was low.

Table F.3: The List of 84 Projects, Their Regions and Sector Boards

Project name	Country	Project ID	Sector Board	Lending instrument	Fiscal year	Date, rev closing	Commitment ($m)
Africa Region							
Borgou Pilot	Benin	P057345	Rural Sector	LIL	1998	6/30/02	4.00
Community-Based Rural Development	Burkina Faso	P035673	Rural Sector	APL	2001	6/30/06	66.70
Urban II	Burundi	P000205	Urban Development	SIL	1989	12/31/96	21.00
SDA/Human Resources	Cameroon	P000405	Social Protection	SIL	1990		21.50
National Livestock Development	Central African Republic	P000474	Rural Sector	SIL	1995	6/30/00	16.60
Public Works and Capacity Building	Chad	P000533	Social Protection	SIL	1994	6/30/99	17.40
Third Education	Comoros	P000603	Education	SIL	1997	12/31/03	7.00
Emergency Recovery/ Community Project	Congo, Republic of	P081924	Poverty Reduction	ERL	2003	12/31/07	41.00

Table F.3: The List of 84 Projects, Their Regions and Sector Boards (continued)

Project name	Country	Project ID	Sector Board	Lending instrument	Fiscal year	Date, rev closing	Commit-ment ($m)
Pastoral Community Development	Ethiopia	P075915	Rural Sector	APL	2003	12/31/08	30.00
AG Services	Gambia, The	P000818	Rural Sector	SIL	1993	3/1/99	12.30
Secondary Schools	Ghana	P000954	Education	SIL	1991	6/30/95	14.70
National Health Development Program	Guinea-Bissau	P035688	Health, Nutrition and Population	SIL	1998	6/30/05	11.70
Sexually Transmitted Infections Project	Kenya	P001333	Health, Nutrition and Population	SIL	1995	6/30/01	40.00
Rural Transport Project	Madagascar	P073689	Transport	APL	2003	6/30/09	80.00
Urban Development Program	Mauritania	P069095	Urban Development	APL	2002	12/31/06	70.00
HIV/AIDS Response Project	Mozambique	P078053	Health, Nutrition and Population	APL	2003	12/31/08	55.00
Community Based Poverty Reduction	Nigeria	P069086	Social Protection	SIL	2001	2/28/06	60.00
Human Resources Development	Rwanda	P045091	Education	SIL	2000	6/30/06	35.00
Rural Water Supply & Sanitation	Rwanda	P045182	Water Supply and Sanitation	SIL	2000	12/31/06	20.00
Quality Education For All	Senegal	P047319	Education	APL	2000	12/31/04	50.00
Social Development Fund	Senegal	P041566	Social Protection	APL	2001	12/31/05	30.00
HIV/AIDS Prevention & Control	Senegal	P074059	Health, Nutrition and Population	APL	2002	9/30/07	30.00
Health Sector Reconstruction & Development	Sierra Leone	P074128	Health, Nutrition and Population	SIL	2003	2/28/08	20.00
Poverty & Social Costs	Uganda	P002966	Health, Nutrition and Population	SIL	1990	9/30/95	28.00
Small Towns Water	Uganda	P002957	Water Supply and Sanitation	SIL	1994	6/30/03	42.30
EMCBP	Uganda	P002978	Environment	SIL	1996	6/30/01	11.80
Pilot RDC	Zimbabwe	P045029	Urban Development	SIL	1997	6/30/00	12.30
Total number of African projects		**27**		**Total from 22 countries**			**848.30**
East Asia & Pacific Region							
Social Fund	Cambodia	P037088	Social Protection	SIL	1995	6/30/00	20.00
Shanxi Poverty Alleviation	China	P003649	Rural Sector	SIL	1996	12/31/03	100.00
Disease Prevention (Hlth7)	China	P003589	Health, Nutrition and Population	SIL	1996	6/30/04	100.00
Anning Valley Agricultural Development	China	P049665	Rural Sector	SIL	1999	12/31/04	120.00

(continued on following page)

Table F.3: The List of 84 Projects, Their Regions and Sector Boards (continued)

Project name	Country	Project ID	Sector Board	Lending instrument	Fiscal year	Date, rev closing	Commitment ($m)
Sustainable Forestry Development	China	P064729	Rural Sector	SIL	2002	8/31/09	93.90
Irrigation Subsector II	Indonesia	P003953	Rural Sector	SIL	1992	7/31/95	225.00
Third Community Health and Nutrition	Indonesia	P003914	Health, Nutrition and Population	SIL	1993	3/31/01	93.50
WSSLIC II	Indonesia	P059477	Health, Nutrition and Population	SIL	2000	6/30/09	77.40
Second Kecamatan Development Project	Indonesia	P073025	Social Development	SIL	2001	12/31/06	320.20
Community Based Resource Management	Philippines	P004595	Rural Sector	SIL	1998	6/30/06	50.00
Kalahi-CIDSS Project	Philippines	P077012	Social Development	SIL	2003	6/30/09	100.00
Agriculture Rehabilitation Project	Timor-Leste	P070533	Rural Sector	SIL	2000	3/15/03	6.80
Small Enterprises Project II	Timor-Leste	P072654	Private Sector Development	SIL	2002	12/31/06	7.50
Second Education Project	Vanuatu	P004823	Education	LIL	2001	6/30/05	3.50
Total number of East Asia and Pacific projects			**14**	**Total from 6 countries**			**1,317.80**
Europe & Central Asia Region							
Natural Resource Management	Armenia	P057847	Rural Sector	SIL	2002	7/31/08	8.30
Highway	Azerbaijan	P040716	Transport	SIL	2001	6/30/05	40.00
Farmer Support Services	Croatia	P008335	Rural Sector	SIL	1996	12/31/02	17.00
Social Safety Net	Kyrgyz Republic	P008515	Social Protection	SIL	1995	4/30/00	17.00
Rural Development	Poland	P058202	Rural Sector	SIL	2000	6/30/05	120.00
SDF 2 (APL 2)	Romania	P068808	Social Protection	APL	2002	8/31/06	20.00
Rural Education	Romania	P073967	Education	SIL	2003	9/15/09	60.00
Rural Infrastructure Rehabilitation	Tajikistan	P058898	Rural Sector	SIL	2000	3/31/06	20.00
Health I	Uzbekistan	P009125	Health, Nutrition and Population	SIL	1999	12/31/04	30.00
Total number of Europe and Central Asia projects			**9**	**Total from 8 countries**			**332.30**
Latin America & Caribbean Region							
Renewable Energy in Rural Markets	Argentina	P006043	Energy and Mining	SIL	1999	9/30/05	30.00
Health Sector Reform	Bolivia	P074212	Health, Nutrition and Population	APL	2001	6/30/06	35.00
Land Management 3 (Sao Paulo)	Brazil	P006474	Rural Sector	SIL	1998	12/31/05	55.00

Table F.3: The List of 84 Projects, Their Regions and Sector Boards (continued)

Project name	Country	Project ID	Sector Board	Lending instrument	Fiscal year	Date, rev closing	Commit-ment ($m)
Basic Education	Costa Rica	P006938	Education	SIL	1992	9/30/00	23.00
Provincial Health Services Project	Dominican Republic	P007015	Health, Nutrition and Population	SIM	1998	6/30/04	30.00
Reconstruction & Local Development	Guatemala	P049386	Social Protection	SIL	1999	6/30/05	30.00
Nutrition/Health	Honduras	P007392	Health, Nutrition and Population	SIL	1993	6/30/01	25.00
PROFUTURO	Honduras	P057350	Environment	SIL	1999	10/31/04	8.30
Fifth Social Investment Fund Project	Honduras	P064895	Social Protection	SIL	2001	6/30/05	60.00
On-Farm & Minor Irrigation	Mexico	P007701	Rural Sector	SIL	1994	3/31/02	200.00
Second Decentralization	Mexico	P007702	Private Sector Development	SIL	1995	6/30/00	500.00
Basic Education Development APL I	Mexico	P040199	Education	APL	1998	12/31/01	115.00
Rural Development in Marginal Areas	Mexico	P007711	Rural Sector	APL	1998	6/30/03	47.00
Rural Development in Marginal Areas II	Mexico	P057530	Rural Sector	APL	2000	6/30/05	55.00
Social Investment Fund	Nicaragua	P007786	Social Protection	SIM	1993	9/30/96	25.00
Basic Education II	Panama	P052021	Education	SIL	2001	6/30/05	35.00
Social Development Fund	Peru	P008062	Social Protection	SIM	1994	6/30/97	100.00
Second Rural Roads Project	Peru	P044601	Transport	SIM	2001	6/30/05	50.00
Caracas Slum Upgrade	Venezuela	P040174	Urban Development	SIL	1999	6/30/05	60.70
Total number of Latin America and Caribbean projects		**19**		**Total from 12 countries**		**1,484.00**	
Middle East & North Africa Region							
Social Fund II	Egypt, Arab Republic of	P043102	Social Protection	SIL	1996	6/30/01	120.00
NW Mountainous and Forest Areas Development	Tunisia	P072317	Rural Sector	SIL	2003	12/31/08	34.00
OT - Emergency Rehabilitation I	West Bank and Gaza	P034112	Transport	SIL	1994	12/31/98	30.00
Palestinian NGO Project II	West Bank and Gaza	P071040	Social Protection	SIL	2001	8/31/05	8.00
Rural Access Improvement Program	Yemen, Republic of	P070391	Transport	APL	2001	12/31/05	45.00
Taiz Municipal Development & Flood Protection	Yemen, Republic of	P070092	Urban Development	SIL	2002	12/31/05	45.20
Total number of Middle East and North Africa projects		**6**		**Total from 4 countries**			**282.20**

(continued on following page)

Table F.3: The List of 84 Projects, Their Regions and Sector Boards (continued)

Project name	Country	Project ID	Sector Board	Lending instrument	Fiscal year	Date, rev closing	Commit-ment ($m)
South Asia Region							
Social Investment Program Project	Bangladesh	P053578	Rural Sector	SIL	2003	6/30/07	18.20
Rural Access Roads	Bhutan	P059481	Transport	SIL	2000	4/30/05	11.60
Population Training (VII)	India	P009940	Health, Nutrition and Population	SIL	1990	6/30/98	96.70
Uttar Pradesh Sodic Lands Reclamation	India	P009961	Rural Sector	SIL	1993	3/31/01	54.70
Andhra Pradesh Forestry	India	P010449	Rural Sector	SIL	1994	9/30/00	77.40
Blindness Control	India	P010455	Health, Nutrition and Population	SIL	1994	6/30/02	117.80
Community School Project	Nepal	P082646	Education	LIL	2003	9/30/06	5.00
Social Action Program	Pakistan	P010456	Education	SIL	1994	12/31/97	200.00
NWFP On-Farm Water Management Project	Pakistan	P071092	Rural Sector	SIL	2001	6/30/06	21.40
Total number of South Asia projects		**9**		**Total from 5 countries**			**602.80**
Total number of projects in sample		**84**		**Total from 57 countries**			**4,867.40**

ANNEX G: OED RATINGS OF COMPLETED PROJECTS

The performance of the completed projects in the portfolio is analyzed using OED ratings for outcome, sustainability, and institutional impact.[1] Of the 3,917 projects approved between fiscal 1989 and fiscal 2003, 2,187 were inactive as of end of fiscal year 2003. To make the comparison between CBD/CDD and non-CBD/CDD projects robust, a few modifications were made that resulted in a database of 1,728 inactive projects (table G.1):

- Adjustment lendings were dropped (only 6 CBD/CDD adjustment lending projects).
- Projects exiting before 1994 were dropped (the first CBD/CDD project exited in 1994).

Table G.1: Project Sets Compared

	CBD/CDD	Non-CBD/CDD
Number of projects approved, 1989–2003	847	3,070
Number of closed projects	336	1,851
Number of closed investment projects	334	1,421
Number of closed investment projects, 1994–2003	334	1,394

Source: World Bank database.

The analysis did not attempt an annual comparison, because only 5 CBD/CDD projects exited in 1994; 9 in 1995, and 4 in 1996. Instead, the entire period from 1994 to 2003 was divided into two phases: 1994–98 (phase 1) and 1999–2003 (phase 2). Of the 334 CBD/CDD projects, 70 projects exited during phase 1 and 264 projects exited during phase 2. Of the non-CBD/CDD projects, 508 exited in phase 1 and 886 in phase 2.

Outcome Ratings for Completed Investment Projects[2]

Overall: About 74 percent of the CBD/CDD projects were rated "satisfactory" on outcome for both phase 1 and phase 2. The corresponding numbers for the non-CBD/CDD projects are 66 percent and 72 percent (figure G.1). Though the CBD/CDD portfolio outperforms the non-CBD/CDD portfolio, the difference between the ratings for fiscal years 1999–03 is statistically insignificant and the trend for non-CBD/CDD is a rising one. Outcome ratings of CBD/CDD projects have been better when they are disbursement-weighted.

This evaluation also found no evidence to support the hypothesis that the CBD/CDD projects in conflict/post-conflict countries outperform the CBD/CDD projects in non-conflict countries for the period 1999–2003 by 4 percentage points (table G.2).[3]

Regional:[4] The Africa Region has the largest CBD/CDD portfolio, but is the lowest-performing Region on outcome. While only 61 percent of the Africa CBD/CDD projects were rated satisfactory for the aggregate period 1994–2003, the Region has improved by 4 percentage points from phase 1 to phase 2 (table G.3). The Latin America and Caribbean Region, with the second-largest portfolio, is the best-performing Region on outcome. However, the percent satisfactory rating in Latin American and the Caribbean on outcome has declined by 10 percentage points for the CBD/CDD projects.[5] The

Figure G.1: Projects—the Gap in Satisfactory Outcome Ratings Between CBD/CDD and Non-CBD/CDD Projects Has Narrowed

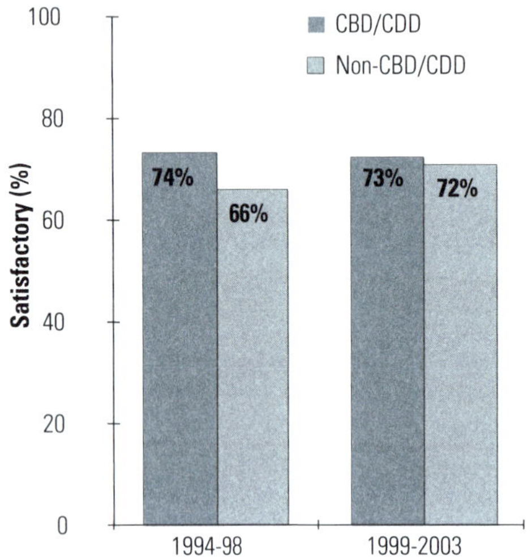

Source: World Bank database.

Note: OED ratings are based on OED reviews of ICRs, 25 percent of which are subsequently revisited through OED field assessments. The outcome ratings of the closed investment projects reveal insignificant differences between CBD/CDD and non-CBD/CDD projects in the two phases. The differences between CBD/CDD and non-CBD/CDD projects were also insignificant for each exit year between fiscal 1999 and 2003.

South Asia Region has maintained its performance over time, but that of the East Asia and Pacific Region has declined (10 percentage points).

Primary Sector: CBD/CDD projects coded under the education sector show the best performance on outcome, followed by projects under the transport, urban development, and social protection sectors. Those under the rural development sector, with the largest CBD/CDD portfolio, performed below average on outcome in aggregate, as did projects under water supply, health, and environment. The CBD/CDD projects under the rural development sector show stable performance; however, those under the social protection sector (second-largest CBD/CDD portfolio) show a marginal decline (table G.4). Projects under the education sector indicate an 11 percentage point improvement, and those under the health sector a 7 percentage point decline.[6]

The non-CBD/CDD portfolio, in aggregate for 1994–2003, performed better than the CBD/CDD portfolio for the environment, health, and transport sectors, and CBD/CDD portfolio for education, rural development, social protection, and water supply outperformed that of non-CBD/CDD portfolio for satisfactory ratings on outcome. However, the differences were not statistically significant between the two groups for any of the sectors.

Sustainability and Institutional Impact

Sustainability. While sustainability ratings have improved for both the CBD/CDD and non-CBD/CDD projects, a significantly lower percentage of CBD/CDD projects were rated "likely" or better on sustainability compared with the non-CBD/CDD portfolio (figure G.2).[7] The Regional variation is somewhat similar, as seen for the outcome ratings—the Africa Region has the smallest percentage of projects rated "likely" or better, and the Middle East and North Africa Region has the highest percentage, followed closely by Latin America and the Caribbean (table G.3). While both Africa and Latin America and the Caribbean (the two Regions with large CBD/CDD portfolios) indicate improving sustainability for CBD/CDD and non-CBD/CDD projects, the CBD/CDD projects in Africa outperform non-CBD/CDD projects in phase 2 and that of non-CBD/CDD projects outperform CBD/CDD projects in Latin America and the Caribbean.

Institutional Development Impact.[8] The percentage of projects rated "substantial" or better on institutional development (ID) impact was

Table G.2: Satisfactory Outcome Ratings Higher for Conflict/Post-Conflict Countries (1999–2003)

	CBD/CDD (%)	Non-CBD/CDD (%)
Conflict/post-conflict countries	76	69
Non-conflict countries	72	73
All countries	73	72

Source: World Bank database.

Figure G.2: Project Sustainability Has Been Consistently Lower for CBD/CDD Projects But Is Improving

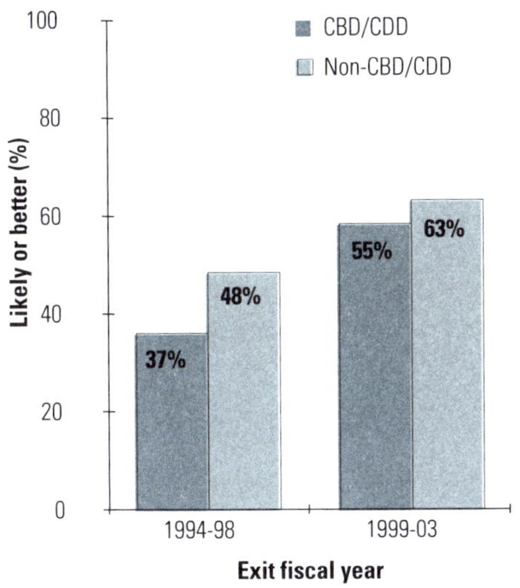

Source: World Bank database.

lower for the CBD/CDD portfolio (29 percent) than for the non-CBD/CDD portfolio (36 percent) for the exit period 1994–98. However, the difference between the two groups was negligible for the exit period 1999–2003. While the performance has improved for both groups, especially for the CBD/CDD portfolio, the percentage for both groups is still low (46 percent).

Table G.3: Regional Variations (1994–2003)

		Region						
		Africa	East Asia & Pacific	Europe & Central Asia	Latin America & Caribbean	Middle East & N. Africa	South Asia	Total
Phase 1 1994–98	Number of projects	26	9	2	21	3	9	70
	Outcome (%)	58	78	50	95	67	78	74
	Sustainability (%)	31	33	50	43	67	33	37
	Institutional development impact (%)	27	33	50	29	67	11	29
Phase 2 1999–2003	Number of projects	89	31	20	65	18	41	263
	Outcome	62	68	75	85	83	78	73
	Sustainability (%)	39	45	55	72	67	66	55
	Institutional development impact (%)	33	29	50	63	61	54	46
Total 1994–2003	Number of projects	115	40	22	86	21	50	333
	Outcome (%)	61	70	73	87	81	78	73
	Sustainability (%)	37	43	55	65	67	60	51
	Institutional development impact (%)	31	30	50	55	62	46	42

Source: World Bank database.

Table G.4: Education Projects Lead in Percentage of Projects Satisfactory on Outcome (1994–2003)

	CBD/CDD				Non-CBD/CDD			
Sector	**No. of projects**	**Phase 1 (%)**	**Phase 2 (%)**	**CBD/CDD (%)**	**No. of projects**	**Phase 1 (%)**	**Phase 2 (%)**	**Non-CBD/CDD (%)**
Education	43	80	91	88	139	85	82	83
Environment	21	0	65	62	44	60	68	66
Health	56	64	57	59	83	65	70	69
Rural development	77	69	69	69	249	61	66	63
Social protection	69	82	81	81	34	77	76	76
Transport	11	100	75	82	183	82	85	84
Urban development	27	100	79	81	76	70	61	64
Water supply	19	50	73	68	66	50	67	62
Grand total	323	74	73	73	874	69	74	72

Source: World Bank database.

ANNEX H: FOCUS ON CBD/CDD AND RELATED ASPECTS IN BANK AND BORROWER STRATEGY

The sample of 84 projects spans 57 countries. Twenty-eight of these countries had completed Poverty Reduction Strategy Papers (PRSPs) as of April 2004. All 28 PRSPs were reviewed to assess the borrower countries' focus on CBD/CDD and CDD-related aspects. The borrower country focus was compared with the CDD focus of the World Bank Country Assistance Strategy for the same country. Only CASs prepared since fiscal 1999 were considered. As a result, 26 CASs were reviewed. The relevant questions and the respective responses are presented in the table H.1. Overall, the review concluded:

- There are significant differences between CASs and PRSPs on three issues related to CBD/CDD approach: donor coordination, enabling environment, and decentralization.
- There is similarity between CASs and PRSPs on many issues, including one basic issue: over four-fifths of each are silent on community management and control of resources as a strategy for the CBD/CDD approach (figure H.1).

To assess the evolution of the focus on CBD/CDD and CDD-related aspects, 58 CASs were reviewed, 2 from each of 29 countries (17 with a PRSP, and 12 without). The selection was made based on the availability of a CAS for a country from two time periods, one from fiscal years 1994–98 and one from fiscal years

Figure H.1: Fewer Than a Fifth of CASs and PRSPs Identify Community Control over Resources

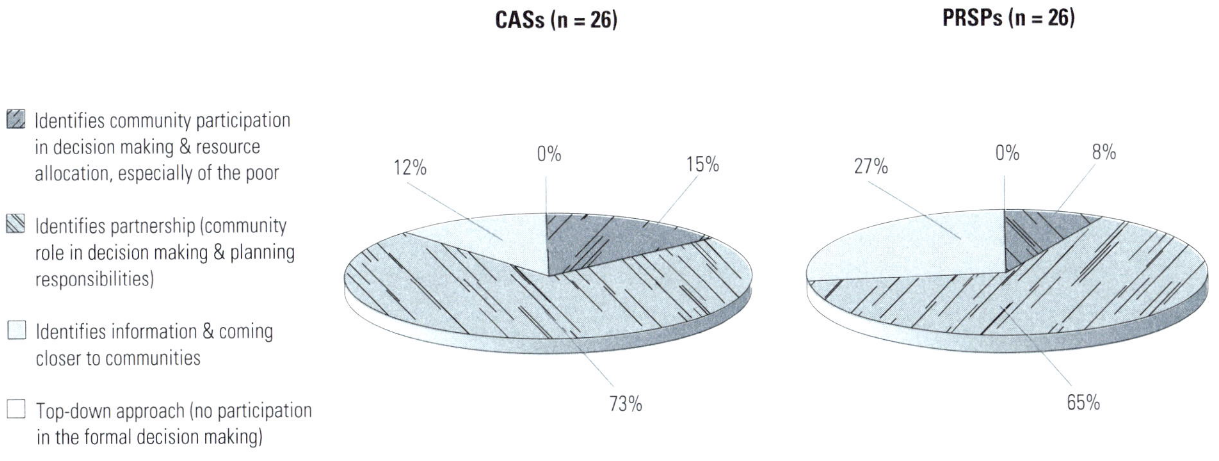

Source: Review of CASs and PRSPs.

1999–2004. The relevant questions and the respective responses are presented in table H.1. Overall, the review concluded:

- The emphasis on the CBD/CDD approach in the Bank's country-level strategy has increased over time (see figure 3.4 in main text).
- Attention has increased over time to issues related to the CBD/CDD approach: capacity enhancement, dissemination, donor coordination, enabling environment, decentralization, and monitoring and evaluation.
- The emphasis on a multisectoral approach in country strategies has changed little over time.

Table H.1: Details of the CAS and PRSP Review (percent)

Does the strategy	Options	CAS	PRSP	CAS FY99–2004	CAS FY94–98
Identify level of community participation as important for poverty alleviation?	In decision making & resource allocation, especially of the poor	15	8	21	0
	In decision making & planning responsibilities	73	65	59	66
	In information sharing & coming closer to communities	12	27	7	7
	No participation in the formal decision making	0	0	14	28
Reflect participatory approach in other economic, macro, sector work and analysis?	Reflects with examples of involvement of all stakeholders	12	12	17	7
	Reflects with examples of local government (+) involvement	46	38	41	14
	Reflects, but without explicit involvement of local government and/or grassroots	38	42	41	31
	Not reflected	4	8	0	48
Emphasize a multisectoral approach?	Yes, with open menu	4	4	3	7
	Yes, with a positive list on the menu	23	12	21	7
	Indicates community choice	31	73	24	21
	No mention of multisectoral approach	42	12	52	66
Link decentralization to participation?	Links to lending and to community participation	15	12	17	3
	Links to community participation	19	54	17	14
	Links without explicit linkage to community participation	58	31	52	31
	Decentralization not addressed as an issue	8	4	14	52
Focus on improving the dissemination of information?	Yes, with emphasis on communities	15	23	21	3
	Emphasis either on how or to who, not both	31	42	41	14
	Some indication; but not on how and to who	35	31	21	17
	No focus on dissemination of information	19	4	17	66
Focus on capacity building (CB)?	Emphasis on community & local government CB	12	4	17	0
	Emphasis on local government or community CB, not both	46	65	59	45
	Refers to capacity building	42	31	24	52
	No focus on capacity building	0	0	0	3

Table H.1: Details of the CAS and PRSP Review (percent) (continued)

Does the strategy	Options	CAS	PRSP	CAS FY99–2004	CAS FY94–98
Focus on building an enabling environment within the country for supporting projects?	Lending programs developed to support enhancing or building an enabling environment for CDD projects	8	0	7	0
	Indication on enhancing or building an enabling environment for CDD projects	27	69	17	7
	Emphasis on enhancing or building an enabling environment for supporting projects	62	27	72	86
	No focus on building an enabling environment within the country for supporting projects	4	4	3	7
Put emphasis on monitoring and evaluation (M&E) of activities?	Links lending to improving M&E and CB to carry out M&E	19	4	14	0
	Emphasis on improving M&E or M&E capacity, not both	58	69	55	21
	Refers to M&E	23	27	28	28
	No emphasis on M&E	0	0	3	52
Address donor harmonization and coordination issues to foster cooperation, and less competition (MDG 8)?	Links lending to strategies (or developing strategies) dealing with donor coordination issues	27	0	28	17
	Developing strategies/multilateral networks to deal with donor coordination issues	54	27	59	52
	Indicates donor coordination; but no explicit strategy/multilateral networks	19	58	10	24
	No explicit suggestion to address donor coordination issues	0	15	3	7
Total number		**26**	**26**	**29**	**29**

Source: Review of CASs and PRSPs.

ANNEX I: CENTRAL GOVERNMENT AND LOCAL GOVERNMENT SURVEYS

Central Government

A structured survey of government officials was conducted in four case countries—Benin, Brazil, Nepal, and Vietnam—and unstructured interviews of government officials were conducted in Egypt, to assess, among other things, the extent to which Bank-supported participatory interventions have been relevant to government and community priorities, and to what extent these interventions helped improve the institutional capacity of the government at both the central and local levels. Unstructured interviews of government officials were also conducted in Turkey in conjunction with an OED project assessment mission.

In Benin, a total of 26 interviews were conducted with different ranking officials based in Cotonou; in Nepal, 16 central government officials based in Kathmandu were interviewed; and in Brazil, 8 state government officials from Natal were interviewed (interviews with the Inter-American Institute for Cooperation in Agriculture (IICA) were not considered). In Vietnam, the Project Management Unit (PMU) director (a high-ranking official from the ministry) for each of the participatory projects was interviewed, for a total of 14 interviews. The most pertinent results for the evaluation are presented below.

The Bank's comparative advantage and expertise: Sixty percent of officials agreed that the Bank has a comparative advantage in advising government on the basis of analytical and evaluative evidence, rather than in working directly with communities. Thus, predictably, nearly 60 percent of the government officials agreed that the Bank should provide resources to the central government to carry out participatory projects rather than undertake these interventions on its own. In Benin and Brazil, about 50 percent of the officials agreed that the Bank has the expertise to build or enhance local government capacity to support participatory interventions; the percentage was much lower in Nepal (only 19 percent).

The Bank's ability in using participatory approaches to address pertinent issues: Fewer than a quarter of the officials surveyed in Nepal and Vietnam and fewer than a third in Benin perceive that the Bank can account for social and cultural factors influencing outcome, ensure sustainable flow of benefits, or ensure downward accountability to the lowest level of government using participatory approaches. In Brazil, although 75 percent of the officials think that the Bank has the ability to ensure downward accountability to the lowest level of government using participatory approaches, only one official indicated that the Bank can ensure a sustainable flow of benefits after projects finish.

The change in coordination between governmental units: A majority of officials in Brazil and Vietnam indicated increased frequency of meetings within the ministry and among ministries since the initiation of the Bank's participatory intervention. In Nepal, however, only 44 percent reported an increase in the frequency of meetings among ministries, compared with 81 percent reporting an increase in the frequency of meetings within ministries.

Responsibility for monitoring and evaluation of Bank-funded participatory projects: In Nepal and Vietnam,[1] a majority of the officials indicated that the responsibility of monitoring and evaluation of Bank-funded participatory projects rests with the central or the regional government. In Benin and Brazil, a large percentage of respondents did not pick any government level or communities to be responsible. A majority had picked others, with 11 to 13 per-

Table I.1: Government Officials Survey Results by Country (percent)

	Benin	Brazil	Nepal	Vietnam	Total
Participation leads to better outcome	65	83	63	86	73
Bank knowledge and expertise. Agree that Bank:					
Has comparative advantage in advising government on the basis of analytical and evaluative evidence rather than work directly with communities	54	63	69		60
Should provide resources to the central government to carry out participatory projects rather than undertaking them directly	50	50	69	64	58
Has the expertise to build/enhance local government capacity to support participatory interventions	50	50	19		40
Bank has substantial ability of using participatory approaches on the following aspects:					
Account for social and cultural factors influencing outcome	15	50	6	14	17
Ensure sustainable flow of benefits after projects finish	23	13	13	21	19
Ensure accountability downward to lowest level of government	27	75	13	21	28
Intra-government coordination. Since the initiation of Bank participatory interventions increase in frequency of meeting:					
Within ministry		75	81	64	74
Between ministries		63	44	64	55
Level of empowerment effective and efficient for development approaches:					
Community is informed and consulted on government development plan	79		25		
Community prepares and/or implements a development plan	0		38		
Community prepares a development plan with the help of gov/NGOs	17		19		
Community has control over decisions and resources	4		19		
More than 75 percent of the communities have the ability to:					
Identify needs and prioritize them		17		21	
Manage financial resources		0		29	
Participatory approaches increase time in involving communities	80	50	81	79	71
M&E responsibility for the Bank-funded participatory projects is with:					
Central government	19	13	56	50	34
Regional government	0	13	13	36	13
Local government	4	0	0	21	6
Communities	8	0	0	7	5
NGOs	0	0	6	14	5
Do not know	12	13	6	7	9
Total number of observations	**26**	**8**	**16**	**14**	**64**

Source: Government Officials Survey.

cent reporting no knowledge of who was responsible for M&E.

Local Government Surveys

Surveys of local government officials were conducted in two countries where more intensive fieldwork was carried out. In Brazil, structured surveys were conducted with 38 local government representatives, while in Benin interviews were conducted with 24 local government representatives to assess, among other things, the extent to which Bank-supported participatory interventions have been relevant to local government and community priorities. It should be noted that because of Benin's Decentralization Program and recent elections, many of the communal representatives were relatively new to their positions.

Among the interesting findings in these surveys: local government representatives in both countries appear to be skeptical about the level of competency of their constituent communities to take charge of their own development. In Brazil, for example, only 33 percent of local government officials surveyed believed that more than 75 percent of communities have the capacity to identify and prioritize their needs; in Benin, the figure was 45 percent. It is worth noting that in Benin, 32 percent of officials said that between 0 and 50 percent of communities have this capacity; in Brazil, the figure was 30 percent, with a full 16.7 percent feeling that none of the communities had this capacity. (See table I.2.)

Officials in both countries also were asked what percentage of communities had the capacity to prepare a development plan. In Brazil, 47 percent said that fewer than 25 percent of communities had this capacity; 24 percent said that none of their communities had this capacity. In Benin, the numbers were similar: 27 percent said that fewer than 50 percent of communities had this capacity and 32 percent believed that fewer than 25 percent did.

Officials in both countries also were asked what percentage of communities had the capacity to implement and maintain a subproject. In Brazil, 57 percent of respondents believed that fewer than half of communities had this capacity; in Benin, the figure was closer to 67 percent.

Table I.2: Percentage of Communities That Can Identify and Prioritize Their Needs

Brazil		Benin	
Range	Percentage	Range	Percentage
Above 75%	33	Above 75%	45
50–75%	37	50–75%	18
25–50%	7	25–50%	18
Below 25%	7	Below 25%	14
None	17	None	0
Total	100	Total	100

Source: Local Government Officials Survey.

When asked how many communities had the capacity to manage the financial resources involved in a subproject, 52 percent of local officials in Brazil estimated that fewer than 25 percent of communities were capable; in Benin, 57 percent of local officials gave this same estimate.

Despite these grim assessments of community capacity by the local government representatives in Benin and Brazil, the survey respondents support the participatory process in general. When asked to what extent they felt the participatory approach should be extended, 60 percent of Brazilian government officials responded "all sectors" and 54 percent responded "all communities." A smaller proportion argued for "some" sectors and communities, and only one respondent responded "none" to either question. In Benin, results were similar: 84 percent believed that the participatory approach should be scaled up to more communities, and 75 percent believed that participatory approaches should be scaled up to all sectors.

The reasons for this dichotomy are unclear. While it may be that local governments were offering a "politically correct" answer to these questions, it is also possible that local governments are looking to either increase or maintain their involvement in local development activities and may be threatened by the notion of complete control of subproject implementation by communities.[2]

Other issues of interest that were raised during local government surveys were:

- **NGO Capacity.** Local officials in Benin were divided on whether NGOs should be involved in the implementation of participatory projects.

A common view expressed was that the quality of NGOs can sometimes be suspect, and thus there seems to be some apprehension about NGOs in general

- **Central/local government coordination.** Local officials in Benin indicated that the level of coordination has increased substantially since the onset of participatory projects in their area. However, in Brazil, only 43 percent of local officials agreed that this was the case, and 24 percent believe that coordination has actually decreased.
- **Increased time needed to involve communities.** The vast majority of local officials in Benin and Brazil agreed that involving communities in participatory development approaches requires an increase in time, which thereby indicates increased costs associated with the approach. In the case of Brazil, it is interesting to note that the response rates to this question at the central level (50 percent) are significantly lower than the response rates at the local level (80 percent). In Benin, response rates to this question between the central and local level were similar, with the 75 percent at the local level and 80 percent at the central agreeing that participatory approaches require more time.

ANNEX J: EFFICIENCY

This annex explores the costs of adopting a CBD/CDD approach to multiple actors and the benefits for poverty impact in an attempt to better understand efficiency in CBD/CDD projects. The data are limited, but CBD/CDD projects seem to cost more to design and implement for all the players, but may provide offsetting savings in infrastructure costs. Whether a sufficient enhanced poverty impact occurs to justify the extra costs incurred is not evident in the cases studied, but poverty impact is not well evaluated.

A typical project has multiple layers of operational costs. These are incurred by the Bank as lender, by the borrower (perhaps at several levels) as implementer, possibly by a contractor, and finally by the households of the community of beneficiaries. An efficient system would be one that, for a given resource transfer and project outcome, would be "least cost," with due social weighting of costs and benefits in favor of any poverty objective. Presumably the system should maximize the incentives down through the chain of actors.

There are four main categories of cost[1] that can be compared between CBD/CDD and non-CBD/CDD interventions:

- Operational costs to the Bank for appraisal and supervision
- Operational costs to the borrower for appraisal and supervision
- Unit costs of project investments, such as costs of contracted construction per kilometer of road
- Opportunity costs to beneficiaries of participation.

Benefits can be divided into primary benefits from investments, such as productivity or welfare gains, socially weighted as appropriate for poverty objectives, and secondary benefits that might arise at a later date from improved capacity. Each of the above will be reviewed in this annex.

Operational Costs to the Bank

The Bank's operational costs have been assessed by three means: (i) actual Bank operational cost data against project commitment size and by type of project—CBD/CDD or non-CBD/CDD; (ii) a staff survey to assess staff perceptions about Bank costs; and (iii) an earlier study that also used staff interviews and actual cost data.

Bank Costs Based on Data

Bank costs for projects with a CBD/CDD approach are higher than for non-CBD/CDD approaches. The Bank cost graphs in the main report (Chapter 3, figure 3.8), read in conjunction with table J.1, show, for the project universe, the lending costs up to Board approval, and the supervision costs thereafter. For the supervision costs, only the completed projects were taken, leaving 1,493 non-CBD/CDD and 374 CBD/CDD from the total of 2,361 and 839, respectively. They also show that CBD/CDD proj-

Table J.1: Mean Bank Operational Costs by Type of Lending (US$'000) for the Mean $50 to $60 Million Commitment Size

	CBD/CDD	Non-CBD/CDD
Average costs to approval	395	355
Average supervision costs	430	356
Total Bank operational costs	825	711

Source: World Bank database and calculations.

ects cost the Bank more to prepare, appraise, and supervise across the whole size range. For Bank costs up to Board approval, at the CBD/CDD project mean commitment size of $50 to $60 million (the average CBD/CDD project is a $57 million commitment), the cost of CBD/CDD is about 11 percent higher than non-CBD/CDD ($430,000 compared with $356,000, a difference of $74,000). For supervision, in the same size bracket, CBD/CDD costs the Bank about 21 percent more ($430,000 compared with $356,000 for non-CBD/CDD). The aggregate difference of operational costs, including costs before and after approval, is 16 percent for the relevant commitment size. These costs include trust funds. To look at it another way, the average non-CBD/CDD project of $100 million commitment could be prepared for about the same cost as a $65 million CBD/CDD project. The cost gap is largely sustained across project commitment sizes. But the gap in supervision costs is narrower for the smaller projects and widens with size, perhaps indicating some added challenge with scaling up of CBD/CDD.

Does the cost difference matter? An average operational cost increase of about 16 percent across the Bank as a whole would certainly be significant.

Staff Perceptions Drawn from Surveys

Staff perceive the costs of CBD/CDD to be higher. The staff survey asked questions about staff perceptions of such relative costs. In response to the statement (Survey Question 6) that implementation costs per dollar lent for CBD/CDD projects are higher than other more traditional types of projects, 41 percent of staff either agreed or strongly agreed, and 27 percent disagreed or strongly disagreed, with 31 percent either neutral or saying they did not know. This suggests that a majority of those taking a position perceived what the data show—that Bank costs are higher for CBD/CDD. In response to the related but more specific statement (Question 7) that CBD/CDD approaches across the whole project cycle, from identification to completion, take more Bank staff resources per dollar of lending than other types of investment projects, 49 percent of staff agreed or strongly agreed, with 23 percent disagreeing or strongly disagreeing. This answer is consistent with the previous answer.

The 1994 Hentschel Paper

Hentschel (1994) found higher costs for participatory projects based both on interviews with staff associated with 21 participatory operations and on data drawn from the Bank management information system. Hentschel compared a sample of 42 participatory projects between 1987 and 1994 with a Bankwide control group. But costs were compared on a per project basis, with no attempt to analyze cost per dollar lent or per dollar of total project cost. Interestingly, the paper stopped short of aggregating the two sets of budget-origin data from Bank and non-Bank, mostly trust fund, sources. This OED study has somewhat extended the analysis. Taking the total resources given in the Hentschel study from all budget sources and for all stages of the project cycle, and assuming that both the participatory and the Bankwide control group projects would be five-year projects, suggests a total of staff weeks for the full cycle of 313 for the participatory sample and 223 for the Bankwide control. Under that assumption, the costs would be about 40 percent higher for CBD/CDD on a per-project basis. The mean project sizes in the Hentschel sample are not given, so it is not possible to normalize for the costs per dollar lent/project size relationship.

Operational Costs to the Borrower

The evidence suggests that costs to the borrower for CBD/CDD operations are higher than for non-CBD/CDD.[2] However, the evidence is scattered and limited. It is drawn from two sources: first, surveys of borrower perceptions in four case study countries and, second, some data from Indonesia and Egypt.

About 80 percent of borrower officials who were asked in case study country surveys whether CBD/CDD projects took more staff time responded "yes" (Benin, 80 percent; Vietnam, 73 percent; Brazil [state], 50 percent; Brazil [municipal], 79 percent; and Nepal, 81 percent). The sample size by country was in the range of 7 to 15. So the perception seems to be quite strong that CBD/CDD costs more in borrower staff time.

Data from the Kecamatan Development Project (KDP) in Indonesia, being assessed by OED, suggest the following:

- At the subdistrict level, the operational costs of the Financial Management Units, which was deducted from the grants, was 5 percent of grants/loans. This proved just enough, but barely, to keep the units funded.
- In addition, $61.9 million was provided for facilitators, implementation technical assistance, and government administrative costs for a grant component of $189 million (about 33 percent). However, a modest portion of the technical assistance costs could be considered outside of the normal operational costs. Nevertheless, including the costs of Financial Management Units, the total operational cost appears to have been not less than 30 percent. This is somewhat higher than typical break-even costs of operating microfinance, which has been found to be around 25 percent globally, including cost of funds at around 7 percent, but which has often ridden on the local institutional support of other community development project expenditures.

The Indonesia KDP cost can be compared with the non-CBD/CDD Indonesia Sulawesi Agricultural Area Development Project, a more traditional project that did not perform well (although it had some elements of consultation in one component). The actual operating costs in that project added to half the consultant costs (since some were technical agriculture support) comes to about 25 percent of the total project costs, notwithstanding its much smaller size. So here there appears to be a difference of at least 5 percent, perhaps more if normalized for size.

In Egypt, drawing from the OED case study analysis, data were limited. However, operating costs as a percentage of the total project costs across 8 CBD/CDD projects lay in the range of 0.9 percent to 8.3 percent, with the modal figure around 6 percent, while for 3 non-CBD/CDD comparators, the operating costs were between 1.0 percent and 3.0 percent, with a modal figure of 2.6 percent. Although a very small sample, this suggests a difference of about 3 percent, with CBD/CDD being the more costly. However, in Egypt it is probable that a number of costs were carried by government outside the defined project funding, making a comparison with Indonesia difficult. Also in Egypt, within the Public Works Program of the Social Funds III Project, the more CBD/CDD-oriented Community Development Program component had administrative costs that, at 8 to 10 percent, were about 6 percent higher than the parallel non-CBD/CDD Public Works Program, at 2 to 4 percent.

Unit Costs of Project Investment

The evidence on the costs of construction provides a mixed picture. In four of the cases reviewed, unit costs of investment, such as village road construction costs, have fallen with participatory approaches. In no study cases have costs risen, although questions have been raised about construction *quality*, and therefore whether it is a fair comparison. In Indonesia, in both the Village Infrastructure 2 Project and the Kecamatan Development Project, the evidence suggests that costs are about 20 to 30 percent lower in community-managed infrastructure than in the same infrastructure built by previous top-down processes, often using public agency force account or poorly supervised or corrupt and colluding contractors. In Brazil, a comparison by OED of the estimated cost per beneficiary of Mossoro Municipality Pipeline with the Northeast Rural Poverty Alleviation Program showed that the investment cost of the latter was about 40 percent of the former.

In Nepal, evidence shows lower subproject unit costs from CBD/CDD projects compared with more traditional government agency projects. For example, quoted rates in person days per cubic meter of earth moved for roads and bridges in ordinary soil was 0.47 for the Rural Community Infrastructure Project and 0.70 for government projects, indicating costs that were about 50 percent higher for the conventional government project. Also, in Nepal,[3] unit costs of service delivery under community programs were found to be significantly lower than under agency programs, exhibiting in many cases over 100 percent differences. However, it is unclear how comparable the different programs were in technical difficulty.

However, OED's 2002 Social Fund Evaluation did not find any clear advantage in cost effectiveness between social funds, local government, other central agencies, and NGOs across the 27 countries studied. It found the data to be highly variable, as might be suggested by the differences between the Indonesia and Egypt data quoted above. There were problems in normalizing for quality. That study warrants being given more weight than the other cases quoted because it represents a larger sample with a comparable methodology across country cases. The study found some indication that unit costs tend to be somewhat lower where community contributions were high and/or where there was community management and contracting. Overhead expenses were found to be in the range of 7 to 14 percent of total program costs.

Opportunity Costs of Beneficiary Participation

Costs of participation are higher by definition in participatory projects; the question is at what level are the costs of participation in relation to the benefits and, at household level, the probability of benefits. No cases were found where the cost of participation had been analyzed either ex ante or ex post. Indeed, in the OED Egypt case study, it was noted that, with the many different participatory approaches being followed, an opportunity had been squandered to compare program efficiency. Given the lack of data, we draw from only one project case.

The OED PPAR for the Indonesia Kecamatan Development Project offers an example of the costs to a representative household of the meetings needed to actively participate in the economic loans component and compared it to the benefits of the group credit provided. (See box J.1.) The costs were substantial. If all meetings in the KDP project were attended, it would be possible to go to about 16.

Box J.1: Costs of Household Time in a KDP Village

In a typical village in North Lampung, Sumatra, for an active participant who took an economic loan, there were 5 decision meetings and a Verification Team meeting. Two of the decision meetings were 2 hours long and involved 1 hour of travel. Three of the meetings were 4 hours long and were farther away, taking 2 hours of travel. The Verification Team meeting was a whole day long plus 1 hour of travel (9 hours total). Thus, the total time was 33 hours, or about 4 working days. At a minimum wage in plantations in this area of Rp21,000 per day, the opportunity cost was Rp84,000. The total time from initiation of the discussions to receipt of grants/loans was 1 year and 4 months. Thus, for an average economic loan size of Rp350,000, this person was spending about 25 percent of the value of the economic loan in meetings, with that investment not paying off in terms of receipt of the money for over a year. However, there is also a probability factor. Since KDP funding was competitive, there was a significant chance of not receiving benefits at all. In this kecamatan, 18 of 42 KDP proposals were accepted in the year in question. Thus, the probability of not getting any reward in this case was about 0.4. Applied to the economic loan size (Rp350,000 * 0.4 = 140,000), this suggests an opportunity cost in terms of time of about 60 percent of the loan size (Rp84,000/Rp140,000). However, there would be other gains on the positive side. Some of the time given would have gained respect and position in the community. Some may have contributed to other infrastructure benefits relevant to the participant's hamlet. Also, there was a probability of not having to repay the loan at all. (In this particular village loan repayments were mostly between 80 and 100 percent, well above the project average.) However, it is concluded that, overall, the costs of full participation were substantial. This probably worked against the full participation of the poorer households who could least afford to give time at the risk of no benefits. While the case given here is a composite individual case, a village-level calculation, assuming the levels of attendance at meetings reported and the types of meetings, generally supports the estimate presented.

Benefits

The primary benefit expected from a CBD/CDD intervention would be its impact on poverty in the broadest sense, which would call for estimating the benefits reaching the lower quintiles and might also place some social weighting on those benefits. Here we explore two types of evidence, the evidence on poverty impact and, more broadly, the project outcome data relative to costs to assess the development efficacy of CBD/CDD projects relative to non-CBD/CDD which, among other things, accommodates the different project objectives.

With respect to poverty, in the four study cases where household surveys were done[4] (Benin, Brazil, and Madhya Pradesh and Uttar Pradesh in India), the impact on the poorest CBD/CDD quintile over the non-CBD/CDD quintile on consumption and expenditure was small. It was statistically insignificant in all cases, except for consumption (but not expenditure) in the Madhya Pradesh case.

With respect to Bank project outcome performance, CBD/CDD has a slight edge over non-CBD/CDD, but only 74 percent satisfactory or better compared with 72 percent (from 1989 to 2003)—not a large difference. Moreover, in recent years CBD/CDD has not improved performance as much as non-CBD/CDD, which has been closing rapidly. This perhaps suggests that the Bank has learned more about how best to design and implement non-CBD/CDD than CBD/CDD. However, it is probably also a function of the fact that CBD/CDD performance was closer to a reasonable ceiling of expectation.

The Net Effect of All Cost Differences between CBD/CDD and Non-CBD/CDD

Costs

The above data are indicative of costs at different levels in the system. What the data appear to show is the following:

- Costs to the Bank are about 16 percent higher for CBD/CDD. Given the large sample, this is a fairly robust figure. Bank operational costs themselves are small compared with those of government or communities. Nevertheless, the extra cost to the Bank is significant: an overall 16 percent increase in Bank costs for the same output across the whole Bank program would be substantial.
- Costs to the borrower at the government level are *perceived* to be higher by most officials, but it has not been possible to find comparable actual cost data. Approximate costs are known in some individual cases, although there are questions about cost categories. They seem to support the perception of higher CBD/CDD operational costs to government, but the sample is very small.
- Costs of construction of subprojects appear to be lower, perhaps typically around 20 percent lower, although there are cases (Nepal) where cost savings are claimed to be much greater than 20 percent, and recent data from Indonesia are showing savings of over 50 percent in some cases compared with government-managed contracts. There is some question about the robustness of the data in some countries.[5]
- Opportunity costs to the beneficiary of time given both for consultation and implementation appear to be significantly higher, in some cases as high as 10 to 20 percent of the investment resources provided to the household, but again the data are very limited.[6]

Based on the above, the reduced unit costs of investment would need to be substantial, perhaps as much as 30 percent, to cover the extra consultation and management costs, or, alternatively, benefits in terms of poverty impact would need to be high. But this conclusion would be different, particularly if operational costs to government are not actually as high as surveyed officials seem to suggest.

Benefits

CBD/CDD projects do not significantly outshine non-CBD/CDD in outcome performance and, so far, there is limited evidence of significant poverty reduction differences. With respect to the outcome rating, CBD/CDD projects were rated satisfactory in 74 percent of cases over the period 1989–2003, compared with 72 percent for non-CBD/CDD. Thus, CBD/CDD has performed marginally better. But this does not offer a decisive outcome performance edge. Moreover, as noted, the performance trend for non-CBD/CDD has gained steadily, while CBD/CDD has remained almost static.

With respect to poverty impact, the case studies and surveys found little evidence that CBD/CDD projects have realized significant poverty impact gains, despite their poverty objectives. As found in the OED Egypt Matrouh Resource Management Project, this is partly because many investments are land-related, so that benefits are almost bound to reflect the existing inequity of land ownership. Although in the Matrouh case OED believed that, because water cisterns were targeted to the poor, there had been some reduction in the level of regressiveness due to the project. In the Turkey Eastern Anatolia Watersheds Management Project, some of the poorer herders, who were not closely linked to the decision communities, appeared to have been losers rather than gainers due to grazing land closure. On the related issue of gender, while there is evidence of some progress, there is still far to go, especially in very conservative situations such as the Egypt Matrouh Project.

CBD/CDD projects only perform 2 percentage points better than non-CBD/CDD on the institutional development (ID) rating (44 percent versus 42 percent). This is a very small difference, and the rating is still low in absolute terms. This is important in assessing CBD/CDD participatory performance, since the performance of community processes is a significant element of the overall ID performance rating. In other words, substantial gains in participatory processes at the community level should partly show up in gains in ID rating.

As noted earlier, secondary benefits to CBD/CDD may be relevant here as well as secondary costs. On the benefits side, there may be improved efficiency in consultative processes with payoffs outside the project. On the costs side, there may be costs such as the cost of diverting an NGO from a more important task to one that is less important, but more immediately rewarding. However, non-CBD/CDD projects that mostly seem to be focused more on growth than equity may have substantial poverty impacts through growth.

Lack of Data

The many data and analysis gaps in the efficiency story need to be filled, particularly regarding borrower costs. Indeed, in the Egypt case study, as noted above, OED pointed out a missed opportunity to compare poverty impact efficiency across a range of Bank-funded project approaches, from the very intensive CBD/CDD approaches to the less-intensive social fund approaches.

ANNEX K: NKAYI DISTRICT FORMAL AND INFORMAL SYSTEMS

The Formal System

In Nkayi District, western Zimbabwe, water is supposedly managed at the community level through formal waterpoint committees, usually made up of three women (representing users) and one man (representing authority). The committee is technically a subcommittee of the village development committee, and is part of a tiered maintenance system involving structures at the ward and district levels. The system is based on the concept of establishing one committee for each waterpoint, representing the users of that point, and great emphasis is placed in training on encouraging a sense of "ownership" for the waterpoint. Training also emphasizes the requirement that committee members are elected, that meetings are held regularly, and that proper minutes are taken. The committee is expected to undertake routine preventive and minor corrective maintenance, and to guide the community in agreeing rules or bylaws relating to the waterpoint. Models of such bylaws are given at training sessions. This formal management system is based on the assumption that people will use and manage one water source only, and that there is a need to restrict irresponsible use of the water source. But research in Nkayi District has uncovered local practices of water use and decision making that are contrary to the formal system as manifested through committee structures.

Local Principles

Many local principles of water use and management are not explicit rules or regulations, but rather customs and conventions, or what people suggest is the "right way of doing things." These often predate (by many decades) the establishment of waterpoint committees.

Open access and the use of multiple water sources: People prefer to maintain access to a number of different water sources over a wide area, not just to the local one that they "own." This is partly because certain sources are preferred for particular purposes. It is also for "insurance" reasons, because if one source dries up, breaks down, or access to it is restricted, the users want to be sure of being able to draw water elsewhere. The Nkayi people believe strongly that everyone should have access to water sources to secure at least the minimum necessary for survival. But such universal access becomes increasingly disputed during dry months. As water sources diminish, some users (often committee members) try to conserve the remaining supplies by restricting access to community members in the immediate vicinity and to those who have participated in implementation. Such action is reinforced in many cases by "ownership" messages introduced by project mobilization and implementation activities.

Scarcity, conventions: People in Nkayi use very small quantities of water for domestic purposes (estimated at a maximum of 8 to 10 liters per person per day in the dry season—a desirable amount would be 15 to 20 1/p/d). Even when water is relatively plentiful (for example, at a fast-flowing borehole), people do not increase the amount they use substantially. There are two likely reasons for this: first, the deeply rooted fear of drought and the perception of water as a scarce resource means that people habitually employ practices that are water conserving. Secondly, water use is partly determined by who and how many in the family can collect water—those households with lots of small children and only one adult to carry water use relatively small quantities.

Water-use preferences: The Nkayi men and women have markedly different priorities where water use is concerned—men want to ensure that they can water their cattle, while women are more preoccupied with having enough water for drinking, washing, and cleaning.

Ownership equals access? As people use multiple water sources over a wide area, the administrative boundaries through which water is managed are not necessarily appropriate. The waterpoint committees are largely established on the basis of village boundaries and are ineffective in area wide resource management, as they have no remit outside their own restricted area. This is the case even if people of that community depend on "external" sources of water (a distant borehole or a dam) for their livelihoods. Attempts to introduce greater "ownership" of new water supplies may result in restricting access. It is generally the poorer households and families living on the outskirts that suffer from such restricted access. So, under such ownership policies, improved management of the waterpoint can on occasion be achieved at the expense of equity. People's preferences regarding different sources of water are complex and their choice of waterpoint not attributable to single factors such as cleanliness or time. Additionally, people do not generally use water sources irresponsibly as their proper use is defined by custom and practice. Project mobilization needs to take account of such complexities and to recognize local cultures of water use.

Decision making: Committees are not necessarily the Nkayi villagers' preferred way of conducting local business. In fact, most decisions of importance (such as restricting access to the water source, or rationing the amount of water available, or deciding to make cash contributions for maintenance), are made at "meetings of the people" nominally held under the auspices of the village development committee. A number of decision-making principles are apparent at community level. The villagers believe that everyone potentially affected by a decision should be present when it is made; therefore meetings of all available adults in the community are held to discuss issues of water-resource management (and other related issues, such as grazing). Wherever possible the use and regulation of local resources is conducted both through informal decision-making and through adhering to custom and practice. Meetings are only held when a problem arises and action taken only when absolutely necessary. Many of the resource use management and decision making arrangements are strongly influenced by the desire to avoid conflict between neighbors.

Source: From Cleaver 1998 (also cited in Kumar 2003).

ANNEX L: RESULTS OF BANK STAFF SURVEY

A survey was conducted to seek the perceptions of selected Bank staff and managers on such issues as CBD/CDD project performance, incentives, process, and resources. A total of 400 surveys were electronically mailed to a select but varied set of staff. The response rate was 38 percent. The following analysis is based on the 152 completed surveys received by OED by the specified date (tables L.1 to L.4). Both response rate and multivariate analysis were conducted. The most pertinent results for the CBD/CDD evaluation are presented below.

Targeting: Fifty-two percent of the respondents indicated that they agree with the statement that the Bank-supported CBD/CDD projects are generally sufficiently targeted at the poorest, 16 percent disagreed with the statement, and 20 percent neither agreed nor disagreed.

Bank strategy, processes, and products: The Bank is increasingly decentralizing its operations to field level. Thirty-nine percent of the respondents were satisfied with the impact of Bank decentralization on the efficacy of Bank support for CBD/CDD projects. However, only 27 percent of the respondents were satisfied with guidance and support from either the management in the region over the project cycle, or the relevant thematic groups, or the Social An-

Figure L.1: Fewer Than a Third of the Respondents Are Satisfied with the Bank's Support and Guidance

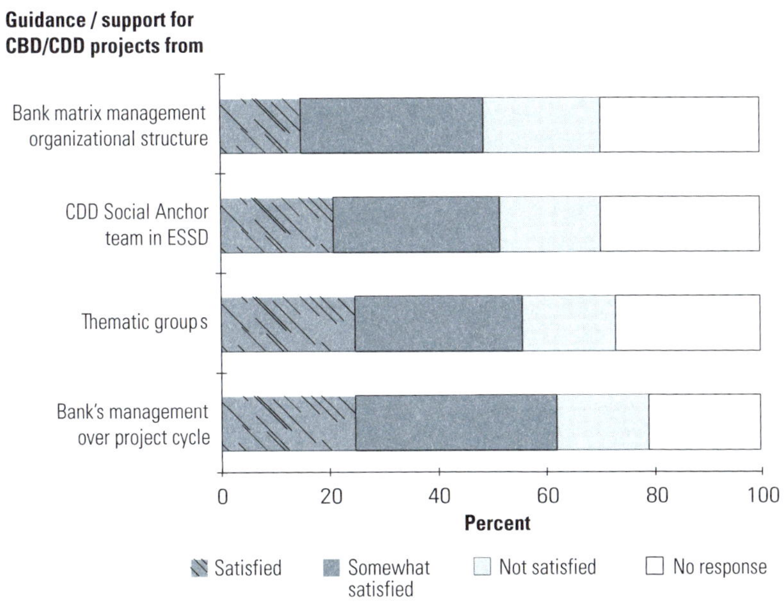

Source: Bank staff survey.

chor team in ESSD, or the matrix-management organizational structure for the needs of CBD/CDD projects (figure L.1). Only 9 percent were satisfied with coordination within the Bank across sectors.[1] There were no significant variations in the response to the above queries by respondent profession/specialty or association with CBD/CDD projects (table L.5).

Cost of doing business: Thirty-nine percent of the respondents agreed that implementation costs per dollar lent for CBD/CDD projects are higher than for more traditional projects (26 percent of the respondents disagreed, and 13 percent neither agreed nor disagreed).[2] Also, only about a quarter agreed that sufficient resources were made available to effectively appraise and implement CBD/CDD projects or address safeguard issues.[3] Despite the lack of resources to effectively implement participatory projects, 35 percent indicated that the Bank has scaled up the project in over 60 percent of the projects.

Sustainability: Only 18 percent of the respondents indicated that they agree with the statement that community maintenance contributions are sufficient to sustain infrastructure investment for Bank-funded CBD/CDD projects. Further, only about a quarter agreed with the statement that the Bank generally contributes funding for CBD/CDD projects long enough to reach a satisfactory level of sustainability of community processes.

Knowledge and skills: Nearly a quarter of the respondents disagreed with the statement that task managers of CBD/CDD projects could monitor fiscal accountability as satisfactorily as in more traditional projects; 36 percent agreed, and 28 percent were neutral. Less than a fifth of the respondents were satisfied with the quantity and quality of training on CBD/CDD over the past 2 years.

Coordination with other players: About a fourth of the respondents indicated that another agency collaboration (NGO or bilateral donor) significantly enhances the quality of the CBD/CDD project in over 60 percent of the projects. Thirty-nine percent of the respondents also agreed with the statement that inadequate donor coordination in a cofinanced project is likely to have a greater negative impact on outcomes in a CBD/CDD project than in a more traditional project (18 percent disagreed and 22 percent neither agreed nor disagreed).[4]

Comparative advantage: Thirty-eight percent of the respondents disagreed that bilateral donors' interventions generally achieve a better CBD/CDD outcome than Bank interventions. Thirty-one percent also disagreed that NGO-supported interventions generally achieve a better CBD/CDD outcome than Bank interventions.[5] Forty-four percent of the respondents indicated that they agree with the statement that the Bank has a comparative advantage over bilaterals to achieve development impact in CBD/CDD interventions; 13 percent disagreed with the statement, and 27 percent neither agreed nor disagreed.

Table L.1: Response Rates for Bank Staff Survey (percent)

	Agree or strongly agree	Neither agree nor disagree	Disagree or strongly disagree
The Bank sufficiently addresses the policy issues needed to support successful CBD/CDD interventions.	38.82	23.03	26.97
Bank CBD/CDD projects generally have been sufficiently targeted at the poorest.	51.97	19.74	16.45
Bank CBD/CDD projects have addressed sufficiently, and had been consistent with, broader institutional and fiscal decentralization.	32.89	22.37	30.26
Sufficient resources (relative to non-CBD/CDD projects) are made available by country directors to effectively appraise and implement CBD/CDD projects.	25.00	21.71	36.18
Sufficient resources are made available by country directors to effectively address safeguard issues related to CBD/CDD projects.	21.71	26.97	30.92
Implementation costs per dollar lent for CBD/CDD projects are higher than other traditional types of projects.	38.82	12.50	25.66
CBD/CDD approaches across the whole project cycle, from identification to completion, take more Bank staff resources per dollar of lending than other traditional types of investment projects.	46.71	12.50	21.71
CBD/CDD projects are more risky than traditional non-CBD/CDD projects.	24.34	21.71	44.74
Task managers of CBD/CDD projects can monitor fiscal accountability as satisfactorily as more traditional non-CBD/CDD projects.	35.53	27.63	23.03
In Bank-funded CBD/CDD projects, community maintenance contributions generally are sufficient to sustain infrastructure investments.	17.76	27.63	36.84
The Bank generally continues funding CBD/CDD projects for long enough (e.g., if necessary, into a second or third phase) to reach a satisfactory level of sustainability of community processes.	24.34	23.68	26.97
Sectoral technical standards (e.g., irrigation or curriculum design standards) in CBD/CDD operations have not been excessively compromised by CBD/CDD approach compared with traditional operations.	43.42	23.03	11.84
Bilateral donor interventions generally achieve a better CBD/CDD outcome than the Bank interventions.	10.53	25.66	38.16
NGO-supported interventions generally achieve a better CBD/CDD outcome than the Bank interventions.	26.32	24.34	30.92
Inadequate donor coordination in a co-financed project is likely to have a greater negative impact on outcomes in a CBD/CDD project than in a more traditional non-CBD/CDD project.	38.82	21.71	17.76
The Bank has a comparative advantage over bilaterals to achieve development impact in CBD/CDD interventions.	44.08	26.97	12.50
Your Region has sufficient CBD/CDD-related skills to achieve satisfactory CBD/CDD project performance.	48.68	15.79	18.42
CBD/CDD projects that use program specific committees to make investment allocation decisions, while perhaps facilitating project implementation in the short term, may often fail in the long term to significantly strengthen decentralized local institutions because they operate—parallel to, rather than integrated with, local government.	44.74	20.39	21.05

Note: Based on 152 responses.

Table L.2: Response Rates for Bank Staff Survey (percent)

	Satisfied or better	Somewhat satisfied	Not satisfied
Understanding by the management in your region of the objectives and design of CBD/CDD projects.	40.13	28.95	15.13
Guidance by the management in your Region over the project cycle on CBD/CDD projects.	26.97	35.53	16.45
Guidance for CBD/CDD work provided by the CDD Social Anchor team in ESSD.	21.05	29.61	19.74
Support for CBD/CDD work from the relevant Thematic Groups.	26.97	29.61	17.11
Support by the current Bank matrix-management organizational structure for the needs of CBD/CDD projects.	13.82	29.61	27.63
Coordination within the Bank across sectors in CBD/CDD interventions.	9.21	34.21	36.18
Coordination within government in borrowing countries for CBD/CDD interventions.	19.08	30.26	30.92
Amount of training on CBD/CDD over the last two years (including clinics, brown-bag lunches, etc. as well as longer training).	19.08	26.97	22.37
Quality of training on CBD/CDD over the last two years (including clinics, brown-bag lunches, etc., as well as longer training).	17.11	23.68	9.87
The impact of Bank decentralization to field offices on the efficacy of Bank support for CBD/CDD projects.	39.47	21.71	12.50
Emphasis placed by the Bank on donor coordination in CBD/CDD projects.	28.29	36.84	14.47
Relevance of current Bank safeguards for CBD/CDD projects.	16.45	35.53	25.66

Note: Based on 152 responses.

Table L.3: Response Rates for Bank Staff Survey (percent)

	More than 80%	60–80%	40–60%	20–40%	Less than 20%
In what percentage has the Bank committed to continuing support to community groups to the point of satisfactory sustainability of those group processes?	9.21	18.42	19.74	17.11	8.55
In what percentage have community groups and associated community processes reached to a level you would rate as "likely" for sustainability?	2.63	25.00	27.63	16.45	9.21
In what percentage has another collaborating development agency (e.g., other donor, NGO, etc.) significantly enhanced the quality of the CBD/CDD elements of design in the project?	6.58	18.42	21.05	11.84	10.53
In what percentage has the Bank scaled up the project?	10.53	24.34	19.74	5.92	9.87

Note: Based on 152 responses.

Table L.4: Response Rates for Bank Staff Survey (percent)

	1-5	6-10	11-15	16-20	20+
In your experience, what would be the average number of years needed for project support of community groups initially formed under the project to reach a level of sustainability of community processes requiring very limited outside support (such as simply a supporting/maintenance visit once a year).	23.68	51.97	11.84	0.00	0.66

Note: Based on 152 responses.

Table L.5: Multivariate Analysis for Bank Staff Survey

	Sufficient resources are made available by country directors to effectively address safeguard issues related to CBD/CDD projects	Implementation costs per dollar lent for CBD/CDD projects are higher than other traditional types of projects	NGO-supported interventions generally achieve a better CBD/CDD outcome than the Bank interventions	Inadequate donor coordination in a co-financed project is likely to have a greater impact on outcomes in a CBD/CDD than non-CBD/CDD project	Support by the current Bank matrix-management organizational structure for the needs of CBD/CDD projects	Coordination within the Bank across sectors in CBD/CDD interventions	Coordination within government in borrowing countries for CBD/CDD interventions	The impact of Bank decentralization to field offices on the efficacy of Bank support for CBD/CDD projects
	Coef.	**Coef.**	**Coef.**	**Coef.**	**Coef.**	**Coef.**	**Coef.**	**Coef.**
Dummy for Africa Region	−0.13	−0.48	−0.74 *	0.07	−0.05	−0.54	0.33	−0.05
Dummy for East Asia & Pacific Region	−0.20	−0.63	0.00	0.12	−0.27	−0.86 *	0.04	−0.12
Dummy for Europe & Central Asia Region	0.98 *	−0.96 **	−0.64	0.39	−0.18	−0.66	0.58	−0.71
Dummy for Latin America & Caribbean Region	0.21	−0.50	−0.80 *	0.51	0.18	−1.04 **	0.54	0.09
Dummy for South Asia Region	0.26	0.22	0.09	0.62	−0.15	−0.39	0.54	0.19
Dummy for CDD specialist	0.31	−0.20	−0.48	0.83	−0.02	−0.67	0.17	0.34
Dummy for economist	−0.60 *	−0.13	0.27	−0.43	0.42	0.06	0.60 *	0.06
Dummy for sectoral technical or thematic specialist	−0.27	−0.15	−0.16	−0.03	0.33	0.05	0.35	0.23
Dummy for sociologist/social anthropologist	0.03	−1.04 **	−0.20	−0.23	0.13	0.45	0.58	0.16
Dummy for manager (sector level or above)	−0.39	1.14 ***	−0.40	0.41	0.76	0.30	−0.27	0.61
Number of CDD projects with >2 weeks of participation	−0.02	−0.08 **	−0.04	−0.11 ***	−0.02	0.04	0.00	−0.02
Ratio of no. of CDD projects task managed and no. of non-CDD projects task managed in past 5 years	0.11	0.26	−0.29	−0.21	−0.09	0.44	0.39	0.12
Days of training in CDD-related topics in last 2 years	0.00	−0.01	−0.04 **	0.01	0.05 **	0.00	0.02	0.01
Observations	121.00	117.00	124.00	119.00	108.00	121.00	122.00	112.00
Pseudo R-squared	0.05	0.07	0.09	0.05	0.05	0.04	0.04	0.03
Chi2	16.42	26.17	31.80	17.69	12.24	10.67	12.50	8.52

Note: * Significant at 10%; ** significant at 5%; ***significant at 1%.

ANNEX M: METHODOLOGY FOR COMMUNITY-LEVEL DATA COLLECTION AND ANALYSIS

Different stakeholders can have different (even opposing) perspectives on the various aspects and outcomes of a project. Hence, it is important to collect information from different stakeholders to get a complete picture of alternative perspectives. Both qualitative and quantitative tools were used to collect data for this evaluation. In each of the four project areas, a total of 30 communities were selected, and roughly 40 households were interviewed per community. Two focus groups and two key informant interviews were also conducted in nearly all communities. This annex is organized in three main sections. The first one presents the methodology used for the selection of communities and households within communities for each of the four project areas. The second presents details of the survey instruments and timing of the fieldwork. The final section describes the methodology adopted for household data analysis.

Four CBD/CDD projects (three of which were CDD) were selected for extensive fieldwork at the community level: the Rural Poverty Alleviation Project (RPAP) in Rio Grande do Norte, Brazil (henceforth Brazil); the Borgou Pilot Project in Benin (henceforth Benin); the Uttar Pradesh Sodic Land Reclamation Project in India (henceforth Uttar Pradesh), and the Madhya Pradesh Forestry Project in India (henceforth Madhya Pradesh). The two projects in India were single-sector interventions, while the projects in Benin and Brazil were multisectoral. Fieldwork in Brazil covered largely water supply subprojects; while in Benin it covered largely primary schools, health facilities, and storage houses.

The community-level data collection was undertaken primarily to assess two issues: first, the association between Bank-supported CBD/CDD interventions and social capital enhancement and empowerment of communities (Annex N); second, the sustainability of project investments (Annex P). The household data was also used to assess the extent to which CBD/CDD project investments met the priority needs of beneficiary communities (figure 3.5, Chapter 3).

Sample Selection

OED's fieldwork adopted a non-experimental evaluation design that compared randomly selected CBD/CDD communities with comparator communities in the four projects using a comparison group methodology. In all four cases the comparator group exhibited similar problems or issues as the project group and had similar socioeconomic and cultural characteristics. The selected comparators varied according to project and country context. In two project areas (Benin and Brazil), the comparison group communities had benefited from similar subprojects as the CBD/CDD communities but through a non-participatory approach adopted either by the government or a religious organization. These two cases allowed the evaluation to assess whether a program that involves communities is more effective than one that does not. In another project area (Madhya Pradesh) comparator communities benefited from a similar activity (forestry) carried out through a participatory approach, but supported by the government in India. Here the evaluation assessed whether there is any difference in outcomes because of the participatory approach pursued by the Bank as compared with the participatory approach pursued by the government. Finally, in the fourth project area (Uttar Pradesh), comparison communities did not benefit from a similar activity as project communities. Here the evaluation assessed the overall outcomes of the Bank

CBD/CDD project, and not only that of its participatory approach.

Community Selection

The process of community selection varied according to the project context and is detailed below. In all four project areas, a larger sample than actually required was selected to allow for replacement of any community that was found not to satisfy the selection criteria after field verification.

Benin

In the Borgou region of Benin, the Bank financed three CBD/CDD projects in the past decade: the Borgou Regional Pilot Project (PAMR); the Social Fund Project (AgeFIB); and the Food Security Project (PILSA). While the focus of the evaluation was on PAMR (hence the focus on the Borgou region), as project documents revealed it to be a CDD project, communities that benefited from AgeFIB and PILSA were also surveyed to allow for comparison among the three projects.[1] The selection of the PAMR, AgeFIB, and PILSA communities required first of all identifying, based on the subproject records of the three projects, communities within the Borgou region that had benefited from only one of these three Bank CBD/CDD interventions.[2] The selection was further restricted to communities that (a) were located in rural areas, (b) benefited from no more than three subprojects, (c) benefited from specific type of investments. For PAMR communities, the selection was restricted to those that benefited from any of the following types of subprojects: construction of a school or other infrastructure (such as well, storage house, hangar, and the like), functional literacy, training in beekeeping, hygiene and nutrition, and provision of essential drugs. The selection of the five comparator communities was undertaken by the local expert contracted for the community-level fieldwork, based on the following three criteria: communities that: (a) did not benefit from any of the Bank CBD/CDD projects; (b) benefited from similar subprojects as the project communities; and (c) were located in rural areas. Comparator communities benefited from non-participatory projects funded by the State and various religious organizations. These communities received investments for the construction of schools (two communities), wells (two communities), and a health center (one community).

Inaccuracies in subproject records required changes to the original sample of communities as well as dropping some communities from the analysis. After verification in the field of the project status of selected communities, a few communities were replaced because they had either benefited from more than one Bank CBD/CDD project, and/or had benefited from more than three subprojects. These communities were replaced with randomly selected communities of the same project status. A few comparator communities were also replaced as they were found to have benefited from one of the three Bank CBD/CDD projects. Further, not all subprojects could be covered in the desired

Table M.1: Coverage of Fieldwork in Benin

	Participatory approaches				Top-down approaches	
	PAMR	AgeFIB	PILSA	Other donor	State-funded	Religious org.
Fieldwork coverage						
Communities	17	7	2	1	3	2
Households	736	304	85	45	118	88
Analysis coverage						
Communities	13	4	2	0	3	2
Households	566	177	85	0	118	88

proportion since it was not uncommon to arrive in a community that had, according to records, received funding for, say, a school, only to find that what was actually funded was a storehouse that had not been accurately registered in the records. The inaccuracies in subproject-level records were detected by visiting sampled communities and asking information of local leaders. However, in some cases, community leaders' recollections also proved inaccurate, as focus group sessions later revealed the presence of other Bank projects that were unknown to local leaders. Such communities, though surveyed, were dropped from the analysis. Further, one comparator community was also dropped from the analysis because it was the only one to have participated in a non-Bank CBD/CDD project. Table M.1 presents the final number of household surveys conducted and the number actually used for the analysis. Two key informant interviews and one mixed (male and female) focus group were conducted in each of the communities.

Brazil

The RPAP (and the follow-on RPRP) adopted three distinct community-driven implementation modalities; in increasing order of decentralization, these were:

- **PAC:** The Community Association (CA) submits a subproject proposal to the State Technical Unit. Using a statewide vetting process, the State Technical Unit chooses the soundest proposals, with some reference to the evenness of distribution among the various municipalities. Once approved, project funds flow directly to a bank account set up locally by the Community Association.
- **FUMAC:** A municipal council (called the FUMAC Council), with representatives of civil society and the government, is set up by the project at the municipal level. The proposals prepared by the CAs are first reviewed and ranked by the FUMAC Council, and only then submitted to the State Technical Unit. The council chooses among subproject proposals with reference to an indicative budget communicated by the State Technical Unit. Vetting by the State Technical Unit is more of a formality compared to PAC; providing the subprojects meet the required technical specifications, the State Technical Unit signs off on the proposal made by the FUMAC Council.
- **FUMAC-P:** The procedures are the same as for FUMAC, except that the FUMAC-P Council is given an annual budget, which it administers itself. The council signs agreements with the CAs, transfers project funds to them, keeps track of receipts, and monitors physical progress. It is accountable to state government auditing procedures. If one CA fails to provide the necessary receipts, disbursements to all other CAs in that municipality may be frozen, paralyzing the project process.

The selection of project communities was based on the project's monitoring and information system (MIS). To keep logistic and transport costs within the budget, fieldwork was restricted to the two regions (out of four) that had the highest number of communities where only one subproject had been financed by the RPAP—Agreste and Oeste Potiguar. The criterion of one subproject per community was chosen for two main reasons. First, 79 percent of the communities that benefited from the RPAP in Rio Grande do Norte received only one subproject. Second, we wanted to avoid comparing communities that had received only one subproject with those that had benefited from more. The selection of project communities was further restricted to those that: (a) were located in the rural areas, and (b) had benefited from one the following investments: water supply, electricity, irrigation, or small bridges.[3] The selection of project municipalities was limited to those that had at least two communities that met the above criteria. A stratified random sample of 11 project municipalities was selected, with each of the three implementation modalities being represented in proportion to the number of municipalities under each modality. A total of 24 communities were selected within these municipalities using a table of random numbers.

The selection of comparator communities required, first of all, identifying municipalities that were targeted by the RPAP and the ongoing RPRP, but that had not yet benefited from either project.[4] Drawing on the MIS data for the RPAP and ongoing RPRP (updated to October 15, 2003), six comparator municipalities were identified—three in each of the two regions. The selection of suitable comparator communities was undertaken by the local expert contracted for community-level fieldwork. Comparator communities had to satisfy four main criteria: (a) they had to have benefited from a similar service as project communities around the same time as these did; (b) they could not have benefited from a Bank-financed CBD/CDD intervention; (c) they had to be located in rural areas; and (d) they had to have more than 40 households at the time of the survey.

Inaccuracies in the project's MIS required changes to the original sample of communities, as well as dropping some communities from the analysis. Two project communities were dropped; qualitative data revealed that one had recently applied for funds under the ongoing RPRP, while the other was the only one to have benefited from a rural electrification investment. The majority of project communities used for the analysis benefited from water supply investments, while three benefited from irrigation investments and two from small bridges. Three of the six comparator communities surveyed were also dropped. The qualitative data revealed that two of them had recently applied for funds under the ongoing RPRP, while one of them was the only one in the sample to have benefited from a government water supply program that had a participatory component. All comparator communities included in the analysis benefited from a government-funded water pipeline constructed at the time when the RPAP was being implemented. None of them benefited from either the RPAP or the ongoing RPRP, while one benefited in 1994 from another Bank CBD/CDD project—the reformulated Northeast Rural Development Program (NRDP; 1993–96). This community was, however, retained for the analysis, as it did not differ from the other two comparator communities, and would therefore not bias the results.[5]

Some of the selected communities were found to have fewer than 40 households. In these cases, a census was taken and, where possible, adjacent CBD/CDD communities that received only one similar subproject were selected to make up for the missing number of respondents. Some municipalities that figured as PAC in the MIS had been "upgraded" to FUMAC under the on-going RPRP. These municipalities continued to be considered as PAC for the purpose of this evaluation only if no subproject had yet been financed through the FUMAC implementation modality. Table M.2 presents the number of household surveys conducted and the number used in the analysis.

Two key informant interviews were conducted in all except five communities, where only the community leader was interviewed. With a few exceptions, two focus group interviews were conducted in each community. In six communities only one focus group interview was carried out, and in two communities no focus group session was held.

Table M.2: Coverage of Fieldwork in Brazil

Modality	FUMAC	FUMAC-P	PAC	Non-Bank
	Fieldwork coverage			
Municipalities	5	2	3	3
Communities	15	8	4	6
Households	514	240	118	225
	Analysis coverage			
Municipalities	5	2	3	2
Communities	14	7	4	3
Households	485	211	118	117

Madhya Pradesh

Twenty project villages were randomly selected from two distinct types of forest zones under the Joint Forest Management (JFM) project in Madhya Pradesh—10 from each zone. One of the zones is characterized by dense forests (ANR), the other by degraded forests (VRDP). In order to keep logistic and transport costs within the budget, fieldwork was restricted to two districts: Betul and Bilaspur, one from the western part of the state and the other from the eastern part (now in the state of Chattisgarh). Bilaspur was chosen because it had been surveyed in March 2000 by the World Bank's Environmentally and Socially Sustainable Development (ESSD) Network. Betul was selected from a list of four districts prepared by the implementing agency based on security concerns because it had a good number of both ANR and VRDP villages. Random selection of villages within each forest zone and district was done using a table of random numbers.

The selection of comparator villages required, first, identifying areas in the districts of Betul and Bilaspur under the government-supported JFM. This strategy was very similar to that supported by the Bank. Under JFM, villagers cooperate to protect forests in exchange for a share in the usufruct and the final harvest. The selection of comparator villages from the government JFM area was undertaken by the project's implementing agency based on the following five criteria: villages that (a) were located in rural areas; (b) did not benefit from any Bank CBD/CDD intervention; (c) were within 5 kilometers of the same forest block as project villages; (d) had similar poverty levels as project villages; and (e) had between 40 and 80 households.

Inaccuracies in subproject records required changes to the original sample of communities, as well as dropping some communities from the analysis. One project village selected in the district of Betul was not found on the map of Betul by the Forest Department. This village had to be replaced by one in the same area with similar forest cover. Another village in the same district, which the records showed as government-JFM, was actually a Bank-JFM village, bringing the total number of project villages to 21. Further, qualitative data revealed that two of surveyed comparator villages did not have government-funded JFM, and were hence dropped from the final analysis. The survey data revealed that villagers did not perceive any difference between a Village Protection Committee, which is set up in degraded forest zone, and a Forest Protection Committee, which is set up in dense forest zone. Hence, data analysis was not differentiated by type of forest zone. Table M.3 presents the number of household surveys conducted and the number used in the analysis.

Two focus group interviews and two key informant interviews were conducted in each village, with the exception of one where no focus group interview was conducted.

Uttar Pradesh

In March-June 2000, the World Bank's ESSD Network surveyed 19 villages in the district of Raibareli, which had benefited from the Bank's Sodic Land Reclamation Project. In order to allow for comparison over time, fieldwork for the OED study was conducted in the same area. The ESSD survey covered villages that were treated during four of the five annual project phases (1993–98); none of the 19 villages was treated during phase II (1994–95). In order to cover all project phases, 4 of the 19 villages were replaced with randomly selected villages within Raibareli district that benefited from the project during phase II. The random selection of these four villages was based on the project's database.

The selection of comparator villages required identifying areas in Raibareli district that faced problems of sodicity of land similar to those faced by project villages prior to the Bank's intervention, but which never benefited from any sodic land reclamation activity. The 11 comparator villages were selected by the implementing agency of the Bank's Sodic Land Reclamation Project (UPBSN) from those that were in the pipeline to be treated if additional funds to address sodicity became available. UPBSN selected comparator villages based on the following three criteria: villages that (a) were located in rural areas, (b) were located in the

Table M.3: Coverage of Fieldwork in Madhya Pradesh

Type of forest	ANR	VRDP	GoMP JFM	Non-JFM
	Fieldwork coverage			
Communities	11	10	7	2
Households	414	393	261	79
	Analysis coverage			
Communities	11	10	7	—
Households	414	393	261	—

same three blocks as project villages; and (c) had similar population size as the project villages. One comparator village was dropped from the analysis, as the comparison of baseline information collected for this study revealed significant difference between this and the other villages. Table M.4 presents the number of household surveys conducted and the number used in the analysis..

Two focus group interviews and two key informant interviews were conducted in each village, with the exception of one where only one of the two key informant interviews was conducted.

Table M.4: Coverage of Fieldwork in Uttar Pradesh

	Project	Comparator
	Fieldwork coverage	
Communities	19	11
Households	757	440
	Analysis coverage	
Communities	19	10
Households	757	400

Household Selection

Wherever possible, 40 households were selected from each community. Two slightly different approaches were adopted for household selection. In communities where the team had the information on the total number of households, these were divided by the number of interviews to be conducted (40) to get an interval of R. The households were then arranged in a concentric manner on the drawing board and a random starting household was selected. Every Rth household was selected until the required number of interviews was complete. In rural dispersed communities where there was low initial knowledge of the number of households, the community was divided in 4 zones, and 10 households were covered in each zone. A similar strategy as above was adopted for each zone, but with a rough estimate from the local leader on number of households in each zone. In communities with 40 or fewer household, all households were surveyed.

Survey Instruments and Timing of Fieldwork

Information was collected at the community level using three instruments. These were all pilot tested in the field in each of the four project areas before being launched.

- First, a pre-coded household questionnaire, which was applied to one adult (25 years or older) from each randomly selected household who had resided in the community for the past eight years. The household survey enquired about respondents': (a) demographic characteristics—age, education, gender, occupation, marital status, etc; (b) household characteristics, including variables capturing economic status at the time of the survey and before subproject implementation; (c) awareness of community problems and participation in community-level project organizations; (d) perception of sustainability of project investments; and (e) perceptions of the levels of and the changes in social capital and empowerment.[6]
- Second, semi-structured focus group interviews held with two groups in each community (one all-female and one all-male) of 10–15 self-selected participants. Focus group sessions attempted to explore, among other things, the following issues: (a) the process of subproject selection, implementation, and operation; (b) communities' access to information; (c) the leadership structure within communities; (d) the levels and changes in empowerment; (e) the priority needs of the community at the time of the survey and before subproject implementation.
- Third, structured key informant interviews held with a community leader and a member of the community organization set up by the project. Key informant interviews used a structured, open-ended questionnaire. The community leader interview consisted of questions about community facilities, ethnic make-up, and the like. The interview with a member of the community organization set up by the project addressed issues of community trust, cohesion, and solidarity, as well as providing

information on the functioning of the community organization set up by project.

In Benin, fieldwork was conducted in October and November 2003 by a team headed by Roch Mongbo from the University of Abomey-Calavi. The fieldwork in Brazil was conducted between November 2003 and January 2004 by a team headed by Alberto Costa from the University for the Development of the Itajaí River Valley. In India, fieldwork was conducted in December 2003 and January 2004 by the Center for Development Economics, Delhi School of Economics. In all four project areas, an OED team member supervised fieldwork activity to ensure quality.

Methodology for Household Data Analysis

Comparison of ex-ante characteristics of project and comparator communities. Respondents' demographic and socioeconomic information before the Bank intervention were aggregated at the community level to provide a general profile of the communities covered by fieldwork. A Student t-test was performed on these aggregated variables to check whether the project and the comparator groups had the same mean. While the difficulty of getting perfect matches between the project and the comparator group must be acknowledged, an attempt was made to get as close a match as possible. As tables M.5–M.8 show, only minimal differences were found between the project and comparator groups in the four project areas. In Benin the project group reported a significantly greater number of children below the age of four than the comparator group. In Brazil, a greater number of women were interviewed in the comparator group than in the project group. In Madhya Pradesh, slightly more respondents in the comparator group reported knowing the chairman of the Farmer's Club, while the project group reported greater ability to organize self-help groups and raise resources from within the community. In Uttar Pradesh, respondents in the project group were slightly older than those in the comparator group, while more respondents in the latter than the former reported knowing local leaders and local elected officials.

Bivariate analysis was used to compare the respondents' perceptions of levels of and changes in social capital and empowerment between the project and the comparator groups. A test of proportion was performed for binary variables and the Kruskall-Wallis nonparametric test of differences for categorical variables (tables N.3–N.6).

Multivariate analysis. In order to control for differences in geographic, demographic, and socioeconomic factors between the project and the comparator groups, multivariate analysis was performed on the variables that capture respondents' perceptions of the changes in social capital and empowerment (see tables M.9–M.12 for the list of dependent and independent variables used in each country). An Ordered Probit model was chosen because the dependent variables are ordinal ranging from least to most, with most capturing greater outcome. The estimation was performed using population weights and adjusting for cluster effects.[7]

Two specifications of the same model were used; with and without interactive terms. The discussion of the overall association between the project and the dependent variables is based on the specification without interactions. The specification with interactions was used in order to explore the association between the dependent variables and the project for women, the poor, and members of project organizations.[8] The results of the specification with interactive variables are presented in full (tables N.9–N.16), while a summary of the results of the project dummies for the specification without interactions is presented in tables N.7–N.8.

As already mentioned, all dependent variables represent changes over time. It is however important to note that there are two types of change variables: (a) changes as perceived and directly reported by respondents, and (b) changes derived from respondents' assessment of the situation in two points in time—before and after subproject implementation. All dependent variables that capture changes in social capital and empowerment are of the first type, with the sole exception of the variable that capture respondents' mobilization skills in the Brazil project, which is of the second type.

The independent variables include community characteristics (such as dummy for regions, population of the community, and the like), household characteristics (such as household size and the index of economic status), and respondent characteristics (such as age, level of education, and so forth). The model used for Benin and Brazil also controls for the type of subproject financed. Household and respondent characteristics were created drawing on demographic and socioeconomic information *before* the Bank intervention as reported by respondents. The model includes two variables representing the respondent's economic status: (a) the index of economic status, and (b) a dummy variable for poor. The reason for including both (a) and (b) is that these are defined differently. While the index for economic status is an absolute figure calculated *across* all respondents, the dummy variable for poor captures the bottom quartile of economic status *within* each community. Therefore, while (a) is a measure of economic status across the entire sample, (b) represents the relatively poor households within each community.

As already mentioned above (pp. 104, 105), the studies conducted in Benin and Brazil included three types of communities that benefited from Bank-supported CBD/CDD projects. In Benin, only PAMR communities were considered as project communities; AgeFIB and PILSA communities were included to elicit differences in performance between the three CBD/CDD projects. In Brazil, the RPAP included three implementation modalities—PAC, FUMAC, and FUMAC-P. These could not be combined in one project group, as they were differently associated with some of the dependent variables.[9] For clarity of exposition, the bivariate analysis reports only the response rate of FUMAC communities, which account for 60 percent of respondents in project communities.

Table M.5: Benin: Comparison of Ex-Ante Characteristics of Project and Comparator Communities

	CBD/CDD	Comparator
Household size (member above the age of 4)	8.75	7.39
Number of children above the age of 4	3.00	2.50
Number of children below the age of 4	1.93	1.07 ***
Schooling of the respondent	0.26	0.33
Age of the respondent	42.71	45.68
Dummy for female	0.31	0.31
Knew community leaders	0.91	0.94
Knew religious leaders	0.86	0.89
Knew the mayor	0.47	0.52
Participation in traditional events	2.86	2.73
Participation in political events	2.33	2.40
Ability to raise resources from within the community	0.58	0.67
Ability to raise funds outside the community	0.38	0.33
Ability to speak freely with community leaders	0.64	0.59
Ability to express community needs to local government officials	0.50	0.55
Blue collar skills	0.46	0.51

Note: Test of significance based on Student t-test. * Significant at 10%; ** significant at 5%; ***significant at 1%.

Table M.6: Brazil: Comparison of Ex-Ante Characteristics of Project and Comparator Communities

	CBD/CDD	Comparator
Municipal Human Development Index	0.62	0.62
Score for community	0.23	0.27
Population of community	59.56	100.00
Household size	4.42	4.83
Number of children	1.56	1.78
Medium consumer durables	1.74	1.80
Large consumer durables	0.23	0.32
Large animals	4.27	1.95
Small animals	7.91	4.14
Schooling of the respondent	2.63	2.80
Dummy for female	0.43	0.71 ***
Age of the respondent	47.55	45.15
Dummy for agricultural laborer	0.56	0.38
Participation in political events	1.91	2.00
Participation in traditional events	1.94	2.05
Ability to raise resources from within the community	0.39	0.36
Ability to raise funds outside the community	0.35	0.30
Ability to speak freely with community leaders	0.50	0.35
Ability to express community needs to local government officials	0.58	0.60

Note: Test of significance based on Student t-test. * Significant at 10%; ** significant at 5%; ***significant at 1%.

Table M.7: Madhya Pradesh: Comparison of Ex-Ante Characteristics of Project and Comparator Communities

	CBD/CDD	Comparator
Population of community	117.76	127.00
Score for community	0.33	0.37
Household size	6.82	6.61
Number of children	2.84	2.99
Land owned	1.58	1.36
Small consumer durables	0.09	0.07
Medium consumer durables	0.45	0.47
Large consumer durables	0.02	0.00
Large animals	2.94	2.83
Small animals	0.71	0.40
Schooling of the respondent	0.36	0.37
Dummy for female	0.47	0.47
Age of the respondent	39.24	38.40
Knew village leader	0.59	0.47
Knew Sarpanch	0.80	0.80
Knew Farmers' Club chairperson	0.02	0.06 ***
Knew local elected officials	0.15	0.16
Knew forest staff	0.63	0.67
Participation in traditional events	3.27	3.20
Participation in non-traditional events	2.27	2.28
Ability to organize self-help groups/raise resources from within the community	0.21	0.12 ***
Ability to raise funds outside the community	0.12	0.10
Ability to express community needs to local government officials	0.37	0.39

Note: Test of significance based on Student t-test. * Significant at 10%; ** significant at 5%; ***significant at 1%.

Table M.8: Uttar Pradesh: Comparison of Ex-Ante Characteristics of Project and Comparator Communities

	CBD/CDD	Comparator
Population of community	276.89	160.50
Score for community	0.62	0.69
Household size	8.18	7.71
Number of children	3.49	3.36
Amount of land owned	81.72	68.72
Small consumer durables	0.26	0.43
Medium consumer durables	0.97	1.10
Large consumer durables	0.04	0.04
Large animals	2.42	2.19
Small animals	0.83	0.51
Schooling of respondent	0.46	0.45
Dummy for female	0.49	0.50
Age of the respondent	44.61	42.42 **
Knew local leaders	0.79	0.90 **
Knew Farmers' Club chairperson	0.01	0.01
Knew local elected officials	0.41	0.60 ***
Participation in traditional events	2.96	2.89
Participation in non-traditional events	2.24	2.10
Ability to raise funds outside the community	0.13	0.09
Ability to express community needs to local government officials	0.45	0.37
Blue collar skills	0.36	0.34

Note: Test of significance based on Student t-test. * Significant at 10%; ** significant at 5%; ***significant at 1%.

Table M.9: Definition of Variables: Benin

Dependent variable	Definition
Change in access to information	Changes in access to information regarding development activities in the community (more=3, same=2, less=1)
Change in mobilization skills	Composite variable equal to the sum of four dummy variables (1=more, 0=everything else) that capture change in the respondent's ability to (a) mobilize community efforts and resources; (b) raise funds outside the community; (c) speak freely with community leaders; (d) express the needs of the community to local government officials.
Change in ability to reach agreement	Change in the community's ability to reach an agreement (more=3, same=2, less=1)
Change in community leaders' responsiveness to community needs	Change in the extent to which community leaders and local government officials listen and respond to community needs (Listen and respond more=4, listen more=3, same=2, listen less=1).
Change in trust	Composite variable equal to the sum of four dummy variables (1=more, 0=everything else) capturing change in trust in: (a) community members, (b) community organizations, (c) local leaders, (d) government officials.
Change in associational life	Composite variable equal to the sum of two dummy variables (1=more, 0=everything else) capturing change in: (a) villagers' participation in groups and associations, (b) cooperation between groups and individuals.
Change in participation in traditional events	Change in the respondent's participation in community's traditional events (more=3, same=2, less=1)
Change in participation in political events	Change in the respondent's participation in community's political events (more=3, same=2, less=1)
Change in circle of friends	Change in the respondent's circle of friends (improved=3, same=2, deteriorated=1)
Independent variable	
PAMR	Equals one if PAMR community, zero otherwise
AgeFIB	Equals one if AgeFIB community, zero otherwise
PILSA	Equals one if PILSA community, zero otherwise
Female in PAMR	Equals one if respondent is a female from PAMR community, zero otherwise
School construction subproject	Equals 1 if school construction subproject, zero otherwise
Training subproject	Equals 1 if training subproject, zero otherwise
Difficult access to community	Equals one if community is geographically difficult to access, zero otherwise
Household size	Number of people living under the same roof
Number of children	Number of children below the age of 16
Dummy for female	Equals 1 if the respondent is a female and zero if male
Schooling	Equals one if the respondent has attended school, zero otherwise
Age	Age of the respondent
Age squared	Age squared
Number of leaders known	Number of leaders the respondent knew prior to the Bank intervention
Participation in traditional events	Frequency of participation in traditional events prior to Bank intervention
Participation in political events	Frequency of participation in political events prior to Bank intervention
Blue collar skills of the respondent	Equals 1 if the respondent was able to do blue collar activities (such as masonry, carpentry, stitching, etc.) prior to Bank intervention
Mobilization skills of the respondent	Number of skills the respondent reported to have prior to Bank intervention. Composite variable equal to the sum of four dummy variables (1=able, 0=everything else) that captures respondent's ability to (a) mobilize community efforts and resources; (b) raise funds outside the community; (c) speak freely with community leaders; (d) express the needs of the community to local government officials.

Table M.10: Definition of Variables: Brazil

Dependent variables	Definition
Change in access to information	Changes in access to information regarding development activities in issues of interest to the community (more=3, same=2, less=1)
Change in mobilization skills	Composite variable equal to the sum of four dummy variables (1=more, 0=everything else) that capture changes in the respondent's ability to (a) raise resources from within the community; (b) raise funds outside the community; (c) speak freely with community leaders; (d) express the needs of the community to local government officials. The dummies for change were derived from respondent's assessment of their skills in two points in time—before and after subproject implementation.
Change in ability to reach agreement	Change in the community's ability to reach an agreement (more=3, same=2, less=1)
Change in leaders' responsiveness	Change in community leaders' responsiveness to communities demands (more=3, same=2, less=1)
Change in trust	Composite variable equal to the sum of four dummy variables (1=more, 0=everything else) capturing change in trust in: (a) community members, (b) community associations, (c) municipal government officials, and (d) state government officials.
Change in associational life	Composite variable equal to the sum of two dummy variables (1=more, 0=everything else) capturing change in: (a) people's participation in groups, (b) cooperation between groups and individuals.
Change in participation in traditional events	Change in the respondent's participation in community's traditional events (more=3, same=2, less=1)
Change in participation in political events	Change in the respondent's participation in community's political events (more=3, same=2, less=1)
Change in circle of friends	Change in the respondent's circle of friends (improved=3, same=2, deteriorated=1)
Independent variables	**Definition**
PAC	Equals 1 if RPAP implemented through PAC modality, zero otherwise
FUMAC	Equals 1 if RPAP implemented through FUMAC modality, zero otherwise
FUMACP	Equals 1 if RPAP implemented through FUMAC-P modality, zero otherwise
Poor in PAC	Equals 1 if respondent is poor and in a PAC community, zero otherwise.
Poor in FUMAC	Equals 1 if respondent is poor and in a FUMAC community, zero otherwise.
Poor in FUMAC-P	Equals 1 if respondent is poor and in a FUMAC-P community, zero otherwise.
Irrigation subproject	Equals 1 if irrigation subproject, zero otherwise
Small bridge subproject	Equals 1 if small bridge subproject, zero otherwise
Agreste region	Equals 1 if Agreste region, and zero if Oeste region
Municipal Human Development Index	Municipal Human Development Index 2000
Score for community	Level of basic infrastructure in a community (such as primary school, basic health post, water supply system, electrification, telephone boots, etc.) prior to Bank intervention (based on village leader interview).
Economic status index	Composite variable equal to the sum of two rebased variables that capture household's ownership of the following items prior to subproject implementation: (a) large animals (horse, cow, and ox), and (b) consumer durables (car, motorcycle, bicycle, freezer, television, satellite dish)
Dummy for poor	Equals 1 if respondent is from the bottom-quartile of the distribution along the Economic Status Index in his/her community, zero otherwise
Household size	Number of people living under the same roof
Number of children	Number of children below the age of 16
Member of CA	Equals 1 if member of Community Association set up by the Bank CBD/CDD project, zero otherwise
Dummy for female	Equals 1 if respondent is a female, zero otherwise

(continued on following page)

Table M.10: Definition of Variables: Brazil (continued)

Independent variable	Definition
Schooling	Level of education attained by the respondent (5=some secondary and above, 4=completed primary, 3=some primary, 2=literate, 1=illiterate).
Agricultural laborer	Equals 1 if the respondent is an agricultural laborer, zero otherwise
Age	Age of the respondent
Age squared	Age squared
Participation in political events	Frequency of participation in political events prior to Bank intervention
Participation in traditional events	Frequency of participation in traditional events prior to Bank intervention
Mobilization skills	Number of skills the respondent reported to have prior to Bank intervention. Composite variable equal to the sum of four dummy variables (1=able, 0=everything else) that captures respondent's ability to (a) raise resources from within the community; (b) raise funds outside the community; (c) speak freely with community leaders; (d) express the needs of the community to local government officials.

Table M.11: Definition of Variables: Madhya Pradesh

Dependent variable	Definition
Change in access to information	Changes in access to information regarding issues of interest to the community (more=3, same=2, less=1)
Change in mobilization skills	Composite variable equal to the sum of three dummy variables (1=more, 0=everything else) that capture change in the respondent's ability to (a) organize self-help groups and raise resources from within the village; (b) raise resources outside the village; (c) express the needs of the village to local government officials.
Change in ability to reach agreement	Change in the community's ability to reach an agreement (more=3, same=2, less=1)
Change in community leaders' responsiveness	Change in the extent to which community leaders listen and respond to community needs (listen and respond more=4, listen more=3, same=2, listen less=1).
Change in trust	Composite variable equal to the sum of five dummy variables (1=more, 0=everything else) that capture change in respondent's trust in: (a) village members, (b) village organizations, (c) village leaders, (d) local government officials, (e) staff of the forest department (implementing agency).
Change in associational life	Composite variable equal to the sum of two dummy variables (1=more, 0=everything else) that capture change in: (a) people's participation in groups, (b) cooperation between groups and individuals.
Change in participation in traditional events	Change in the respondent's participation in community's traditional events. (more=3, same=2, less=1).
Change in participation in political events	Change in the respondent's participation in community's non-traditional events. (more=3, same=2, less=1).
Change in circle of friends	Change in the respondent's circle of friends (improved=3, same=2, deteriorated=1)
Independent variable	
Project village	Equals 1 if project village, and zero if comparator
Poor in project village	Equals 1 if respondent is poor and in a project village, zero otherwise
Betul district	Equals 1 if Betul district, and zero if Bilaspur district
Score for community	Level of basic infrastructure in a community (such as primary school, basic health post, wells, hand-pumps) and distance to the closest market prior to Bank intervention (based on village leader interview)

Table M.11: Definition of Variables: Madhya Pradesh (continued)

Independent variable	Definition
Economic status index	Composite variable equal to the sum of three rescaled variables that capture household's ownership of the following items prior to subproject implementation: (a) land (linear log), (b) large animals (horse, cow, and ox), (c) consumer durables (car, bicycle, fan, radio)
Dummy for poor	Equals 1 if respondent is from the bottom-quartile of the distribution along the Economic Status Index in his/her community, zero otherwise
Household size	Number of people living under the same roof
Number of children	Number of children below the age of 16
Member of forest committee	Equals 1 if member of forest committee set up by Bank CBD/CDD project, zero otherwise
Dummy for female	Equals 1 if respondent is female, zero otherwise
Age	Age of the respondent
Age squared	Age squared
Schooling	Equals 1 if the respondent has attended school, zero otherwise
Number of leaders known	Number of leaders a respondent knew prior to the Bank intervention
Participation in traditional events	Frequency of participation in the traditional events prior to Bank interventions
Participation in non-traditional events	Frequency of participation in the non-traditional/political events prior to Bank interventions
Mobilization skills	Number of skills the respondent reported to have prior to Bank intervention. Composite variable equal to the sum of three dummy variables (1=able, 0=everything else) that captures respondent's ability to (a) organize self-help groups and raise resources from within the village; (b) raise resources outside the village; (c) express the needs of the village to local government officials

Table M.12: Definition of Variables: Uttar Pradesh

Dependent variable	Definition
Change in access to information	Changes in access to information regarding issues of interest to the community (more=3, same=2, less=1)
Change in mobilization skills	Composite variable equal to the sum of three dummy variables (1=more, 0=everything else) that capture change in the respondent's ability to (a) organize self-help groups and raise resources from within the village; (b) raise resources outside the village; (c) express the needs of the village to local government officials.
Change in ability to reach agreement	Change in the community's ability to reach an agreement (more=3, same=2, less=1)
Change in community leaders' responsiveness	Change in the extent to which community leaders listen and respond to community needs (listen and respond more=4, listen more=3, same=2, listen less=1)
Change in trust	Composite variable equal to the sum of five dummy variables (1=more, 0=everything else) capturing change in trust in: (a) village members, (b) village organizations, (c) village leaders, (d) local elected officials, (e) implementing agency
Change in associational life	Composite variable equal to the sum of two dummy variables (1=more, 0=everything else) capturing change in: (a) people's participation in groups, (b) cooperation between groups and individuals
Change in participation in traditional events	Change in the respondent's participation in community's traditional events (more=3, same=2, less=1)
Change in participation in non-traditional events	Change in the respondent's participation in community's non-traditional events. (more=3, same=2, less=1).

(continued on following page)

Table M.12: Definition of Variables: Uttar Pradesh (continued)

Dependent variables	**Definition**
Change in circle of friends	Change in the respondent's circle of friends (improved=3, same=2, deteriorated=1)
Independent variable	
Project village	Equals 1 if project village, and zero otherwise (if comparator)
Poor in project village	Equals 1 if respondent is poor and in project village, zero otherwise
Female in project village	Equals one if the respondent is a female in a project village, zero otherwise
Amawa block	Equals 1 if Amawa block, zero otherwise
Maharajganj block	Equals 1 if Maharajganj block, zero otherwise
Rural community	Equals 1 if it is a rural community, zero if rural dispersed
Score for community	Level of basic infrastructure in a community (such as primary school, basic health post, wells, hand-pumps) and distance to the closest market prior to Bank intervention (based on village leader interview)
Economic status index	Composite variable equal to the sum of three rescaled variables that capture household's ownership of the following items prior to subproject implementation: (a) land (linear log), (b) large animals (horse, cow, and ox), (c) consumer durables (car, bicycle, fan, radio)
Dummy for poor	Equals 1 if respondent is from the bottom-quartile of the distribution along the Economic Status Index in his/her community, zero otherwise
Household size	Number of people living under the same roof
Number of children	Number of children below the age of 16
Member of SIC	Equals 1 if member of village organization set up by the Bank CBD/CDD project, zero otherwise
Dummy for female	Equals 1 if respondent is a female, zero otherwise
Age	Age of the respondent
Age squared	Age squared
Schooling	Equals 1 if the respondent has attended school, zero otherwise
Number of leaders	Number of leaders the respondent knew prior to the Bank intervention
Participation in traditional events	Frequency of participation in the traditional events prior to Bank interventions
Participation in non-traditional events	Frequency of participation in the non-traditional/political events prior to Bank interventions
Blue collar skills of the respondent	Equals 1 if respondent was able to do boring, construct field drains, link drains and/or construct irrigation channels prior to Bank intervention
Mobilization skills of the respondent	Number of skills the respondent reported to have prior to Bank intervention. Composite variable equal to the sum of three dummy variables (1=able, 0=everything else) that captures respondent's ability to (a) organize self-help groups and raise resources from within the village; (b) raise resources outside the village; (c) express the needs of the village to local government officials

ANNEX N: ENHANCING COMMUNITY CAPACITIES

One of the premises of the CDD approach is that it fosters the formation of social capital at the community level and empowers communities to take charge of their own development.[1] The assessment of the extent to which the CDD projects supported by the World Bank have improved communities' capacity focuses on these two processes. This annex presents the findings of community-level fieldwork undertaken for this evaluation in the Borgou region of Benin (henceforth Benin); the state of Rio Grande do Norte in Brazil (henceforth Brazil); the Betul and Bilaspur districts in Madhya Pradesh, India (henceforth Madhya Pradesh); and Raibarelli district in Uttar Pradesh, India (henceforth Uttar Pradesh). Three of these projects were CDD and one was CBD. Henceforth, when reference is made to the four projects, the broader term CBD/CDD is used. In addition, where relevant, this annex draws on a review of appraisal documents of 84 sampled CBD/CDD projects and on the literature on participatory development.

The field research at the community level included household surveys, focus group interviews, and key informant interviews (see Annex M for details). The methodology adopted for the analysis of the household data as well as details of the model used for multivariate analysis are also discussed in Annex M . Results of the bivariate analysis are presented in tables N.3–N.6, while those of the multivariate analysis are presented in tables N.7–N.16.[2] It should be noted that in the first two sections, discussion of the results of the multivariate analysis refers to the model without interactive terms, while the last two sections draw on the model with interactive terms (Annex M). As already mentioned in Annex M, the results of the specification with interactions are presented in full (tables N.9–N.16), while a summary of the results of the project dummies for the specification without interactions is presented in tables N.7 and N.8. Unless otherwise specified, the discussion of the statistical significance is always based on the probability value of the regression coefficients of the relevant specification.

Empowerment

The World Bank's (2002d) sourcebook on empowerment and poverty reduction identifies four key elements for a successful empowerment strategy: (a) inclusion and participation, (b) access to information, (c) accountability, (d) and local organizational capacity. This understanding of empowerment has informed data collection for this study, which explores both the levels of empowerment at the time of fieldwork and respondents' perceptions of changes in empowerment before and after subproject implementation. While a comprehensive assessment of the levels of empowerment and the empowering effects of the Bank's CBD/CDD initiatives at the community-level was beyond the scope of this study, our analysis focuses on some aspects of the four above-mentioned elements. It should also be noted that empowerment is multidimensional and it is hence possible for a person to experience empowerment in one dimension and disempowerment in another.

Inclusion and Participation

CBD/CDD projects are operationalized at the community level through community organizations. While at times these predate CBD/CDD interventions, new ad hoc organizations are often created by CBD/CDD projects, as was the case in Benin, Brazil, Madhya Pradesh, and Uttar

Pradesh.[3] Because these organizations constitute the locus of decision making at the local level, becoming a member (or attending meetings) is extremely important in order to attain inclusion in decision making. This, however, is not in itself sufficient. Drawing on the literature on participatory development, we make a distinction between formal inclusion, which concerns the extent to which community members are able to enter decision-making arenas, and substantive inclusion, which captures the extent to which different participants are able to exert influence over decisions.[4] While assessing formal inclusion is a fairly simple exercise, assessing substantive inclusion is far more complex, as it requires a detailed analysis of the very process through which decisions are made. This type of investigation was beyond the reach of our field research. However, based on our data, we can assess the extent to which villagers were likely to attain substantive inclusion in decision making.

Our household data reveal that in Benin, a large share of respondents attained formal inclusion in subproject decision making, while the opposite holds for Brazil and Uttar Pradesh. In Madhya Pradesh the picture is somewhat mixed. As figure N.1 shows, in Benin, 72 percent of respondents attended the meetings for subproject selection, while in Brazil, only 37 percent of respondents in FUMAC communities attended these meetings, and in Uttar Pradesh only 16 percent of respondents were members of project organizations and only 13 percent attended meetings regularly.[5] In Madhya Pradesh, over half of the respondents were members of project organizations, but only a third of respondents attended meetings regularly. In Brazil, the majority of respondents were also likely to have exerted only minimal influence over subproject decision making. Only 22 percent of the respondents in FUMAC communities spoke during the meetings (figure N.1), and a large share of respondents would refrain from expressing grievances with the subproject being implemented if this risked losing projects funds or compromising relations with other villagers.[6] The OED Social Fund Evaluation (OED 2002b) reports similar results; only around 15 percent of the beneficiaries reported speaking at the meetings in the four countries surveyed. Focus group sessions held with villagers across the four project areas indicate that decision-making processes relative to the Bank-funded subproject lacked broad community participation.

It can be argued that a low level of inclusion in community organizations responsible for subproject selection and management is not in itself problematic. It is unrealistic and perhaps inefficient to expect communities to collectively undertake such activities, and a group of villagers could instead be chosen to do so on behalf of the community. Though valid, this argument raises concerns regarding the ways in which community representatives are selected and the inclusion of weaker social groups. In three of the four project areas for which information is available, respondents who were members of community organizations set up by the Bank intervention had a higher socioeconomic profile, including greater mobilization skills and a more extensive social network than non-members prior to subproject implementation.[7] Similarly, a large share of focus group interviews in India and Benin pointed out that decision making regarding the subproject was largely controlled by local leaders (figure 3.6 in Chapter 3). Various studies in the literature on participatory development also point out that the better-educated members of the community and the relatively better-off are often the ones who represented the community in participatory intervention (Desai 1996; Gibson and Marks 1995; van der Linden 1997; Ribot 1998).[8]

Access to Information

As the World Bank's (2002d) sourcebook on empowerment puts it, "information is power.... Without information that is relevant, timely, and presented in forms that can be understood, it is impossible for poor people to take effective action." Ensuring people's access to information is particularly important in CDD projects, in which communities are expected to take a proactive role in initiating the subproject cycle. A review of the appraisal documents for our sample of 84 interventions reveals that fewer than half of them included an extensive campaign to disseminate

Figure N.1: Beneficiaries' Inclusion and Participation in Subproject Decision Making

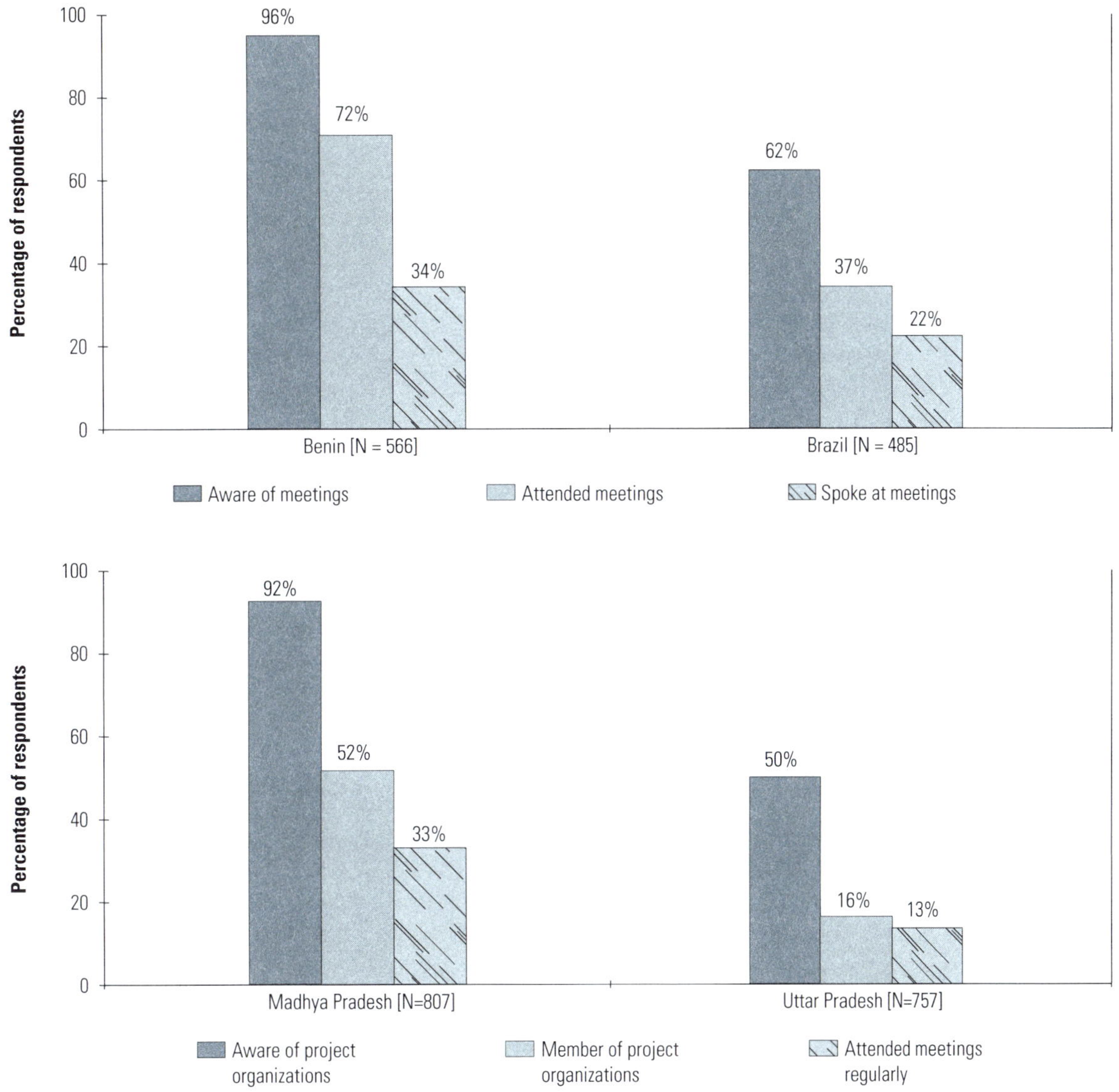

project information.[9] When information is not disseminated widely, communities are likely to be dependent on a few informed individuals for accessing development opportunities, and as the focus group interviews in Benin and India reveal, these tend to be the local leaders. Controlling information reinforces the position of power of these leaders, and creates opportunities for strengthening their clientelistic network (Kumar and Corbridge 2002; Desai 1996; Das Gupta and others 2000).

Household data also reveal communities' lack of information regarding the subproject implemented. In Benin and Brazil, the vast majority of respondents in project communities had no information on the cost of the subproject—86 and 82 percent, respectively.[10] Evidence from the literature on northeast Brazil supports these findings (Tendler 2000).[11] Communities' lack of information on the subproject affects the ability of the community to hold to account the people who managed the subproject investments on its behalf, and provides further evidence of the general lack of broad-based community participation in Bank-funded initiatives.

In addition to exploring the level of information at the time of our fieldwork, the household surveys also captured respondents' perceptions of the change in access to information on issues of interest to the communities before and after subproject implementation. Our findings reveal a mixed picture (figure N.2). A significant positive association was found between the Bank's CBD/CDD projects in Madhya Pradesh and respondents' access to information on issues of relevance to the community, while no significant association was found in Benin and Uttar Pradesh. In Brazil, respondents in comparator communities reported a significantly higher increase in access to information than did respondents in FUMAC communities.[12]

Accountability

The notion of accountability has a range of connotations. It is used here to refer to citizens' ability to hold local leaders and public officials accountable. The availability and accessibility of information are critical for accountability, and the findings discussed above on access to information already indicate weak accountability to communities. Although necessary, access to information is not in itself sufficient, as it does not automatically result in accountability; citizens must act upon the information they acquire (Jenkins and Goetz 1999). While it was beyond the scope of our field research to explore accountability issues extensively, a few aspects of these issues were captured by our questionnaires.

A large share of respondents in project communities in Benin, Uttar Pradesh, and Madhya Pradesh and over half of those in FUMAC communities in Brazil agreed that if dissatisfied with the performance of community leaders, villagers would call a meeting to discuss it. More than half of the respondents in project communities in Benin and Madhya Pradesh also agreed that if dissatisfied with community leaders, the community would replace them. Fewer respondents agreed with this statement in project communities in Uttar Pradesh and FUMAC communities in Brazil—respectively 42 and 24 percent. Our household data also capture respondents' per-

Figure N.2: The Bank's CBD/CDD Projects and Access to Information

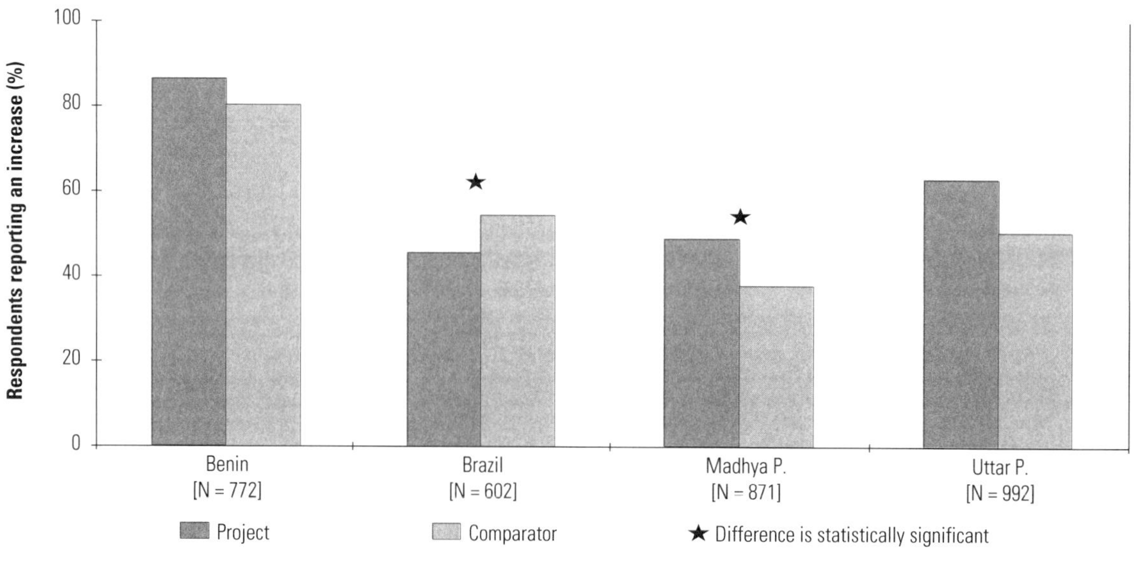

Note: Statistical significance based on the model without interactions.

ceptions of the changes in community leaders' responsiveness to community needs before and after subproject implementation. Multivariate analysis indicated no statistically significant association between the Bank's projects in Benin and Madhya Pradesh and community leaders' responsiveness to community needs. In Brazil, respondents in all three types of project communities reported a significantly smaller increase in community leaders' responsiveness than did respondents in comparator communities.

Local Organizational Capacity

According to the Bank's empowerment sourcebook, local organizing capacity "refers to the ability of people to work together, organize themselves, and mobilize resources to solve problems of common interest" (World Bank 2002b). In order to assess the extent to which the Bank's interventions succeeded in fostering communities' organizational capacity, our surveys captured respondents' perceptions of the changes in their mobilization skills, and in the ability of the community to reach an agreement before and after subproject implementation.[13] A third aspect relevant to local organizational capacity (which is also a dimension of social capital) is the change in associational life, which captures changes in respondents' participation in community groups and changes in cooperation between community groups.

Multivariate analysis indicated no statistically significant association between the Bank's projects and the changes in respondents' mobilization skills, with the exception of Uttar Pradesh, where respondents in project communities reported a significantly greater increase in mobilization skills than did respondents in comparator communities. The relation between Bank's CBD/CDD projects and communities' ability to reach an agreement was mixed (figure N.3). The projects in Benin and Uttar Pradesh were positively associated with communities' ability to reach an agreement, while no statistical association was found in Madhya Pradesh. In Brazil, respondents in all three types of project communities reported a significantly smaller increase in their ability to reach an agreement than did respondents in comparator communities. A more positive picture emerges from the

Figure N.3: The Bank's CBD/CDD Project Communities' Ability to Reach an Agreement

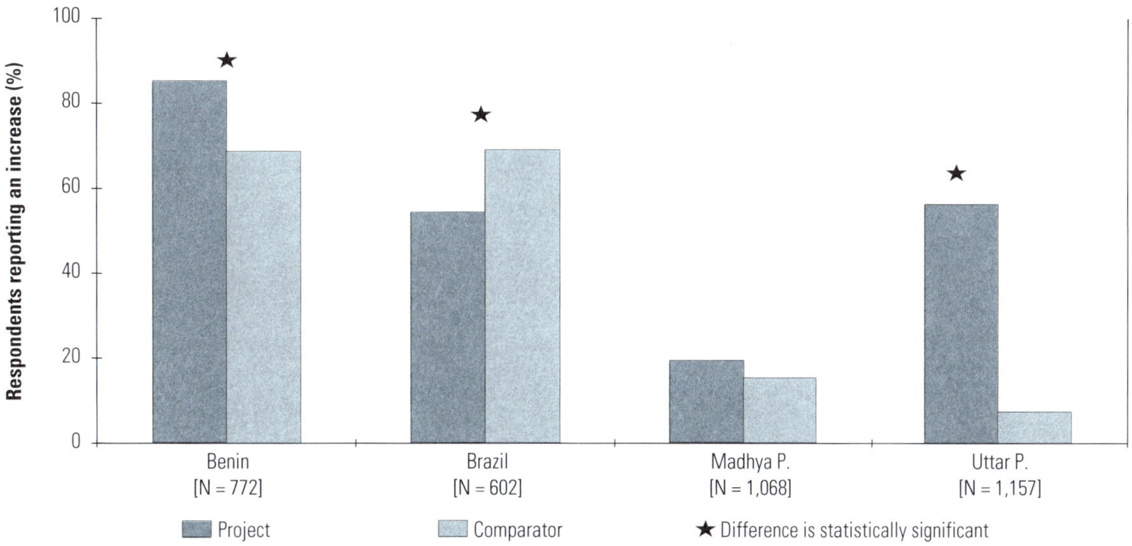

Note: Statistical significance based on the model without interactions.

analysis of the changes in associational life (figure N.4). All four Bank's projects are positively associated with respondents' perceptions of the changes in associational life.[14]

Figure N.4: The Bank's CBD/CDD Projects and Social Capital

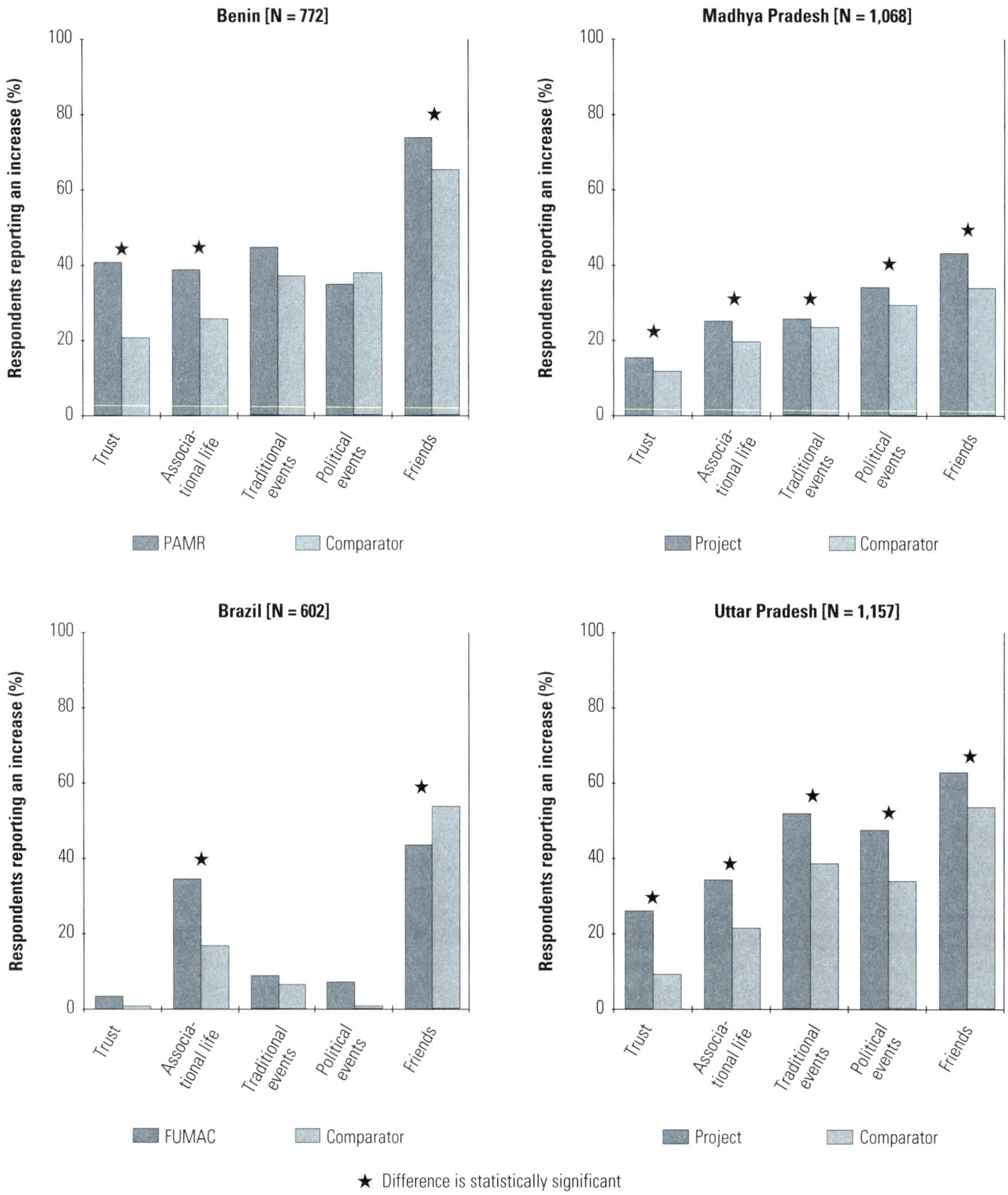

Note: Statistical significance based on the model without interactions.

Social Capital

Social capital refers to the norms and networks that enable collective action.[15] By drawing people together to collectively decide and manage project activities and outputs, these projects are expected to expand the depth and range of communities' social networks. In order to assess the extent to which Bank-funded interventions have succeeded in enhancing social capital at the community level, we draw on five variables, which capture respondents' perceptions of the changes in (a) trust, (b) associational life, (c) participation in traditional events, (d) participation in non-traditional/political events, and (e) circle of friends before and after subproject implementation.[16] It is important to bear in mind that these variables capture only some of the multiple dimensions of social capital and that our analysis of the association between Bank-supported projects and social capital was limited to the changes observed in these five dimensions.

Multivariate analysis indicated a statistically significant and positive association between the projects in Uttar Pradesh, Madhya Pradesh, and Benin and respondents' perceptions of the changes in social capital.[17] Results for the Brazil projects are mixed. While respondents in project communities reported a significantly greater increase in associational life than did respondents in comparator communities, the opposite holds for respondent's perceptions of changes in their circle of friends (figure N.4).[18] There are three reasons for the different levels of change in social capital in the four project areas, which might also explain the differences in the changes in empowerment. First, communities in the four project areas are likely to have different capacity levels; therefore, the change that can be expected as a result of exposure to a Bank intervention is also likely to be different. Second, the socio-political setting in which these initiatives are implemented affects their impact on social capital enhancement. The literature notes that the pervasive clientelism in the northeast of Brazil creates a social system in which vertical ties of mutual dependence prevail, and hinder the development of strong horizontal links of solidarity between communities (Costa and others 1997; Tendler 2000). This probably explains the lack of influence on social capital of the Bank's initiative in Rio Grande do Norte. Third, a lengthy engagement with a consistent capacity-building strategy with the same communities is likely to yield better results than a brief one. This might explain why the Borgou Pilot Project, which was introduced in communities where the Bank's Village Level Participatory Approach had been implemented in the 1990s and shared its approach, outperformed the Social Fund (AgeFIB) and the Food Security Project (PILSA).[19]

Bank's Projects and Members of Community Organizations

As already mentioned above, new ad hoc community organizations were created by the Bank's projects for their operationalization at the community level (see endnote 3). This section explores the institutional development impact of the CBD/CDD projects in Brazil, Madhya Pradesh, and Uttar Pradesh on the members of these organizations. In order to do so, a variable interacting membership in project organizations and the project dummy was included in the model. This variable estimates the association between the dependent variable and membership in project organizations relative to the project dummy.

The multivariate analysis indicated a statistically significant and positive association between the projects in Brazil, Madhya Pradesh, and Uttar Pradesh, and the changes in empowerment reported by members of community organizations set up by these projects (table N.1). In Brazil, members reported a greater increase in access to information and community leaders' responsiveness to community needs than non-members. In Madhya Pradesh, members reported a greater increase in access to information and mobilization skills than non-members, while in Uttar Pradesh, they reported a greater increase in mobilizations skills and communities' ability to reach an agreement. A statistically significant and positive association is also found between the projects in Madhya Pradesh and Uttar Pradesh, and respondent's perceptions of the changes in social capital. These two Bank projects are positively associated with four of the five dimensions of social capital considered in this study (table N.2). A weaker association is found between the Brazil

Table N.1: Empowering Members of Community Organizations

Change in...	Brazil	Madhya Pradesh	Uttar Pradesh
Access to information	positive	positive	
Mobilization skills		positive	positive
Ability to reach agreement			positive
Community leaders' responsiveness to community needs	positive		

Table N.2: Enhancing the Social Capital of Members of Community Organizations

Change in...	Brazil	Madhya Pradesh	Uttar Pradesh
Trust in individuals/organizations		positive	positive
Associational life	positive	positive	positive
Participation in traditional events			
Participation in non-traditional/political events		positive	positive
Circle of friends		positive	positive

Note: Results for the dummy for members of project organizations in CBD/CDD communities estimated in the model with interactions (tables N.10–N.16).

project and changes in social capital, with members of Community Associations reporting a greater increase in only one of the five dimensions of social capital considered—associational life.

While encouraging, these findings raise important concerns, because, as pointed out earlier (see endnote 7), respondents who were members of project-induced community organizations had a higher socioeconomic profile, including greater mobilization skills and a more extensive social network than non-members prior to subproject implementation.

Bank's Projects and Vulnerable Groups

Bank's CBD/CDD projects are aimed at empowering and enhancing the social capital of vulnerable groups, including women and the poor (endnote 1). Two interactive variables were included in the regression model in order to explore the associations between the changes in social capital and empowerment and the poor in project communities, on the one hand, and women in project communities, on the other. The first variable interacts belonging to the bottom quartile of the index of economic status with the project dummy, while the second interacts being a women with the project dummy. These variables estimate the association between the dependent variable and women or the poor in project communities relative to the project dummy.

The multivariate analysis indicated that the poor in project communities in Madhya Pradesh reported a significantly greater increase in two dimensions of social capital—trust and associational life—as well as a greater increase in their mobilization skills than did the relatively better-off in project areas. In Uttar Pradesh, the association between changes in empowerment and the poor in project communities is mixed. While the poor in project areas reported a greater increase in the community's ability to reach an agreement than did the relatively better-off in CBD/CDD communities, they also reported a significantly smaller increase in their access to information. In Brazil, no significant association is found between changes in social capital and empowerment and the poor in project communities.

The projects in Benin and Uttar Pradesh, which explicitly targeted women, do not appear to have enhanced women's capacities over and above other respondents in project communities. The only exceptions are women in project areas in Uttar Pradesh who reported a significantly greater increase in their mobilization skills and associational life than did men in project communities.

Table N.3: Benin: Bivariate Analysis of Variables Relevant to the Discussion on Empowerment and Social Capital (percent)

		PAMR, 566 observations	Comparator, 206 observations
Change in access to information	Worse	1	2 **
	Same	12	17
	Better	86	80
Change in mobilization skills	Same	10	16 **
	Increase in 1 of 4	10	8
	Increase in 2 of 4	16	14
	Increase in 3 of 4	20	29
	Increase in all 4	45	34
Change in ability to reach an agreement	Worse	1	9 ***
	Same	14	22
	Better	85	68
Change in community leaders' responsiveness to community needs	Less	3	1 **
	Same	25	35
	Listen more	44	40
	Listen and respond more	28	24
Change in trust in individuals and organizations	Same	32	43 ***
	Increase in 1 of 4	11	12
	Increase in 2 of 4	17	24
	Increase in 3 of 4	26	12
	Increase in all 4	14	8
Change in associational life	Same	18	25 ***
	Increase in 1 of 2	43	50
	Increase in 2 of 2	39	25
Change in participation in traditional events	Less	9	8
	Same	47	55
	More	44	37
Change in participation in political events[a]	Less	12	11
	Same	54	50
	More	35	38
Change in circle of friends	Less	1	2 **
	Same	25	32
	More	74	66
Express grievances if this risks losing project funds or compromising relations with other villagers	No	50	58
	Yes	49	42
If unhappy with community leaders, villagers call a meeting to discuss it[b]	Disagree	6	9 ***
	Somewhat disagree	5	6
	Somewhat agree	15	23
	Agree	74	62
If unhappy with community leaders, villagers replace them[c]	Disagree	19	27 ***
	Somewhat disagree	11	13
	Somewhat agree	13	13
	Agree	57	47

(continued on following page)

Table N.3: Benin: Bivariate Analysis of Variables Relevant to the Discussion on Empowerment and Social Capital (percent) (continued)

		PAMR, 566 observations	Comparator, 206 observations
Participation at community meetings for subproject selection	Unaware of meetings	4	
	Aware of meetings	96	
	Attended meetings	72	
	Attended and spoke at meetings	34	

Note: Significance based on a test of proportion for binary variables and the Kruskall-Wallis test for categorical variables. * Significant at 10%; ** significant at 5%; ***significant at 1%.

a. No. observations: project = 562

b. No. observations: project = 561

c. No. observations: project = 555; comparator = 202

Table N.4: Brazil: Bivariate Analysis of Variables Relevant to the Discussion on Empowerment and Social Capital (percent)

		FUMAC, 485 observations	Comparator, 117 observations
Change in access to information [a]	Worse	16	3 ***
	Same	38	41
	Better	46	56
Change in mobilization skills	Same	60	53
	Improve in 1 of 4	20	33
	Improve in 2 or more of 4	20	14
Change in ability to reach an agreement	Worse	13	2 ***
	Same	32	27
	Better	54	69
Change in community leaders' responsiveness to community needs[b]	Less	19	9 *
	Same	53	58
	Listen more	28	32
Change in trust in individuals and organizations	Same	66	59
	Increase in 1 of 4	22	34
	Increase in 2 and above of 4	12	7
Change in associational life	Same	49	58 ***
	Increase in 1 of 2	16	25
	Increase in 2 of 2	34	17
Change in participation in traditional events [c]	Less	18	17
	Same	73	76
	More	9	7
Change in participation in political events [d]	Less	13	2
	Same	80	97
	More	7	1
Change in circle of friends	Less	4	3 *
	Same	51	44
	More	44	54

Table N.4: Brazil: Bivariate Analysis of Variables Relevant To the Discussion on Empowerment and Social Capital (percent) (continued)

		FUMAC, 485 observations	Comparator, 117 observations
Express grievances if this risks losing project funds	No	66	77 **
	Yes	34	22
Express grievances if this risks compromising relations with other villagers	No	61	66
	Yes	39	33
If unhappy with community leaders, villagers call a meeting to discuss it[e]	No	38	44 ***
	Yes	56	14
If unhappy with community leaders, villagers replace them[e]	No	64	49 ***
	Yes	24	4
Participation at community meetings for subproject selection	Unaware of meetings	38	
	Aware of meetings	62	
	Attended meetings	37	
	Attended and spoke at meetings	22	

Note: Significance based on a test of proportion for binary variables and the Kruskall-Wallis test for categorical variables. * Significant at 10%; ** significant at 5%; ***significant at 1%.

a. No. observations: project = 482; comparator = 115

b. No. observations: project = 452; comparator = 96

c. No. observations: project = 481; comparator = 117.

d. No. observations: project = 474; comparator = 117

e. No. observations: project = 484; comparator = 111.

Table N.5: Madhya Pradesh: Bivariate Analysis of Variables Relevant to the Discussion on Empowerment and Social Capital (percent)

		Project, 807 observations	Comparator, 261 observations
Change in access to information [a]	Worse	16	21 ***
	Same	35	41
	Better	49	38
Change in mobilization skills	Same	35	40 *
	Improve in 1 of 3	31	34
	Improve in 2 of 3	19	14
	Improve in all 3	15	12
Change in ability to reach an agreement	Worse	23	25
	Same	29	31
	Better	19	15
Change in community leaders' responsiveness to community needs [b]	Less	17	16
	Same	37	38
	Listen more	20	27
	Listen and respond more	19	15
Change in trust in individuals and organizations	Same	62	67 *
	Increase in 1 of 5	15	12

(continued on following page)

Table N.5: Madhya Pradesh: Bivariate Analysis of Variables Relevant To the Discussion on Empowerment and Social Capital (percent) (continued)

		Project, 807 observations	Comparator, 261 observations
	Increase in 2 of 5	8	9
	Increase in 3 of 5	5	4
	Increase in 4 of 5	5	3
	Increase in all 5	6	4
Change in associational life	Same	60	67 **
	Increase in 1 of 2	15	13
	Increase in 2 of 2	25	20
Change in participation in traditional events[c]	Less	9	13
	Same	65	63
	More	26	23
Change in participation in non-traditional events[d]	Less	11	8
	Same	55	63
	More	34	29
Change in circle of friends[e]	Less	10	12 ***
	Same	47	54
	More	43	34
Express grievances if this risks losing project funds	No	48	46
	Yes	43	47
Express grievances if this risks compromising relations with other villagers	No	40	34 *
	Yes	52	59
If unhappy with community leaders, villagers call a meeting to discuss it[f]	Disagree	14	17
	Somewhat disagree	6	3
	Somewhat agree	19	20
	Agree	61	59
If unhappy with community leaders, villagers replace them[g]	Disagree	23	26
	Somewhat disagree	8	7
	Somewhat agree	17	21
	Agree	51	47
Participation in community organizations set up by the bank project	Unaware of project organizations	8	
	Aware of project organizations	92	
	Member of project organizations	52	
	Member and attended meetings regularly	33	

Note: Significance based on a test of proportion for binary variables and the Kruskall-Wallis test for categorical variables. * Significant at 10%; ** significant at 5%; ***significant at 1%.

a. No. observations: project = 653; comparator = 218.

b. No. observations: project = 581; comparator = 191.

c. No. observations: project = 790; comparator = 260.

d. No. observations: project = 787; comparator = 258.

e. No. observations: project = 716; comparator = 249

f. No. observations: project = 688; comparator = 229.

g. No. observations: project = 667; comparator = 227.

Table N.6: Uttar Pradesh: Bivariate Analysis of Variables Relevant to the Discussion on Empowerment and Social Capital (percent)

		Project, 757 observations	Comparator, 400 observations
Change in access to information[a]	Worse	8	8 ***
	Same	29	42
	Better	63	50
Change in mobilization skills	Same	22	33 ***
	Improve in 1 of 3	21	31
	Improve in 2 of 3	27	21
	Improve in all 3	30	16
Change in ability to reach an agreement	Worse	24	46 ***
	Same	15	39
	Better	56	8
Change in community leaders' responsiveness to community needs	Less	26	
	Same	27	
	Listen more	23	
	Listen and respond more	22	
Change in trust in individuals and organizations	Same	33	51 ***
	Increase in 1 of 5	24	25
	Increase in 2 of 5	17	15
	Increase in 3 of 5	14	7
	Increase in 4 of 5	8	3
	Increase in all 5	4	0
Change in associational life	Same	53	68 ***
	Increase in 1 of 2	13	11
	Increase in 2 of 2	34	22
Change in participation in traditional events	Less	12	20 ***
	Same	36	42
	More	52	38
Change in participation in non-traditional	Less	12	15 ***
	Same	40	52
	More	47	34
Change in circle of friends[b]	Less	5	4 ***
	Same	32	42
	More	63	54
Express grievances if this risks losing project funds	No	45	36 ***
	Yes	54	64
Express grievances if this risks compromising relations with other villagers	No	33	30
	Yes	65	70
If unhappy with community leaders, villagers call a meeting to discuss it[c]	Disagree	11	11 *
	Somewhat disagree	5	4
	Somewhat agree	19	27
	Agree	63	55

(continued on following page)

Table N.6: Uttar Pradesh: Bivariate Analysis of Variables Relevant to the Discussion on Empowerment and Social Capital (percent) (continued)

		Project, 757 observations	Comparator, 400 observations
If unhappy with community leaders, villagers replace them[d]	Disagree	25	25
	Somewhat disagree	7	7
	Somewhat agree	21	28
	Agree	42	37
Participation in community organizations set up by the bank project	Unaware of project organizations	50	
	Aware of project organizations	50	
	Member of project organizations	16	
	Member and attended meetings regularly	13	

Note: Significance based on a test of proportion for binary variables and the Kruskall-Wallis test for categorical variables. * Significant at 10%; ** significant at 5%; ***significant at 1%.

a. No. observations: project = 686; comparator = 306.

b. No. observations: project = 705; comparator = 386.

c. No. observations: project = 728; comparator = 393.

d. No. observations: project = 722; comparator = 393.

Table N.7: Coefficients and Significance of Project Dummies in the Model without Interactive Terms: Change in Empowerment (Ordered probit)

	Change in access to information (Coef.)	Change in mobilization skills (Coef.)	Change in ability to reach agreement (Coef.)	Change in community leaders' responsiveness to community needs (Coef.)
Benin (PAMR)	0.19	0.25	0.73 ***	0.13
Brazil (PAC)	–0.04	–0.44	–0.53 ***	–0.42 *
Brazil (FUMAC)	–0.40 ***	–0.11	–0.50 ***	–0.38 *
Brazil (FUMAC-P)	–0.37 **	–0.42 ***	–0.83 ***	–0.65 **
Madhya Pradesh	0.27 **	0.13	0.19	0.07
Uttar Pradesh	0.08	0.61 ***	0.93 ***	—

Note: Weighted estimation (except for Benin) adjusted for cluster effects. * Significant at 10%; ** significant at 5%; ***significant at 1%.

Table N. 8: Coefficients and Significance of Project Dummies in the Model without Interactive Terms: Change in Social Capital (Ordered probit)

	Change in trust in individuals & organizations (Coef.)	Change in associational life (Coef.)	Change in participation in traditional events (Coef.)	Change in participation in non-traditional/ political events (Coef.)	Change in circle of friends (Coef.)
Benin (PAMR)	0.35 ***	0.27 **	0.17	0.08	0.35 ***
Brazil (PAC)	−0.27	−0.26	0.11	−0.08	0.07
Brazil (FUMAC)	−0.09	0.27 *	0.13	−0.10	−0.27 ***
Brazil (FUMAC-P)	−0.34 **	−0.57 **	0.01	−0.32 **	−0.45 ***
Madhya Pradesh	0.36 ***	0.36 **	0.34 **	0.20 **	0.26 ***
Uttar Pradesh	0.55 ***	0.48 *	0.50 ***	0.25 **	0.34 **

Note: Weighted estimation (except for Benin) adjusted for cluster effects. * Significant at 10%; ** significant at 5%; ***significant at 1%.

Table N.9: Benin: Change in Empowerment (Ordered probit)

	Change in access to information (Coef.)	Change in mobilization skills (Coef.)	Change in ability to reach agreement (Coef.)	Change in community leaders' responsiveness to community needs (Coef.)
Dummy for PAMR	0.19	0.16	0.73 ***	0.08
Dummy for AgeFIB	0.01	−0.11	0.54	0.05
Dummy for PILSA	−0.46 *	0.37	−0.19	−0.11
Dummy for female in PAMR	0.01	0.26	−0.01	0.16
Dummy for school construction subproject	0.32 ***	0.05	−0.07	0.09
Dummy for training subproject	1.23 ***	0.07	1.43 ***	0.51 ***
Dummy for difficult access to community	−0.05	−0.05	−0.16	−0.07
Household size	0.02	0.01 *	0.00	0.02 ***
Number of children	−0.03	−0.01	0.01	−0.01
Dummy for female	−0.22	−0.36 **	−0.15	−0.14 *
Schooling of the respondent	−0.07	0.09	−0.11	0.01
Age	0.00	−0.04 ***	−0.03	−0.01
Age square	0.01	0.18	0.27	0.10
Number of leaders known	0.17 ***	0.11 **	0.15 **	−0.03
Participation in traditional events	0.21 ***	−0.03	0.13 *	−0.02
Participation in political events	0.00	0.05	−0.02	0.12 ***
Blue collar skills of respondent	0.13	−0.05	−0.10	0.10
Mobilization skills of the respondent	−0.11 ***	0.38 ***	0.01	−0.02
Observations	1,028	1,028	1,028	1,028
Pseudo R-squared	0.08	0.12	0.09	0.02
Chi^2	472.67	489.58	276.21	361.93

Note: Estimation adjusted for cluster effects. * Significant at 10%; ** significant at 5%; ***significant at 1%.

Table N.10: Brazil: Change in Empowerment (Ordered probit)

	Change in access to information (Coef.)	Change in mobilization skills (Coef.)	Change in ability to reach agreement (Coef.)	Change in community leaders' responsiveness to community needs (Coef.)
Dummy for PAC	–0.25	–0.44	–0.62 ***	–0.44 *
Dummy for FUMAC	–0.62 **	–0.23	–0.55 ***	–0.51 *
Dummy for FUMACP	–0.62 **	–0.51 **	–0.95 ***	–0.69 **
Dummy for poor in PAC	0.43	–0.09	0.17	–0.10
Dummy for poor in FUMAC	0.11	0.25	–0.04	0.11
Dummy for poor in FUMACP	0.31	0.20	0.21	–0.27
Dummy for irrigation subproject	–0.05	0.04	–0.05	–0.39
Dummy for small bridge subproject	0.06	0.53 **	–1.04 ***	–0.67 ***
Dummy for Agreste region	0.08	–0.02	–0.34	–0.43 ***
Municipal Human Develop Index	1.35	–2.44	–6.33 **	0.85
Score for community	–0.80	–0.91 *	–0.65	–0.31
Economic status	0.44	0.66 ***	0.37	0.07
Dummy for poor	–0.25	–0.09	–0.07	0.01
Household size	0.01	0.04	0.05	0.00
Number of children	0.01	–0.04	–0.04	0.01
Dummy for member of the CA	0.49 ***	0.13	0.19	0.26 **
Dummy for female	0.04	–0.10	0.11	–0.17
Schooling of the respondent	0.04	–0.04	0.03	0.08
Dummy for agricultural laborer	–0.26 **	–0.24	0.01	–0.13
Age	–0.01	–0.01	0.02	–0.01
Age square	0.03	0.02	–0.23	0.12
Participation in political events	0.10	–0.22	0.11	–0.02
Participation in traditional events	0.14	0.11	0.08	0.26 ***
Mobilization skills of the respondent	0.01	–0.09 **	0.03	0.06 *
Observations	916	925	915	771
Pseudo R-squared	0.05	0.03	0.06	0.07
Chi^2	1,636.00	418.59	2,147.15	3,005.88

Note: Weighted estimation adjusted for cluster effects. * Significant at 10%; ** significant at 5%; ***significant at 1%.

Table N.11: Madhya Pradesh: Change in Empowerment (Ordered probit)

	Change in access to information (Coef.)	Change in mobilization skills (Coef.)	Change in ability to reach agreement (Coef.)	Change in community leaders' responsiveness to community needs (Coef.)
Dummy for project village	0.22	0.01	0.21	0.05
Dummy for poor in project village	0.11	0.30 **	−0.13	0.11
Dummy for Betul district	0.27 *	0.12	0.55 ***	0.38 **
Score for community	−0.25	−0.48	−1.42 ***	−1.20 ***
Economic status	0.21	0.05	0.17	0.04
Dummy for poor	−0.08	−0.22 *	0.00	−0.09
Household size	-0.03	0.02	0.01	−0.02
Number of children	0.08 **	0.00	−0.01	0.06
Dummy for member of forest committee	0.28 ***	0.35 ***	0.06	−0.02
Dummy for female	−0.14	−0.11 *	−0.03	−0.07
Age of respondents	0.01	0.00	0.04 *	0.00
Age square	−0.05	−0.11	−0.51 **	0.07
Schooling of the respondent	0.34 ***	0.34 ***	0.18	0.10
Number of leaders known	0.00	0.04	0.00	0.03
Participation in traditional events	0.05	0.17 ***	0.31 ***	0.19 ***
Participation in non-traditional events	−0.04	0.05	0.03	−0.07
Mobilization skills of the respondent	−0.06	0.18 ***	0.02	−0.08
Observations	859	1,046	756	712
Pseudo R-squared	0.05	0.07	0.10	0.05
Chi^2	155.53	490.72	216.07	289.32

Note: Weighted estimation adjusted for cluster effects. * Significant at 10%; ** significant at 5%; ***significant at 1%.

Table N.12: Uttar Pradesh: Change in Empowerment (Ordered probit)

	Change in access to information (Coef.)	Change in mobilization skills (Coef.)	Change in ability to reach agreement (Coef.)	Change in community leaders' responsiveness to community needs[a] (Coef.)
Dummy for project village	–0.09	0.34 **	0.80 ***	—
Dummy for poor in project village	–0.28 *	0.23	0.42 ***	–0.17
Dummy for female in project village	0.37	0.34 ***	–0.05	–0.04
Dummy for Amawa district	0.25	0.08	0.14	0.49 ***
Dummy for Maharajganj district	–0.17	–0.29	–0.25	0.22 ***
Dummy for rural	–0.52 **	–0.16	–0.25	–0.34 ***
Score for community	–0.25	0.06	0.74 *	–0.17
Economic status	0.17	–0.25	–0.75 *	0.19
Dummy for poor	–0.11	–0.48 **	–0.66 **	—
Household size	0.02	0.01	0.00	0.01
Number of children	–0.08	–0.05 **	–0.02	–0.04
Dummy for member of SIC	0.25	0.25 **	0.32 **	0.30
Dummy for female	–0.20	–0.41 ***	–0.24 **	—
Age of the respondent	–0.03	–0.01	0.02	–0.07 ***
Age square	0.20	0.02	–0.29	0.71 ***
Schooling of respondent	0.29 **	0.37 ***	0.00	–0.01
Number of leaders known	0.19 ***	0.35 ***	0.07	0.19 ***
Participation in traditional events	0.07	–0.05	0.03	—
Participation in non-traditional events	0.17 **	0.24 ***	–0.03	—
Blue collar skills of respondent	–0.02	0.18	0.40 ***	—
Mobilization skills of the respondent	0.14	0.18 ***	0.12	–0.04
Observations	986	1,148	1,082	747
Pseudo R-squared	0.09	0.10	0.13	0.03
Chi^2	757.04	2,022.38	2,407.09	408.07

Note: Weighted estimation adjusted for cluster effects. * Significant at 10%; ** significant at 5%; ***significant at 1%.

a. This question was only asked in project villages. Three variables were dropped from this regression because in order to be estimated adjusting for cluster effects, the model requires the number of clusters to be greater than the number of constraints. The variables dropped were found not significant in the model estimated without adjusting for cluster effects.

Table N.13: Benin: Change in Social Capital (Ordered probit)

	Change in trust in individuals & organizations (Coef.)	Change in associational life (Coef.)	Change in participation in traditional events (Coef.)	Change in participation in political events (Coef.)	Change in circle of friends (Coef.)
Dummy for PAMR	0.33 ***	0.29 **	0.12	0.01	0.34 ***
Dummy for AgeFIB	0.28 **	0.05	0.07	–0.04	–0.14
Dummy for PILSA	0.30 ***	0.32 *	–0.08	0.03	–0.06
Dummy for female in PAMR	0.07	–0.06	0.13	0.23	0.03
Dummy for school construction subproject	0.43 ***	1.32 ***	–0.12	–0.01	0.19
Dummy for training subproject	0.16	0.03	–0.01	–0.36 ***	0.45
Dummy for difficult access to community	–0.10	–0.25	–0.09	–0.18 *	–0.34 **
Household size	0.02 ***	0.00	–0.02 **	–0.01	0.01
Number of children	–0.02	–0.01	0.04 ***	0.02	0.00
Dummy for female	–0.16	–0.17	–0.01	–0.11	–0.13
Schooling of the respondent	–0.08	0.03	–0.01	0.11	0.08
Age	–0.04 **	–0.01	0.00	0.01	–0.01
Age square	0.34 **	0.10	0.00	–0.18	0.11
Number of leaders known	0.13 *	0.20 ***	0.04	0.08	0.14 **
Participation in traditional events	–0.05	0.11 **	0.06	–0.03	0.14 ***
Participation in political events	0.11 **	–0.01	0.10 *	0.39 ***	–0.06
Blue collar skills of respondent	0.06	0.15	–0.25 **	–0.35 ***	0.02
Mobilization skills of the respondent	0.05	0.02	–0.05	–0.03	–0.01
Observations	1,028	1,028	1,028	1,026	1,028
Pseudo R-squared	0.03	0.15	0.02	0.08	0.04
Chi^2	151.03	629.10	491.85	303.81	768.10

Note: Estimation adjusted for cluster effects. * Significant at 10%; ** significant at 5%; ***significant at 1%.

Table N.14: Brazil: Change in Social Capital (Ordered probit)

	Change in trust in individuals & organizations (Coef.)	Change in associational life (Coef.)	Change in participation in traditional events (Coef.)	Change in participation in political events (Coef.)	Change in circle of friends (Coef.)
Dummy for PAC	−0.21	−0.23	0.07	−0.17	0.20
Dummy for FUMAC	−0.10	0.24	0.15	−0.14	−0.37 ***
Dummy for FUMACP	−0.28	−0.70 **	−0.05	−0.39 **	−0.61 ***
Dummy for poor in PAC	−0.23	−0.35	0.18	0.28	−0.49 **
Dummy for poor in FUMAC	0.03	−0.37	0.02	0.11	0.14
Dummy for poor in FUMACP	−0.22	0.01	0.28	0.23	0.38 *
Dummy for irrigation subproject	0.01	0.08	−0.25	−0.36	−0.25
Dummy for small bridge subproject	0.35	−0.69 ***	−1.19 ***	−0.54	−0.81 ***
Dummy for Agreste region	0.00	−0.55 **	−0.21	−0.04	−0.23
Municipal Human Develop Index	−2.37	−8.18 **	−4.90 **	−1.73	−4.65
Score for community	−0.68	0.17	0.22	0.11	−0.90 *
Economic status	0.33	0.55 **	−0.47 **	0.05	0.42
Dummy for poor	0.11	0.34	−0.31	−0.17	−0.10
Household size	0.05 *	0.05	0.05 *	0.02	0.02
Number of children	−0.04	−0.07	−0.09 **	−0.02	−0.03
Dummy for member of the CA	0.00	0.38 **	−0.06	0.02	0.17
Dummy for female	−0.13	0.02	−0.11	−0.16	0.08
Schooling of the respondent	−0.05 *	0.01	0.08 *	0.05	−0.07 **
Dummy for agricultural laborer	−0.43 **	0.16	0.00	−0.10	−0.02
Age	−0.01	−0.01	−0.01	−0.02	0.01
Age square	−0.04	0.00	0.02	0.20	−0.10
Participation in political events	−0.22	0.04	0.00	0.00	0.12
Participation in traditional events	0.12	0.17	0.20 ***	0.17 ***	0.20 ***
Mobilization skills of the respondent	0.03	0.00	0.11 ***	0.06 **	0.06 **
Observations	925	925	919	909	917
Pseudo R–squared	0.03	0.07	0.05	0.03	0.05
Chi^2	1,043.50	986.26	1,945.22	283.91	874.42

Note: Weighted estimation adjusted for cluster effects. * Significant at 10%; ** significant at 5%; ***significant at 1%.

Table N.15: Madhya Pradesh: Change in Social Capital (Ordered probit)

	Change in trust in individuals & organizations (Coef.)	Change in associational life (Coef.)	Change in participation in traditional events (Coef.)	Change in participation in non-traditional events (Coef.)	Change in circle of friends (Coef.)
Dummy for project village	0.25 *	0.20	0.41 ***	0.11	0.20 *
Dummy for poor in project village	0.33 *	0.54 **	−0.25	0.22	0.11
Dummy for Betul district	0.13	0.18	−0.01	0.26 **	−0.09
Score for community	−0.83 **	−0.50 *	0.33	0.05	0.21
Economic status	0.17	−0.03	0.37 *	−0.13	−0.27 *
Dummy for poor	−0.38 *	−0.50	0.31	−0.22	−0.37 **
Household size	−0.02	−0.01	0.00	−0.02	0.01
Number of children	0.03	0.01	0.05 **	0.04 *	0.03
Dummy for member of forest committee	0.33 ***	0.29 ***	0.13	0.30 ***	0.22 **
Dummy for female	−0.18 **	−0.21 *	−0.15 *	−0.20 **	−0.11
Age of respondents	0.00	−0.01	0.07 **	0.04	−0.02
Age square	−0.06	0.12	−0.76 ***	−0.43 *	0.18
Schooling of the respondent	0.45 ***	0.26	0.00	0.19	0.17
Number of leaders known	0.00	−0.02	−0.03	−0.03	0.03
Participation in traditional events	0.00	0.11 *	−0.04	0.00	0.03
Participation in non-traditional events	0.02	0.03	−0.02	0.00	0.05
Mobilization skills of the respondent	0.05	0.12 ***	0.00	−0.14 **	−0.11 **
Observations	1,046	1,046	1,045	1,042	956
Pseudo R-squared	0.06	0.06	0.03	0.04	0.04
Chi^2	721.66	113.39	80.62	100.59	327.13

Note: Weighted estimation adjusted for cluster effects. * Significant at 10%; ** significant at 5%; ***significant at 1%.

Table N.16: Uttar Pradesh: Change in Social Capital (Ordered probit)

	Change in trust in individuals & organizations (Coef.)	Change in associational life (Coef.)	Change in participation in traditional events (Coef.)	Change in participation in non-traditional events (Coef.)	Change in circle of friends (Coef.)
Dummy for project village	0.44 ***	0.18	0.33 **	0.09	0.15
Dummy for poor in project village	0.19	0.26	−0.10	0.05	0.22
Dummy for female in project village	−0.01	0.31 *	0.31	0.17	0.10
Dummy for Amawa district	0.24 **	0.15	0.09	−0.12	−0.09
Dummy for Maharajganj district	−0.13	−0.31 *	0.04	−0.24	−0.09
Dummy for rural	−0.09	−0.08	0.14	−0.09	0.15
Score for community	−0.29	0.65	1.09 ***	0.10	0.31
Economic status	−0.11	−0.10	−0.13	−0.25	0.17
Dummy for poor	−0.24	−0.31 **	−0.06	−0.30 *	−0.28 ***
Household size	0.01	0.00	−0.01	0.01	0.02
Number of children	−0.02	−0.05 *	−0.01	−0.04	−0.04
Dummy for member of SIC	0.37 **	0.45 ***	0.25	0.35 ***	0.61 ***
Dummy for female	−0.05	−0.31 *	0.08	0.10	0.08
Age of the respondent	−0.02	−0.02	−0.03	−0.01	−0.02
Age square	0.26	0.18	0.27	0.11	0.13
Schooling of respondent	0.44 ***	0.30 ***	0.04	0.03	0.03
Number of leaders known	0.18 ***	0.14	0.14	0.11	0.21 ***
Participation in traditional events	0.04	−0.13 **	0.04	0.02	−0.03
Participation in non–traditional events	0.01	−0.08	0.10	0.16	0.14 ***
Blue collar skills of respondent	0.13 **	−0.09	0.01	0.07	0.28 ***
Mobilization skills of the respondent	0.07	0.12	−0.03	−0.03	0.08
Observations	1,148	1,148	1,148	1,144	1,083
Pseudo R-squared	0.06	0.07	0.03	0.03	0.06
Chi^2	1,120.56	218.88	194.52	511.74	2,091.91

Note: Weighted estimation adjusted for cluster effects. * Significant at 10%; ** significant at 5%; ***significant at 1%.

ANNEX O: POVERTY TARGETING

Poverty Targeting Mechanisms

Bank projects use a variety of methods to target project beneficiaries. The most popular method is geographic targeting. A project can focus on a poor region or province, usually using government figures/criteria, or at a more local level such as a municipality or community, often using the results of participatory planning processes. Another mechanism that has been increasingly used, especially in social funds, is self-targeting. In this method the project supports basic infrastructure and services that are likely to be among the priority needs of poor communities or households, such as basic schools, health posts, water pumps, and similar infrastructure. A third mechanism becoming popular with CDD projects is social targeting, whereby the project targets particular social groups (women, handicapped, disadvantaged, small and marginal farmers, herders, and others).

The approach to poverty targeting for any project is largely based on the project objectives, availability of data, and institutional considerations. For example, the development objective of the Natural Resources Management and Poverty Reduction Project for Armenia (approved in fiscal 2002) was to adopt sustainable natural resource management practices and to alleviate rural poverty in mountainous areas where degradation is now reaching a critical point. Provincial-level geographic targeting alone was sufficient given the nature of the project: the project selected two marzes in the poorest mountainous regions of Armenia. In contrast, the development objective of the Rural Development in Marginal Areas Project in Mexico (fiscal 1998) was to improve the well-being and the income of smallholders in about 24 targeted marginal areas—among the poorest of the country—through sustainable increases in productivity and better food security. Clearly, project objectives required geographic targeting to identify marginal areas, social targeting to focus on smallholders, and self-targeting to focus on subprojects that define basic needs of the poor (food security). The project used a combination of all three poverty-targeting mechanisms. Over time, Bank-supported CBD/CDD projects are employing increasingly sophisticated mechanisms to target beneficiaries.[1]

Poverty Targeting for CBD/CDD Projects Covered by the Fieldwork

The evaluation studied in depth four targeted CBD/CDD projects, one each in Benin and Brazil, and two in India. One or more targeting mechanisms were adopted in all of them.

- The Borgou Pilot Project in Benin applied geographic targeting in 250 villages using a participatory diagnosis. The eligibility criteria for beneficiaries included the definition of clear priorities, as established by the Comité Villageois de Concertation, and the capacity of the community to contribute financially to certain types of investments. Specific emphasis was to be placed on women's groups and Fulani herders.[2]
- The RPAP project in Brazil's Rio Grande do Norte was to apply three targeting methods: (a) geographic by poverty level and other characteristics of the municipality; (b) geographic within municipalities to target rural settlements and communities; and (c) community-based selection of poor beneficiaries and particularly vulnerable groups by the project Municipal Councils. The communities themselves, through their majority participation in

the Councils, were to determine where project resources would best be applied.

- In the Forestry Project in Madhya Pradesh, India, the target group consisted of tribal peoples and forest fringe villagers. The group was to be to be identified by the government forest department. The project incorporated specific measures to safeguard the interests of the landless and women.
- The Sodic Land Reclamation project in Uttar Pradesh, India, was to target small and marginal farmers or previously landless allottees in the sodic land area identified by the government agency. Women were to be targeted and supported as a special group.

Disaggregated data were not available for most projects (except for Brazil) to allow comment on the success with which the project targeted the poorest and most disadvantaged. In Brazil, although the project was a targeted intervention, 136 of the 166 municipalities in the state were covered. The justification for the vast coverage was that all of the rural areas of the state were deemed sufficiently poor to warrant inclusion in the project. Only the state capital and its surrounding area were considered ineligible. Using a Municipal Human Development Index (MHDI), the evaluation attempted to assess whether municipalities with lower MHDI received more Bank funds compared to municipalities with higher MHDI. There was no relation between the level of MHDI and per capita investment in the municipality as a whole. In other words, there appears to be no concerted effort to target greater resources (subprojects) to poorer municipalities.

ANNEX P: EVIDENCE FROM FIELDWORK ON SUSTAINABILITY

This annex draws on the household surveys and the qualitative data gathered in four project areas in the context of this evaluation to explore issues relevant to sustainability of subprojects funded by Bank interventions.

Benin

Both the PAMR and AgeFIB projects provided support for construction of small infrastructure, a very large percentage of which was primary schools, in hundreds of communities. Typically, the government pays the salaries of certified schoolteachers for village primary schools. However, the fieldwork in the Borgou region reveals that the government has not been in a position to provide for paid certified teachers in the numerous schools that have been constructed under both the projects. Interviews with village leaders revealed that over 50 percent of PAMR schools and 80 percent of AgeFIB schoolteachers were community teachers, in comparison with comparator villages, where only a third of the teachers were community teachers. Because of a shortage of government teachers, the communities have been forced to hire teachers and pay their salaries from their own resources. The fieldwork was undertaken shortly after the projects closed, and new infrastructure generally does not entail significant maintenance costs. It is not clear whether poor communities will be able to bear the cost burden of maintenance and teachers' salaries from their own resources over the long run. The expectation among the communities is that the government will be responsible for the salary portion of the provision of education services. The majority of the household survey respondents considered repairs to be a responsibility of parent-teacher associations, but considered staff salaries a central government responsibility. These interventions have put a resource burden on the communities, which they may not have anticipated and may find difficult to sustain.

There is also the issue of the quality of education services imparted, which requires coordination with the education department in terms of adherence to a centrally planned curriculum, among other things. In the absence of certified schoolteachers, it is not clear how education in these schools will conform to a national standard. Poor communities may not be able to pay adequate salaries and benefits to attract qualified teachers.

Brazil

In Brazil, project communities benefited from three types of investments: water supply (20 communities), irrigation (three communities), and small bridges (two communities); while the three comparator communities benefited from a government water pipeline. The comparison between project and comparator communities is restricted for the analysis on sustainability to those project communities that received water supply investments.

Water supply investments: The RPAP financed a variety of water supply systems, including wells, cisterns, and small dams. While the majority of these systems are community-based, and hence require the community to collectively organize for its O&M, three communities benefited from household-based water supply systems, such as household water tanks and boxes, whose O&M falls solely on the individual household. These three project communities were dropped from the comparative analysis between the project and the comparator group. As figure P.1 shows, a larger share of respondents in comparator

Figure P.1: User-Fee Payments and Satisfaction Rates with Water Services in Project and Comparator Communities in Rio Grande do Norte

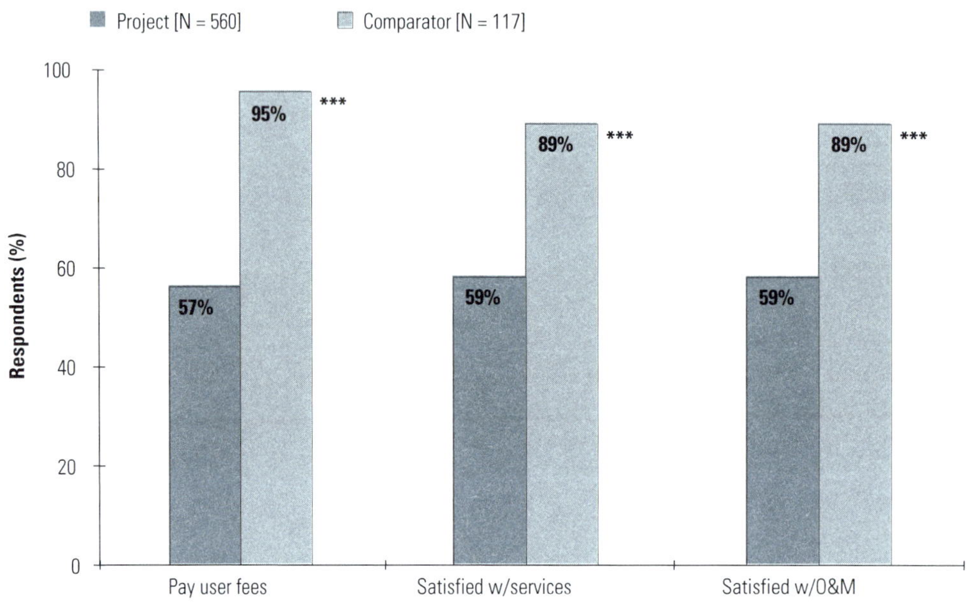

Note: Significance level based on test of proportion. * Significant at 10%; ** significant at 5%; ***significant at 1%.

communities than in project communities paid user fees, and were satisfied with the services provided and with O&M of their water system. However, these aggregated figures hide pronounced differences among project communities. As the qualitative data reveal, while almost half of them collect monthly fees to cover the cost of the electricity, and in some cases maintenance of the equipment, a few have yet to set up adequate O&M systems, and others have transferred the system to the state water company, which is now responsible for O&M. The quantitative data reflect this great variation among project communities. The percentage of respondents that pay user fees varied widely, from 100 percent in four communities to zero percent in six communities. Similarly, satisfaction with the services provided and with O&M varied, respectively, between 8 and 94 percent and 5 and 100 percent. Conversely, variation between comparator communities is very limited, and all display similarly high level user-fee payment and satisfaction with the services provided and with O&M.

Irrigation investments: Fewer than half of the respondents who are members of the three community associations (CA) that benefited from irrigation investments pay user fees.[1] Only 37 percent of them rated the services provided as good, while they hold divergent opinions on O&M, with 42 percent rating it as poor and another 42 percent rating it as good. These aggregate figures, however, hide pronounced differences among the three CAs. In one of them, the subproject is paralyzed by the high cost of electricity to operate the pump, while another is temporarily suspended by a shortage of water. A large share of the CA members interviewed where the irrigation system is functional and where it has been temporarily suspended rated the service provided and O&M as good. While the majority in the former pay user fees, half in the latter do so.

Small bridges: Fifty-seven percent of the respondents in the two communities that benefited from the construction of a small bridge are satisfied with the service provided by the infra-

Table P.1: Declining Forest Cover (percent)			
Forest cover	Less than before	Same as before	More than before
Bank-JFM	35	10	22
Govt.-JFM	62	14	16
Non-JFM	90	3	1

structure, while 52 percent rated O&M as poor. None of the respondents pays any kind of fees for the upkeep of the small bridges. As the qualitative data reveal, the choice of these investments, which did not result from a process of broad community participation, is not perceived as a solution to one of their main priorities.

Madhya Pradesh

The World Bank project aimed to assist implementation of the government strategy for development of the forest sector using joint forest management (JFM). The Bank project also provided improved information, extension services, and complementary investments in communal infrastructure to give villagers an incentive to cooperate. The appraisal document identified the need for the Bank to support the forest sector in the state for about 10 years with investments that could total more than US$200 million. Actual support provided was about a quarter of this amount over a period of four years. The Bank did not follow through with a second intervention in the state.

It appears that this is the main reason why it has not been possible to build the elements of sustainability in this short time. While household data indicate that Bank JFM villages seem to have experienced less of a decline in forest cover than comparator communities (table P.1), this gain has not been sufficient to provide adequate returns to the communities. At the time of the survey only a small percentage of the beneficiaries from Bank JFM communities reported collection of forest products, a large percentage reported having less access to forest products than previously, and a very small percentage reported collection of the forest products for income (table P.2). Focus group sessions reveal increasing hardship and lack of income-generating activities in the Bank JFM villages. Further, communities that have received support from the Bank appear to be receiving less support from the government for other development activities. Nearly two-thirds of the Bank beneficiaries report no micro-project in their village, compared with a third of government beneficiaries.

Uttar Pradesh

The World Bank project aimed to remove sodicity of land. The project also provided gypsum and other inputs, helped construct boring for irrigation, set up formal extension services, and introduced loans for cropping. Maintenance of drains, especially the main drains, is critical to the sustainability of reclaimed lands. Most respondents from the Bank project communities characterized maintenance of the drains as "bad," and said that O&M of the drains had deteriorated over time (figures P.2 and P.3). Focus group sessions reiterated these findings, emphasizing dysfunctional main drains. An interesting fact revealed by the open-ended discussion was that most farmers no

Table P.2: Forest Product Use

Forest product	Percent reporting collection of forest products: Bank	Percent reporting collection of forest products: Government	Percent reporting decline in collection: Bank	Percent reporting decline in collection: Government
Fuelwood	65	94	47	52
Fodder	16	22	15	13
Tendu	47	54	39	34
Mahua	36	43	29	26
Amla	8	15	13	16
Grass	6	11	10	15

Figure P.2: O&M for Drains Is Bad

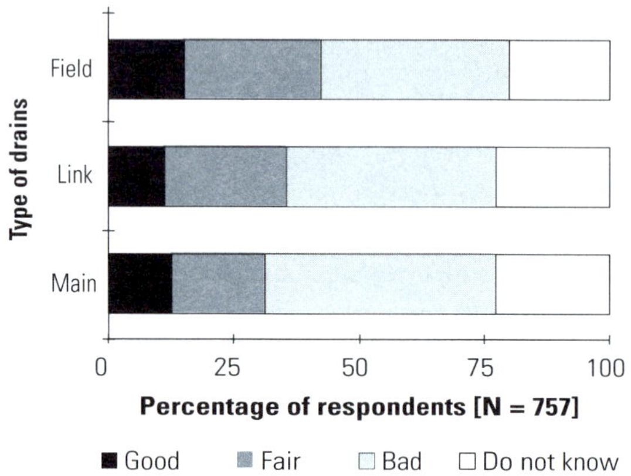

Figure P.3: O&M for Drains Deteriorating

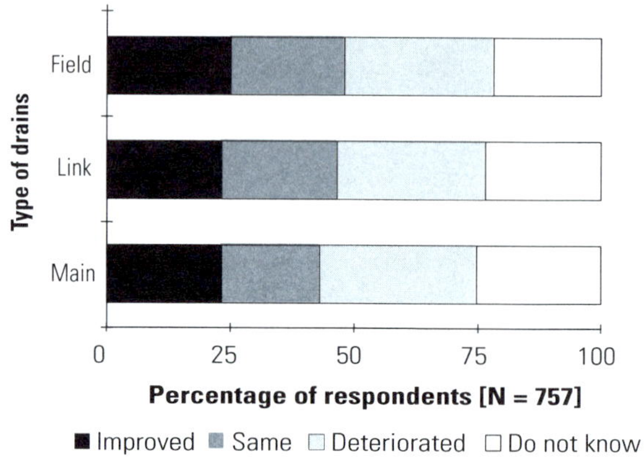

longer have field drains. Farmers have used that part of the land for cropping and are using irrigation channels for drainage purposes.

The Irrigation Department is responsible for maintaining the main drains, the village organization is responsible for link drains using internal funds, and farmers are responsible for field drains. The OED assessment notes that the implementing agency believed that political pressure from farmers would ensure that the government provides sufficient resources to the Irrigation Department for this activity. However, most beneficiaries are not even aware of the critical importance of drainage for containing sodicity, or that it is the responsibility of the Irrigation Department to maintain the drains. Over 80 percent of the respondents thought that continuous application of gypsum and water supply for irrigation will prevent the land from becoming sodic. Further, fewer than 4 percent of the respondents were aware that the responsibility of O&M of main drains lies with the Irrigation Department, and that responsibility of O&M of link drains lies with the village organization (table P.3).

Table P.3: Many Unaware of Who Is Responsible for Drains (percent)

	UPBSN/ Irrigation Department	Village leaders	Beneficiaries/ villagers	Do not know
Main drains	15	20	14	36
Link drains	9	17	28	32
Field drains	5	9	51	24

The project constructed many borings, and most respondents agree that O&M of that boring is the responsibility of the pump owner. However, most water pump owners indicated that the money received from farmers for water rights was insufficient to maintain the pump. At the same time, a majority of the respondents who pay the pump owner for water for their fields believe they pay enough to cover the O&M of the pump. Eight of the 18 village leader interviews indicated that boreholes have not helped improve irrigation; and the other 10 raised concerns about the continued flow of service from the borings because of erratic water supply, prohibitive costs of diesel, temperament of the pump owners, and deteriorating conditions of some boreholes.

The project committee (site implementation committee) setup is functional in only one of the project villages, according to interviews with project committee members in each of the project villages. Focus group sessions revealed that most respondents were also unaware of the existence of any MK/MMK.

ANNEX Q: SAFEGUARD THEMATIC STUDY: A SUMMARY

The Safeguards Policy Review is one of two thematic studies conducted for the OED evaluation of the World Bank's support for community-based and community-driven development. The study reviewed project appraisal, supervision, and completion documents for a sample of 84 projects to assess their compliance with the Bank's safeguard policies.[1] The desk reviews were supplemented by interviews with task team leaders, the Quality Assurance and Compliance Unit team, and Regional safeguards coordinators in selected cases. Selected items of direct relevance from the literature on safeguard policies and CBD/CDD projects were also reviewed.

Detailed findings on each project were condensed into a set of ratings on quality of compliance and analyzed with respect to: environmental assessment (EA) category, sector, Region, project type, and age. Findings and recommendations were developed from this analysis. Examples of best practice and missed opportunities were also identified. A special review was made of the 10 CBD/CDD projects in Benin as part of a country study. Finally, 473 headquarters and field staff were sent a questionnaire that included questions on safeguard issues to assess Bank performance in the area of CBD/CDD projects and how Bank capacity to undertake CBD/CDD interventions has evolved.[2]

Because of the broad definition of CBD/CDD used, which includes some projects with only minor CBD/CDD aspects, the sample projects are heterogeneous. Therefore, the projects were divided into two broad groups:

- **CBD/CDD with subprojects (CBD/CDD-S)** (76 percent of the sample): CBD/CDD projects for which the majority of investment funding is for a large number of small and scattered subprojects. Such subprojects may be multisectoral or may be limited to a single sector, such as health or education.
- **Other Projects (CBD/CDD-NS)**: Projects that have CBD/CDD aspects or components but do not fit the definition above.

Quality at Entry

The study found that the EA category was correctly assigned for 80 percent of the sample projects but, given the nature and extent of potential impacts, it was judged that 9 percent of Category Bs should have been As and 38 percent of Cs should have been Bs (see box 5.1 in Chapter 5 for definitions of these categories). The quality of appraisal was rated moderately satisfactory and above for 70 percent of the total sample, with newer projects scoring higher. The quality of EA documents was mixed: only two of the five A projects and 74 percent of B projects were rated moderately satisfactory or above. The special requirements for IDA B projects with a separate EA report were generally observed. The quality of Resettlement Action Plans and Indigenous Peoples Development Plans was generally high. The number of cases where the potential applicability of one or more of the safeguards policies should have been discussed but was not was high—about equal to the cases where policies were triggered. Compliance with the public disclosure and consultation requirements of the safeguard policies was good for resettlement and indigenous peoples issues, but less so for EAs. In contrast, provisions for capacity building were well developed, with monitoring somewhat less so.

Overall, quality at entry was rated moderately satisfactory and above for 70 percent of the sample. The small group of FI (Financial Intermediary) projects were rated much better than average, while As were distinctly worse than average. Newer projects are markedly better than the older group—81 percent versus 54 percent moderately satisfactory and above. CBD/CDD-S projects also score better than CBD/CDD-NS—77 percent versus 50 percent moderately satisfactory and above. Adjustable Program Loans (APLs) scored somewhat better than conventional projects. In terms of Regions, Africa, Europe and Central Asia, and the Middle East and North Africa have the highest percentages of moderately satisfactory and above, while Latin America and the Caribbean and South Asia have the lowest. Among sectors, transport, social, and environment had the best results, while the ratings for the rural and urban sectors were well below average.

The study found that internal guidance on the use of the FI category and, consequently, the practices of the Regions have not been entirely consistent since that category was introduced in January 1999. Discussion about the assignment of the FI category for most CBD/CDD projects is ongoing, but full guidance has yet to be issued.

Quality during Implementation

Despite format changes in the Project Status Report (PSR) that encourage detailed reporting on the implementation of safeguard measures, such reporting remains sparse and inadequate. This is true especially for Category A projects, which should receive particular scrutiny during implementation, and FIs, where the real work of screening subprojects and designing mitigation measures falls into the project implementation phase. There was no specialist follow up for cases where the dam safety and pest management policies were triggered. There was almost no reporting on capacity building or monitoring systems. Most of the Implementation Completion Reports (ICRs) were also less than satisfactory on reporting safeguard compliance, with the majority containing no discussion at all. Of the four Project Performance Assessment Reports (PPARs) available for this sample, two provided good analysis of safeguard issues, while the other two said nothing.[3]

The overall quality of implementation was rated moderately satisfactory and above for only 35 percent of cases, with A projects at 40 percent. While newer projects score much better than older ones, at 44 percent moderately satisfactory and above, they are still far from meeting Bank standards. As at appraisal, CBD/CDD-S projects are distinctly better than CBD/CDD-NS (38 percent versus 25 percent). In contrast to the quality at entry ratings, East Asia and the Pacific and South Asia score highest for quality of supervision of safeguard issues, with Latin America and the Caribbean and the Middle East and North Africa scoring lowest. Sectorally, water supply and sanitation and transport had the best record, with energy, mining & private sector, social, and education scoring lowest.

Overall Project Quality

When the ratings for entry and implementation are combined, the overall proportion of projects moderately satisfactory and above is 70 percent, the same outcome as for quality at entry. However, this disguises the fact that the projects rated (fully) satisfactory and above slip from 52 percent at entry to 17 percent when implementation is considered, and those rated unsatisfactory and highly unsatisfactory climb from 20 percent to 33 percent. Regardless of statistical quirks, the result of 70 percent falls well below Bank expectations. Between EA categories, the result for the small FI sample is 100 percent moderately satisfactory and above, while Bs and Cs are close to the average. The main concern is the very low percentage of A projects (40 percent) that is being handled well. Nevertheless, newer projects are closer to compliance than the older group—87 percent to 45 percent. While 87 percent is an encouraging result, it includes 65 percent in the moderately satisfactory category, indicating considerable room for improvement. The Europe and Central Asia and Middle East and North Africa Regions achieved the best results overall, with the other Regions close to each other at a lower level. Among the sectors, transport, social, and environment scored highest, and urban lowest.

The review also found that difficulties exist in applying the safeguard policies to multicomponent projects and that the potential for cumulative impacts from large numbers of small subprojects is sometimes overlooked. The importance of adequate collection and disposal of medical waste was not recognized in some earlier health projects, but recent practice has improved.

The review found that 6 of the 11 projects rated unsatisfactory on overall quality were in the Bank's largest borrower countries.

The survey of Bank staff showed that only a quarter of respondents agreed that resources for addressing safeguard issues were sufficient, though about half felt that current policies were relevant for CBD/CDD projects.

Conclusions

Four broad themes emerge from the analysis:

- Although there has been clear improvement, safeguard compliance in CBD/CDD projects does not yet fully meet Bank standards.
- While quality at entry needs improvement, safeguards compliance during implementation warrants much greater attention by the Bank and borrowers, and may indicate the need for greater allocation of supervision resources.
- Gaps in the compliance system may be leading to significant environmental and social impacts, which may not be caught by the monitoring and reporting systems typically used.
- The Bank appears to have particular difficulty in ensuring safeguard compliance in its largest borrowers.

Based on its findings and conclusions, the Review makes the following recommendations.

At the level of policy development, Regional coordination, staff guidance, and training:

- Guidance is urgently needed on the appropriate EA categorization of CBD/CDD projects, especially on the use of the FI category and on the special requirements for IDA B projects with a separate EA report.
- Training of task teams in the application of the safeguard policies to CBD/CDD projects should be intensified and should rely heavily on "best practice" examples, of which this Review has identified some.
- A thematic study of the environmental and social implications of changes in land use may be warranted.
- In any planned revision of Operational Policy 4.01 (and/or the other safeguard policies), special attention should be given inter alia to: streamlining the IDA B with separate EA report procedures; defining "financial intermediary"; dealing with multicomponent A projects; defining standards for supervision and completion reporting on safeguards compliance; and a possible mandated role for the Regional environmental and social units in the supervision of A projects.
- The experience of the Poland: Rural Development Project should be thoroughly reviewed for examples of the issues that may arise from the use of country systems for safeguards compliance.

At the level of Regional safeguards compliance assurance:

- Evaluating the recent transfer of sign-off authority for Category B and FI projects in light of the above findings and those of other OED studies, including staffing and budgeting issues.
- Ensuring full compliance at entry with safeguard policies, especially in the Bank's largest borrower countries.
- Ensuring that policies other than Operational Policy 4.01 are triggered in appropriate cases and necessary follow up actions taken.
- Obtaining resources for and carrying out special reviews of safeguard compliance for CBD/CDD projects under supervision, with special attention to the adequacy of agreed provisions, the effectiveness of their implementation, and the success of capacity building and monitoring activities.
- Developing standard document packages (cf. procurement documents) for safeguard instruments such as EAs, Environmental Management Plans, Resettlement Action Plans, and Indigenous Peoples Development Plans.

- Reviewing the potential for delegation of safeguard management authority to national agencies.

At the level of project development, approval and supervision:

- Identification of potential safeguard issues, for example, by use of Strategic Environmental Assessment.
- Mainstreaming environmental and social safeguards into the preparation process for CBD/CDD projects, for example, in developing, planning, programming, and monitoring programs, as well as staff training.
- Collaborating closely with the Regional environmental and social units in assigning EA categories appropriately and in using the Integrated Safeguards Data Sheet as a "contract" for actions needed between the project concept development and appraisal stages.
- Being sensitive to the special disclosure and consultation requirements of Categories A and B (and agreeing with management on commonsense waivers where process requirements may impede project quality or timeliness).
- Obtaining sufficient financial and staff resources to allow adequate supervision of the implementation of agreed safeguard measures, especially for As and Bs with an EMP, including periodic review of a sample of subprojects.
- Using the comment boxes in the PSR form to explain the reasoning behind the ratings given, the progress of capacity building or monitoring programs, and any unforeseen problems encountered, with special attention to Category A projects.
- Using the Midterm Review to look in greater depth at safeguard compliance, with the assistance of environmental and/or social specialists.
- Following the guidelines for the ICR in reporting on safeguard compliance at project completion.

ANNEX R: ADVISORY COMMITTEE COMMENTS

Robert Chambers

The OED team deserves congratulations on the effort put into the monumental task of this evaluation. The subject matter is vast, scattered and difficult to assess. The documents made available to the Advisory Committee and our discussions in December 2004 made it clear that the research was carried out with conventional rigour and care, and that the conclusions are credible, based on and emerging from careful and balanced analysis of the evidence. The extensive and valuable literature review also drew on and collated much other relevant experience. Other aid agencies would do well to conduct evaluations similar in their independence, breadth and depth as those of the OED. The conclusions, as far as they go, resonate with and are confirmed by my own experience. The recommendations, however, fall short of what the evidence implies.

I note that CBD/CDD approaches with HIV/AIDS are not included and are the subject of a separate evaluation. Given the delicacy and complexity of AIDS-related issues, and my participation in a Bank-led workshop on CDD and HIV/AIDS in Africa, I expect its findings to be even more negative than those presented in this present evaluation.

There is much in the report which merits endorsement, presenting aspects which are both positive and negative. Rather than list such points, let me highlight four issues which qualify the conclusions of the evaluation. I do not make these comments with any pleasure, or lightly, but given what I have experienced, and given the Bank's commitment to professionalism in the service of poor people, I have to make them. All four suggest that this evaluation is over-favourable:

1. Picking winners. This is not a criticism of the selection of the large sample of projects where I agree with the points about this made by Norman Uphoff. There are two other points.

First, success with "indigenously matured organisations" is the result of no doubt rational cherry-picking by the Bank. These were outstanding organisations with exceptionally high calibre, continuity and commitment of management with charismatic and inspiring leaders and which had existed for a decade or more and already successfully gone to very large scale: for example, AKRSP Pakistan, the NDDB in India, and SEWA in Gujarat. They were highly successful before the Bank became involved. They are correctly distinguished as a separate category from other CBD/CDD. Their performance is irrelevant to the evaluation of other CBD/CDD projects, which are by far the majority. In earlier stages of their development they did not need, and might have been hampered by, support from the World Bank.

Second, the Matrouh Project in Egypt is world-renowned as perhaps the most famous Bank flagship participatory project. It is several times mentioned. We know that it benefited from exceptional continuity of exceptional staff and high-level support from James Wolfensohn. But even it, one of the most favoured and best examples that could be found, is noted in this evaluation for its serious downsides, including the effects of creating a parallel organisation and overlooking changes in land tenure which harmed the Bedouin. If one of the very best cherries has such flaws, one may wonder about the rest.

2. Positive bias. Any evaluation of Bank projects involving interviews with Government staff and NGO beneficiaries of Bank funding is vulnerable to positive biases. The power and prestige of the Bank, the careful respect with which it is treated, and the tendency to try to please with favourable feedback, present systemic difficulties in knowing what is really happening. All power deceives (see Chapter 5 of my book *Whose Reality Counts?*). However careful the research, there will always be questions about prudent, deferential and self-serving responses. It is as much as some officials' jobs are worth to say anything negative about the Bank.

3. Hidden negative externalities. The following negative effects are either not mentioned or understated. The fact that they are half-hidden to conventional research does not make them any less plausible or less real. Some of them are part of another and more inclusive research agenda.

- Diversion of progressive NGOs (both INGOs and NNGOs) from rights-based and empowering activities which would do more for poor people than the provision of infrastructure which does less, and/or may even be negative, and/or may drag the NGOs back into activities they were attempting to move on from. (36 per cent of projects had some form of NGO involvement). In pro-poor terms, this is likely to reduce NGO additionality, leaving poor people net losers.
- Undermining other more participatory, less target- and disbursement-driven, less infrastructure-focused, and more sustainable programmes supported by other organisations in neighbouring areas. ("Why should we do it ourselves when our neighbours are getting so much done for them or for free?")
- Diversion of government recurrent funds, staff and materials from other places and services (schools, clinics etc) to the new infrastructure, with hidden costs to services in those other places. With schools and clinics, for example, resources are most likely to be diverted to communities which are accessible to government and Bank staff inspection, to show success. Where government staff and recurrent funds are, as so often, limiting, this will deprive poor communities that are less accessible.
- Risks and costs associated with top-down time-bound disbursement-driven capital projects. These include scope for petty and not so petty corruption, and the proliferation of opportunistic NGOs as noted on page 35.
- The long-term disempowering effects of dependence and disillusion created at the community level (see, e.g., box 4.2). Communities become, as so many have, less self-reliant and more inclined to lobby, beg, and wait

These are general tendencies. There will be exceptions. But together on balance they mean that the findings of the evaluation should be more negative. Given the goodwill, energy and commitment of many Bank staff, I regret having to say this. But it is quite possible that, overall, the Bank's CBD/CDD initiatives do more harm than good to poor communities and people. In addition there are the opportunity costs of alternatives foregone.

4. The comparative disadvantages of the Bank. While the conclusions of the report follow from the evidence and analysis, they do not adequately confront the comparative disadvantage of the Bank with CBD/CDD, nor the full range of what would be required if performance were to justify continuing to try to support it. This is alarming, especially when CBD/CDD-related lending, far from prudently diminishing, is increasing beyond its already remarkably high level.

The comparative disadvantages are institutional and paradigmatic and related to:

- Reliance on loans, the future repayment of which may impact adversely on government services and so on poor people. If loan-based rather than grant-based projects are to be justified, repayments will be at the cost of other government expenditure. The bar, therefore, has to be higher.
- Disbursement pressures and the typical one-year sub-project cycle (pp. 20–21) with top-

down one-shot interventions, an approach antithetical to participation and to assuring benefits to those who are poorer. We know and do not need to learn again how badly this works.
- The management and staff-intensity of empowering and participatory development. The extra cost of preparation of CBD/CDD projects is only 10 percent higher than non-CBD/CDD. For effective pro-poor participation, it would need to be far higher than this.
- The staff incentive system of the Bank which rewards high and fast disbursements. This was a major factor which emerged from a participatory workshop for task managers which I facilitated a few years ago. Nothing I have heard suggests that this has changed significantly.
- Inability to learn and change. That the ratings of CBD/CDD projects are stagnating suggests that institutional learning and change are not taking place. A likely reason is that the Bank is not looking hard enough at itself or is simply unable to perceive, learn, and change.

These factors combine to disable the Bank, making it inherently difficult for it to do well with CBD/CDD. The question then is whether they can be changed.

The report correctly points to the need for radical institutional change in government bureaucracies: "The literature shows that the institutionalization of a CBD/CDD approach requires a radical reorientation in the way governments and bureaucracies operate." This applies if anything more to the Bank itself, as the dominant partner, than to governments and their bureaucracies. This is not rocket science. It is common sense and common experience. In practice, the disabling culture, incentives, procedures and imperatives of the Bank are passed on "downwards" to governments and NGOs. It is no good saying "Do as I say but not as I do." The Bank may not be able to become more participatory. But unless it does, it cannot expect the CBD/CDD it funds to be cost-effective in empowering and benefiting poor people. This means that the Bank itself must walk the talk, and take on board "physician heal thyself" and "do no harm."

The Recommendations

The recommendations in this final version of the evaluation fall far short of what is demanded by the evidence. If the Bank is serious about poverty and empowerment, more radical action is required. In effect, the recommendations as they stand leave the door open to going on with more of much the same. The evidence of this OED evaluation, combined with other studies and insights, shows the CBD/CDD initiatives of the Bank to be of such questionable value that the approach now should be damage limitation, intensive learning and finding out whether change is possible in the Bank. I hesitate to say what I believe the Bank should do, but the stakes for poor people and communities are so high and on such a scale that it would be wrong for me not to do so. I have agonised over this. And I recognise that there is no way I can assess fully the implications or modalities for what follows. But on the basis of the evidence of this evaluation and of other experience, my own best judgement is that it the Bank should now, and decisively:

- Rein back on and/or slow down existing CBD/CDD projects, where this is legally and ethically feasible.
- Impose a moratorium on new ones.
- Learn more about what happens and what might be made to happen by selecting ongoing projects for intensive learning through action research, including investigating hidden externalities.
- As part of this examine the Bank itself—its culture, procedures, norms, incentives and behaviours—and its impact on governments, NGOs and communities, and analyse the contradictions between these and empowering, pro-poor community development and how these play out.
- And then review how the Bank must change if the short and long-term effects for poor people, communities and countries of Bank-driven CBD/CDD are to be positive and to justify the costs, and whether and how such change could be achieved.

Robert Chambers
5 September 2005

Norman Uphoff

This evaluation is originally planned to evaluate ***World Bank support for community-driven development (CDD) projects***. However, when reviewing earlier drafts of this report, this and the other reviewers saw some problem with characterizing these projects "community-driven." This terminology had been was introduced within the Bank to distinguish newer, more participatory project initiatives from what were being called "community-based" development projects. The term "CDD" seemed rather grandiose to the reviewers for what was actually happening in these projects. They were hardly "community-driven" when the project design, what kinds of things could be done, within what time frame, on what financial terms, were all decided unilaterally by Bank staff. The projects themselves were not open to local participatory inputs, only subprojects. The main decisions left to communities were whether or not they would make a proposal to gain access to Bank project funds for something they wanted to do (within the non-negotiable framework set by Bank or government personnel) and how they would carry out the work once it was approved. This issue of how these projects should be described does not make the evaluation that has been done less relevant or meritorious, since the purpose of the assessment was to learn more about the Bank's approach to this kind of development, no matter what it is called.

The projects have in common an aspiration (and enabling provisions) for delegating to communities (or their representatives) responsibility for taking initiative to plan and implement certain improvements in infrastructure and/or services at community level. But "community-driven" means only community-initiated, -implemented and -managed, within externally-set parameters. The first point in the Executive Summary makes clear that only participation in "subprojects" is covered by the study. There is nothing wrong with this, and it can be preferable to more conventional top-down efforts for local development, *depending on results*.

The evaluation of results found that what were called CDD projects, meeting certain criteria for a community role in activity initiation and implementation, *did not perform much better, and sometimes less well*, than conventional projects with similar objectives and environments. This could be because there is nothing inherently superior in CDD-type project, or what were called CDD projects were not planned and carried out in ways that gave them any advantage. From my experience of over 30 years working on participatory development, I would think the latter explanation is more apt, and indeed, the evaluation team identified many ways in which the way the Bank operates "got in the way" of carrying out the projects included in this study so that they did not perform noticeably better. Possibly if they had been carried out properly, they might still have shown no performance advantage. But we can't know that until the CDD concept has at least been properly introduced. Can CDD deliver more benefits to the poor? More cheaply? More reliably? We don't know and can't say because it hasn't really been properly tried.

The overall hypothesis guiding this evaluation was, essentially, that CDD projects (as supported by the Bank) would produce more and better outcomes. The evidence assembled and assessed does not support the hypothesis; so we are left with the **null hypothesis**. However, as someone who has worked on participatory development, several times as a consultant for the Bank on this subject, I must say that I am not surprised, because I have seen the Bank's efforts, however well-intended, to be continually well behind the "state-of-the-art." Although there are some ways in which some of the CDD projects have given superior results, there is no basis for concluding that *on average*, the Bank would get better results by doing more of its projects in what it has been considered and created as a CDD mode.

This said, the converse is also true: there would be no significant degradation of the Bank's portfolio by expanding CDD efforts even as currently supported by the Bank. The increased cost associated with CDD project design and sometimes in implementation can probably be justified by some subsequent cost reductions to the government as communities take more financial responsibility, or by more rapid implementation once the planning has been completed, or from better post-project utilization and maintenance of project services and facilities, not all the time, but sometimes. Such a conclusion is based on the evidence provided in the evaluation. It does not take into account the various **external costs** that Robert Chambers delineates very persuasively in his comments on the evaluation. Such broader considerations that go beyond the terms of reference and the framework of this evaluation could justify his suggestion that there be a moratorium on CDD efforts until the Bank figures out how to pursue them more effectively.

There is little to find fault with in the way that the evaluation itself has been done, or in the way that it is reported. The evaluators have used both quantitative methods and qualitative description and summarization quite satisfactorily. There is not much to critique on methodological grounds. However, this does not make the evaluation itself irreproachable, because the state-of-the-art followed has some shortcomings that should be noted. The following comments refer to the way in which formal evaluations are done these days by institutions like OED, rather than to the way that this particular evaluation was done.

Sample size and statistical significance. One area where the evaluation could have been more informative is to have disaggregated the CDD sample more in terms of the *kinds of development work* being fostered. This was not done because that would have reduced subsample sizes and impaired the scope and validity of statistical analysis. However, by lumping diverse experiences together in one pool, or making only a few gross disaggregations, the validity and value of the generalizations are diluted for the sake of being able to use statistical methods and offer assessments of (statistical) significance. If the analysis had been done on smaller but more homogeneous subsamples, what could be said with statistical confidence would have been reduced—but we would know more about whether CDD approaches (as the Bank has been supporting them) would be more productive and sustainable in some sectors than in others, in some Regions, within certain time periods, etc. The OED team made a defensible decision to analyze internally heterogeneous samples. But more "less rigorous" analysis could have revealed some operationally useful insights, not being "shackled" by statistical analysis conventions.

Ontological assumptions. In this analysis, as in most such evaluations these days, there is a certain "reductionism" that obscures more than it reveals. There is an implicit assumption that there is an "essence" of CDD that is the same in all cases that are characterized as CDD, and that this quality is rather equally represented in all such cases. Then there is a concomitant assumption that this "essence" of CDD, whatever it is, has *independent, rather than contingent, causal effects.* Such assumptions are common throughout development studies, and indeed in most social science analyses, which try to draw broad generalizations (about often ethereal characteristics) rather than stick to more disaggregated, concretely specified assessments. This kind of reliance on abstractions is at the root of many of the failures in development efforts, and it is one reason why so much of our social science is so irrelevant to real-world decision making and action. This comment is not a critique of this evaluation, but rather of the broader enterprise.

The Bank's CDD approach has sought to bring more participation and more flexibility into World Bank projects. This is commendable and moves the Bank toward what can be thought of as the "state-of-the-art." This evaluation documents that the Bank's procedures, staff incentives and orientation, borrower-country predispositions and capabilities, and still other factors have kept "CDD" projects from achieving the degree of community assumption of responsibility that was anticipated and hoped for, and the amount of improvement in the lives of poor people that was expected. What is evaluated in this report is, at most, "partial CDD," and some of the case studies suggest this was even "minimal CDD." When local people say that the project did not address their priority needs (see 3.9) or they are not willing to maintain the facilities or services beyond life-of-project (4.30), it does not appear that this is an evaluation of truly "community-driven" processes. Such processes are directed to meeting priority needs, and if what is created is of value to people, they will find ways to maintain the facilities or services somehow, anyhow.

An earlier draft of the report described the Bank's Adaptable Program Loans (APLs) and Learning and Innovation Loans (LILs) as "allowing (!) communities greater choice in the selection of activities" and as "providing them opportunities to control investment decisions and resources during project implementation." This underscores the extent to which the process is in Bank or borrower government hands. These are community-proposed (not community-selected) projects, and they are community-managed (within often complicated and burdensome terms).Few people would understand this to be "community-driven development."

The concept of **"community"** that underlies this effort is also questionable. Endnote 1 to Chapter 1 in the report says: in a World Bank project, a community is considered a "unified, organic whole." This is dubious thinking, suggesting that the Bank has learned little from the hundreds of social science assessments of "community" written over the past half century. These have stressed the pitfalls of internal divisions, conflicting interests, etc. among any given set of households that is delineated on the basis of residential area. Even when there are ethnic or other kinds of homogeneity, village residents often find personalistic or other bases on which to factionalize. Some communities will have a high degree of solidarity and significant potential for collective action. But this is a *variable* rather than a *defining characteristic*. (The Bank's own efforts to bring some rigor to the concept of "social capital" have help to clarify this matter, because this concept does not take village solidarity for granted, but rather examines different levels, kinds, and activation.)

Assuming that the Bank is serious about **poverty reduction** and **empowerment**, two of the most attractive justifications for its existence and for its support by member governments, there is much more that could be done to improve prospects for better CDD outcomes. My own experience with a USAID project introducing participatory irrigation management in Sri Lanka in the early 1980s has demonstrated that there can be significant measurable benefits from truly community-driven development. The incremental rice production possible in a single season, the 1997 dry season, alone covered 4–5 times the total cost of the participatory component, for example (see article by Uphoff and Wijayaratna in *World Development*, November, 2000). And such investments in social infrastructure and social capital can be sustainable; the community organizations established in 1981-85 are still functioning well 25 years after end of project, and they became the model for a national program improving management of the whole sector. (On the strategy and implementation of this effort, see Uphoff, *Learning from Gal Oya*, Intermediate Technology Publications, 1996.) The Bank has approached the introduction of CDD in a rather self-referential manner, trying to learn mostly from its own experience, which is a limited "slice' of what is known and what has been done, rather than look beyond its institutional boundaries.

One of the most interesting and relevant findings of the evaluation concerns the value of recognizing and working with **informal organizations** (pp. 39-40, and the very instructive Annex K), not just with formal organizations. We saw this clearly in the Sri Lanka experience mentioned above. One of the "hypotheses" we tested and confirmed was that it would be most effective to **begin with *informal* organization**, creating a **demand** for formal organization rather than **begin with supply** and then try to create a local demand for it, the usual approach. Our strategy was: work first, organize second. More could be said and done along these lines, but this last paragraph "flags" this issue as one where the Bank could usefully focus some attention.

Norman Uphoff
Cornell University

Paiboon Wattanasiritham

The Revised report has taken into account the Advisory Panel's concern about the World Bank's use of the term "Community Driven Development" (CDD) and has made changes which make the report read better on the whole.

In particular, the reference to the participation of communities in development as either "community-based development" (CBD) or "community-driven development"(CDD) appears more appropriate and more easily understood.

Realizing the many difficulties in evaluating the effectiveness of World Bank support for community development, the evaluation attempt has done well in gathering information from several angles, making logical analyses and interpretations, and finally coming up with reasonable and credible conclusions and recommendations.

The difficulties in evaluating CBD/CDD effectiveness in the context of World Bank programs stem partly, as pointed out in the report, from the fact that the Bank has not , until recently, systematically identified and tracked its portfolio of CBD/CDD projects and therefore has lacked a comprehensive understanding of the evolution and scope of its work on community development. Further, the Bank has not been sufficiently clear about the objectives of using CBD/CDD approaches, criteria for choosing between different community development approaches, or how to measure the results. But evaluating CBD/CDD effectiveness in World Bank programs is also difficult because, for CBD/CDD, and especially for CDD, to be effective , a complex set of factors have to be at work. Government policies and programs, national and local administrative structures, relevant laws and regulations, attitudes and capacities of officials who can have impact on CBD/CDD effectiveness, the economic, social , cultural and human capacity settings of communities in the country, all contribute to how easy or difficult it is for CBD/CDD programs to be effective, as well as how long it would take for the cumulative effects to be realized. World Bank projects or programs, therefore, may be more or less effective depending, to a significant extent, on the nature of the programs' interrelationships with the many relevant factors just mentioned.

Utilizing a "systems thinking" approach should be useful in undertaking such an evaluation as well as in drawing conclusions and making recommendations.

A country or society—comprising communities, institutions ,organizations, etc.—is a highly complex and dynamic "system." World Bank programs, therefore, are but a small "part" or "component" of a very big, complex "whole", especially when considering that "sustainable poverty reduction" is the ultimate objective of those World Bank programs. In this context of "systems thinking", it should be added, CBD/CDD is more than "poverty reduction", and "sustainable poverty reduction" is more than CBD/CDD. Furthermore, the differentiation and comparison between CBD/CDD and non-CBD/CDD programs cannot be too clear-cut since both, as well as the many other relevant factors, are very much inter-related and intertwined in a complex and dynamic manner. Indeed, CBD/CDD and non-CBD/CDD programs can, and perhaps should also, be complementary. Although they may be different in nature and may aim at different outputs and even outcomes, the ultimate objective, or final impact, should be the same, that is, sustainable development which includes poverty reduction and improvement in people's quality of living.

The purpose of evaluation is (or should be) "to learn and improve." This OED evaluation should be a useful point of departure, or point of reference, for both learning and improvement efforts, both of which are mutually reinforcing.

Much "learning" can be gained from such processes as "knowledge management" (KM) which in turn may be organized under one or more, or all, of the following contexts :

- KM within a World Bank program
- KM among World Bank programs
- KM within a country
- KM among countries
- KM within the World Bank

- KM among a number of organizations including the World Bank
- KM under any other contexts or combinations.

For the World Bank in particular, appropriate knowledge management, or some other learning systems, should be useful for executives and staffs, not only in understanding and appreciating the true essence of CBD/CDD, but also in being able to come up with innovations and / or creative developments that will be beneficial for all concerned, including the World Bank itself.

As a "development partner" of the its member countries (particularly developing countries), the World Bank may find it constructive and beneficial, both to the member countries and to the Bank , to have an assessment study undertaken as to the relevant situations and factors that have bearing on each country's potentials for higher degrees of community empowerment, including community-driven development.

Such a study would be particularly relevant in the case where the World Bank is to have a development lending program in a country, be it a CBD/CDD-related programs or a non-CBD/CDD program. The outcome of the study should then be useful is helping shape the concept and the design of the program in such a way that it is conducive to the improvement in community empowerment or community-driven development (CDD) efforts. For this purpose, it should be borne in mind also that true and effective community empowerment or CDD need to involve a comprehensive, integrated development agenda of the country, not just the World Bank program. In addition, adequate time will be needed for the many relevant parts and factors to be in place and become rooted firmly enough to make the empowerment or CDD sustainable. In this context, therefore, it may be useful for the World Bank to be clear from the beginning about the purpose, nature, scope, etc., of its program in a country, particularly whether the program aims at CDD as the main thrust or only a supplementary feature, and so on.

The concept of CBD/CDD, especially in the form of CDD, logically points to the principle of "holistic country-driven development " (HCDD), about which an in-depth study as well as a knowledge management process should be undertaken, which could lead to a significant change in the way World Bank programs, especially country programs, are conceptualized, designed, and managed.

A number of possible outcomes of such a study (and / or knowledge management process) can be envisaged. For example, more emphasis may be given to "holistic country-driven development" programs as opposed to ordinary programs or the so-called "country assistance" programs. In such a "holistic country-driven development" (HCDD) program, "community-driven development" (CDD) should automatically be a significant part, or even a crucial part, of the total package.

Paiboon Wattanasiritham
2 September 2005

ANNEX S: MANAGEMENT RESPONSE

Introduction

Management welcomes a review of the effectiveness of Bank support for community-driven development (CDD)[1] and projects that include community participation (covering CBD by OED's definition).[2] Management is encouraged by the evidence that CDD and CBD operations have in aggregate, higher development outcome ratings than non-CBD and non-CDD operations and have proven to be an effective tool for client countries. Management notes that this review reinforces findings from previous OED reports including the OED Review of Social Development[3] that community participation contributes to overall project success and sustainability. Given the demand from client governments, these types of operations are expected to remain an important component of the Bank's assistance to client countries.

Areas of Agreement. Management concurs with the OED Review that sustainability, monitoring and evaluation, and local leadership are issues of particular importance to the Bank's work on community development. Accordingly, for some time management has been devoting increasing resources to address these issues to improve the quality of its support for community development interventions. These issues are discussed in more detail below.

Areas of Divergence. Management, however, has questions regarding the relevance, rigor, and clarity of some aspects of the OED Review. In particular, management would like to note:

a. The potential for misunderstanding the Bank's role in CDD operations and borrowing countries' ownership of the CDD agenda, as evidenced by a growing demand. The OED review talks about "Bank projects" and the "Bank-subproject cycle" and contrasts "Bank projects" with government programs, not noting that CDD operations are all government programs. The Bank's role is to provide support.
b. The analysis and findings related to safeguards and fiduciary aspects of CDD that lead OED to recommend more guidance and oversight. Data from OED's own reviews of compliance with safeguard policies have never highlighted CDD or "CBD/CDD" operations as having more problems than other types of projects. On the contrary several other types of projects were highlighted. Data from the Quality Assurance Group (QAG) indicate that CDD operations do better in assuring compliance with Bank policies than the average for all other operations, both during preparation and implementation. This is not surprising, given the extensive training programs, thematic reviews, and operational guidance already available to staff.
c. The suggestion that the Bank should do more up-front analysis and move more slowly on "CDD/CBD" operations; while great care is important in working with client countries on the preparation of all operations, Management does not see evidence of a need to slow down its processing of CDD operations, given their better quality at entry and better outcomes that the average for all other projects.

This remaining divergence likely results from the scope and methodology of the OED review. Management tracks CDD operations and operations that involve participation broadly, including community participation. For its review, OED created a set of operations as discussed in Annex E of the report. The methodology includes text searches and OED staff judgment. That set of operations differs significantly from either of the sets that Management tracks. Much of the evidence OED presents for "CDD" concerns operations that do not meet the definition of CDD used broadly, including by Management.[4] Further, Management has questions concerning the methodology used, including the data sources, fieldwork, and surveys (for more details see Annex I).

The Approach Paper. As outlined in the Approach Paper,[5] the original focus of the review was on CDD. It stated that the objective of the review was to "assess the relevance, efficacy, efficiency, institutional development impact, and sustainability of the World Bank's CDD interventions" (para. 6).[6] While the Approach Paper clearly stated that the evaluation would also look at other forms of community participation, the three primary evaluation questions and the six sub-questions included in the approach paper focused on CDD.[7] In management's view, a review with a focus on CDD would have been particularly useful, given the growth in the CDD portfolio in recent years and the increased corporate attention to CDD over the past five years.[8] Management believes that a review of the now substantial set of closed CDD projects (56 operations at the end of fiscal year 2005) would have been more appropriate. When invited by OED to comment early in the review process, management expressed its concerns with how the Approach Paper defined the scope of OED's inquiry and with the proposed methodology. In retrospect, management should have shared those concerns officially in writing with OED and with executive directors.

Management Comments

The management comments that follow refer to the main issues of agreement and provide an expanded set of comments on the evolution of Bank community-driven development operations. As noted above, the OED review highlights three areas that, while important for all operations, are particularly pertinent to effective CDD operations: sustainability, monitoring and evaluation, and local leadership. For some time management has been directing attention to these issues in CDD operations. The impetus for the establishment of a Bank-wide CDD Steering Group and a corporate Anchor unit in FY01 was to draw on global experiences in order to enhance the quality and effectiveness of community-driven development operations. Client Governments have embraced CDD as a valuable approach to deliver public services to poor people, to strengthen the capacity of people's organizations to participate in development, and to build the assets and capabilities of poor women and men so as to improve their well-being. Given the heightened interest of client governments, management has invested significantly in ensuring that ongoing and new programs benefit from global lessons learned through improved guidance and technical support.

Key Area of Agreement: Sustainability

The review attests to overall improvements in sustainability of the "CBD/CDD" portfolio, albeit with scope for further improvement (para. 4.27). When CDD operations and programs are carefully designed and well implemented, with clear exit strategies, the likelihood of sustainability increases. OED's Social Development review found that "giving the participants the responsibility for structuring their involvement in the project increases the likelihood of success and sustainability."[9] The Social Development evaluation emphasized the value of quality participation in the success of Bank-supported operations and noted that "best practice" projects were likely to have attributes such as involvement of beneficiaries in project design and implementation and securing of community contributions to the project and its future maintenance (Annex D). All are attributes found in most CDD operations. A combination of top-down and bottom-up measures is critical for sustainability of any type of project. These typically include line ministry budgetary resources and inputs, appropriate technical standards, community-led maintenance and local government involvement.[10]

Community-Level Sustainability. At the community level, sustainability efforts and project exit strategies revolve around dynamics of linkages between communities and external support institutions, most notably local governments. Design characteristics of CDD operations place considerable emphasis on embedding community initiatives in permanent institutional frameworks, including local government systems. Evidence from the field suggests that CDD initiatives with these design characteristics are more likely to be sustainable; for example, schools built through a CDD approach have more and better teachers than schools built without (Zambia) and child mortality declined more in areas that have involved communities than in areas that have not (Bolivia).[11]

Aid Dependency and Sustainability. Despite this evidence of trends showing increasing sustainability, the OED review mentions lower than average sustainability ratings for "CBD/CDD" operations. This rating covers a number of issues beyond sustainability of the service and infrastructure created. Specifically, for several operations rated as non-sustainable, OED noted in their rationale for the rating the issue of whether the implementing agency will be able to continue absent donor funding. While these issues of aid dependency are valid and important for all donor assistance, they are different from the issue of sustainability of outputs and outcomes at the community level.

Constant Attention to Sustainability Issues. Overall, what is required is constant attention during design and implementation to sustainability of community impacts. To this end, Management has augmented its internal quality control functions and scaled up its technical guidance through project Quality Enhancement Reviews, CDD quality clinics and peer reviewing.

Key Area of Agreement: Monitoring and Evaluation

Management agrees with OED that monitoring and evaluation (M&E) is of utmost importance. Management's approach to monitoring results emphasizes the identification and tracking of the impact of Bank-financed operations and learning from approaches that are most successful. Given that borrowing governments increasingly rely on CDD approaches to address community empowerment objectives, Management has for some time been strengthening monitoring and evaluation of the CDD portfolio.

Guidance on M&E. Consistent with OED recommendations to promote learning by doing, Management has been encouraging clients implementing CDD programs to test out different approaches, to build robust systems to monitor implementation for rapid and operationally relevant feedback, and to emulate best practice. The operational manuals that guide client implementation give practical guidance for setting up Management Information Systems to track results of decentralized local initiatives. Innovative beneficiary assessment approaches collect real time feedback from those directly involved in community initiatives, so that information about successes and challenges can be quickly relayed to implementing agencies.

Evaluating the Impact of CDD Approaches. As OED notes, while real-time information flow is crucial to success, it is also important to evaluate the impact of CDD approaches. As part of its efforts to improve impact evaluation across the Bank portfolio, management has placed particular emphasis on CDD. Given the institutional development objectives and decentralized implementation of CDD approaches, it is particularly challenging to evaluate CDD impact. Nonetheless more than 50 impact evaluations have been carried out for 36 CDD operations (see Annex II).[12] In addition several evaluations have been done that use the most sophisticated techniques available, that are more robust than those used in the past by essentially any development evaluators, including OED. They use randomized treatment and control sampling and differences in difference techniques (for example, the randomized studies of the Bolivia Social Fund and the Indonesia Kecamatan Development Program). Several additional sophisticated evaluations are currently underway. To measure the institutional effects of CDD operations, Management has developed and supported extensive quantitative and qualitative techniques for understanding changes in social capital, such as those applied recently in the Philippines, Indonesia, and Thailand.

Cost-Benefit Analysis. In addition to impact evaluation studies, Management also agrees with OED that it is important to do cost-benefit analysis of CDD operations—where feasible and at reasonable cost. Besides provisional ex-ante cost-benefit analysis (such as that carried out in the Philippines), many operations undertake some ex-post cost-benefit analyses; some examples include Bank support to the Cambodia SEILA program and the Indonesia Kecamatan Development Project. Operational manuals for CDD operations contain guidance on how to carry out economic analysis. As would be expected when communities are able identify and support operations that are their highest priorities, the internal rates of return for such operations are high. For example, in the Indonesia case, two independent cost-benefit analyses point to internal rates of returns in excess of 60 percent for rural roads built using CDD approaches. That said, ex-ante cost-benefit analysis of social sector operations is rare (and not required by Bank procedures), given the intrinsic difficulties, and social sector activities supported by CDD operations are no exception. OED is correct in noting that for the majority of interventions in client "CBD/CDD" operations supported by the Bank there was no ex-ante cost-benefit analysis of the project itself. OED fails to note, however, that individual sub-projects were subjected to economic analysis.[13]

Key Area of Agreement: Local Leadership

Management agrees with OED on the importance of supporting client countries in working effectively with local leadership. Communities are not homogenous. As management has learned from extensive experience in support of community initiatives, it is critical to ensure buy-in from diverse social groups within a given community. The role of elites needs to be carefully considered, but practice suggests that they can act benevolently and play a positive leadership role, as the OED review points out (para. 3.19, footnote 27). CDD programs, through capacity development, promote inclusive decision-making and collective action and strive for the type of institutional change that underlies participatory local governance. These programs are extensively engaged in dealing with the challenge of how to most effectively work with local leadership. The degree to which they have succeeded is reflected in part by assessments of perceptions of choice and relevance of investments. Evidence suggests that most benefits accrue to poor people; reviews of beneficiary assessments from eight countries "were uniform in their finding that beneficiaries consistently felt that...projects reflected priority needs of the community."[14] The quality of program design, including the role of community facilitators and local transparency and accountability measures, have a major bearing on a program's impact on community inclusion and community empowerment.

Evolution of CDD Programs

The CDD approach builds on a rich history of innovations in participatory development, predominantly accumulated from outside the Bank. The composite of CDD programs also reflect lessons from earlier efforts by the Bank in support of community-based development (CBD) initiatives of client countries. There are several CDD operating principles that are markedly different from CBD program mechanisms; these were conceived directly in response to perceived shortcomings in earlier CBD efforts. Of particular relevance are current CDD design features for institutional arrangements, the role of local government, and broader governance linkages.

The CDD Portfolio Today. The current CDD portfolio comprises iterative and evolving programs that build on lessons from across the portfolio—from prior operations in-country, similar operations in comparable environments (for example in post-conflict countries), and operations that address related technical and operational issues, such as decentralization reform and public-private partnerships. The CDD portfolio includes a host of long-standing, transformative CDD programs which have evolved over time. In these programs in particular, the areas of sustainability, local leadership challenges, and M&E have been of critical interest. Management will continue to put resources into learning in these areas and continue to exercise vigilance in enhancing operational guidance to staff. Some examples of client operations supported by the Bank that have contributed to and benefited from lessons learned include the following.

Andhra Pradesh (AP) CDD Operations, India

The AP District Poverty Initiatives Project (APDPIP) and AP Rural Poverty Reduction Project are two statewide community-driven rural poverty reduction projects under implementation in Southern India with World Bank support since the year 2000. These programs build on the AP Government's cumulative investments in women's self-help groups over the last 10 years. The APDPIP supports the development of self-managed grass-roots level institutions of poor rural women and their federations; it has supported half a million groups and 800 federations in 29,000 villages covering 80 percent of all rural poor households (6.4 million) over last five years. The key project investments include institution building, capacity building and local leadership development of community organizations, an investment risk fund in key livelihood sectors and livelihood support services for the poor. The project uses a learning-by-doing approach and employs process monitoring and other M&E mechanisms to develop mid-course corrections and make adjustments in project design and procedures. The current design features reflect this evolution.

Scaled-Up Investments in the Poor. An outcome of institutional development and the empowerment and skill enhancement of communities has been the willingness of public and private sector agencies, including commercial banks, to scale up their investments in the poor. Annual credit to poor households and household groups has increased twelve-fold from $23 million in 2000 to $276 million in 2005. The total credit flow from commercial banks to these groups is expected to reach $1 billion by the time the project closes. World Bank investment has proved to be catalytic and mobilization of other sources of finance has been key to ensuring sustainability of investments.

Fiduciary Aspects. The APDPIP project has invested in the development of adequate fiduciary and auditing systems to ensure accountability and transparency in a program of this scale, including building up auditing and financial management capacity among 800 federations of self-help groups. These federations have developed capacity to train village-level bookkeepers in financial management and provide auditing services. The project has initiated the development of a rating system jointly with financial institutions to provide performance data on village groups to banks and agencies investing in communities. The project commissions independent agencies to undertake process monitoring to give feedback on process, institutional and empowerment aspects.

Zambia Social Investment Fund (ZAMSIF)

This fund was conceived as a two-phase program to support, over a ten-year period, two main strategic objectives of the Government of Zambia (a) decentralization and empowering local authorities to improve governance and efficiency in service delivery; and (b) increasing access to basic social services through direct poverty interventions. It followed on two social recovery projects (SRP) designed in the late 1980s, and is a classic example of a CDD program that has evolved over time, based on country context and lessons learned. The earlier SRP projects worked directly with communities (and deconcentrated technical staff of central ministries) to deliver quick impacts and open up space for anticipated macro-level reforms. ZAMSIF also strove to support the implementation of critical aspects of the decentralization process and introduced a process for strengthening local government capacity and performance.

Learning and Design Evolution during Implementation. The project devised a process of graduation that would align a local government's capabilities with its responsibilities in each of two ZAMSIF components: a community investment fund financing community sub-projects and a district investment fund financing capacity building and providing funds for district-level subprojects serving multiple communities managed by local governments. Over time, the project was restructured and its development objectives modified in the face several structural challenges, including delays by the government in enacting supportive decentralization policies—notably new laws providing for elected local governments and policies to increase the limited administrative, technical and fiscal capacity of nominated local governments.

Kecamatan Development Project (KDP), Indonesia

This project is an example of a CDD program built on rigorous social and institutional analysis, adapted to country context, which includes mechanisms for poverty targeting and inclusion. In 1996, prior to the Asian economic crisis, a local level institutions study portrayed the rich variety of organizations and associations at that level capable of planning and managing a broad range of development projects. It also illustrated that development resources rarely reached local groups, and instead were channeled through public sector institutions that crowded out local initiatives in favor of government and elite controlled "user groups." With the onset of the economic crisis, economic gains vanished, poverty worsened, and both government policies and institutions were discredited. In this context, a rapid response to poverty was required that would by-pass weak and ineffective line agencies, establish transparent systems to deliver financial resources to communities to be used for high priority social and infrastructure projects, and develop institutional mechanisms at the local level that were more inclusive and community driven.

Targeting Financial Resources. To achieve its objectives, the project's financial resources were targeted to the poorest sub-districts in rural areas where poverty was most highly concentrated, and mechanisms were built in to ensure that poor people, and especially poor women, were incorporated into decision making about priorities and project proposals. Although originally intended to be small, the project was scaled up to permit financial flows to a large number of poor areas. Among the most innovative aspects of the program were mechanisms for transparency (such as access to public records, media involvement, and NGO scrutiny) and to encourage institutions to respond quickly to proposals and be responsive to community needs. The first KDP project covered about 30 percent of the rural sub-districts in the country and it has benefited more than 15,000 villages. Ongoing evaluations have determined that KDP investments are more cost-effective than other mechanisms for delivering similar services.

Learning During Implementation. As an example of learning by doing, Management encouraged, supported, and financed (along with DFID) a path-breaking study on monitoring possible corruption (as measured by price versus cost indicators) across different models of KDP interventions. The study found that increasing grass roots participation in monitoring village-level KDP interventions altered the method of possible corruption (it substantially reduced the theft of villagers' wages) but had relatively minimal effects on the overall level of possible corruption. However, KDP interventions that also included an announced increased probability of a government audit substantially reduced the level of possible corruption.[15] Because there are no other such careful analyses of corruption for non-CDD operations it is not possible to benchmark whether the amount of corruption observed in the CDD operations is greater or less that in other operations.

OED Recommendations

The following paragraphs provide Management's specific comments on the review's recommendations.

> ***Recommendation 1.*** *The Bank should provide operational guidance for the application of Bank safeguard policies and fiduciary oversight of CBD/CDD projects and for the strengthening of cost-benefit analysis and M&E [monitoring and evaluation] systems; and should commission an audit of the fiduciary aspects of a rep-*

resentative sample of CDD projects for submission to the Board within a year.

Operational Guidance on CDD Safeguards and Fiduciary Oversight. Management notes that it has been engaged for some time in providing additional operational guidance and fiduciary oversight and that CDD and "CBD/CDD" operations have benefited as a result. The Quality Assurance and Compliance Unit (QACU), the Rural Development anchor, and the CDD anchor have been conducting specialized training programs on safeguards in CDD operations. Additionally, the Regional safeguard teams routinely carry out thematic reviews of CDD operations to assess the level of compliance. The results of these studies have been used for development of staff guidelines for application of safeguard policies in CDD operations. The CDD anchor will continue to collaborate with QACU and Regional teams in providing operational guidance for the application of Bank safeguard policies during the preparation and implementation of CDD operations. There is no evidence from OED's evaluations of environmental and social safeguard compliance, nor from work by QACU or QAG that indicate that those operations perform less well than the rest of the World Bank's portfolio in terms of safeguard implementation. The "CBD/CDD" operations sampled by OED for this study and reviewed by QAG do better on safeguards and fiduciary aspects than the average in QAG reviews for all operations.[16] The OED review's findings on medical waste do point out difficulties with the application of the Environmental Assessment policy in health projects. However this is an issue for health projects in general and not specifically for CDD or "CDD/CBD" projects. Similarly the report raises the issue of dams. However, all the dams financed were below the height that triggers the Operational Policy on Dam Safety.

Cost-Benefit Analysis. As indicated above, Management agrees with OED's recommendation that it is important to do good economic analysis (including but not limited to cost-benefit analysis) of all operations including CDD operations and continues to work with implementing agencies in borrowing countries to improve such analysis. There are fundamental challenges in undertaking ex-ante cost-benefit analysis for operations that involve decentralized community activities. These are principally related to the difficulties in profiling with any degree of exactitude in advance the type and proportion of a large number of dispersed sub-projects. However, all project manuals, the client-produced documents that the World Bank appraises, include guidance on how to carry out cost-benefit analysis where appropriate. Management notes that QAG reviews and OED reviewed implementation completion reviews tend to rate Bank performance in project preparation and supervision higher for CBD and CDD operations than for overall Bank-supported operations.[17]

Monitoring and Evaluation. Management notes that through its results agenda, much effort is being directed at assisting countries in improving M&E systems across its portfolio. Concerning impact evaluation of CDD operations, Management notes significant commitment to conduct cutting edge research to understand the impact of these initiatives and is pleased to note that there are several impact evaluation efforts underway. The Bank's Development Economics (DEC) vice presidency intends to produce a Policy Research Report in FY07 on CDD operations, once a number of impact analyses of sufficient quality have been undertaken to provide accurate and operationally relevant evidence.

Fiduciary Aspects of CDD Projects. All CDD operations have audits built into them, most using both the borrower's regular independent audit system as well as special systems for independent audits of sub-projects. However, given the concerns raised in the OED report Management will conduct a review of audits of a representative sample of CDD operations by the end of the year, with independent input into the choice of the sample, and on the basis of the review findings will determine what course of action to take. That said, Management notes that IAD's extensive risk analysis in setting up its

FY06 work program did not raise CDD as a priority concern for auditing. QAG data indicate no special issue with fiduciary aspects in CDD operations; in fact the "CBD/CDD" operations sampled by OED tend to score higher on fiduciary aspects than other operations both in QAG quality at entry and quality of supervision assessments.[18]

> ***Recommendation 2.*** *Future CASs should show how they have analyzed and addressed linkages not only between various CBD/CDD projects to be undertaken in the country but also between CBD/CDD and relevant non-CBD/CDD projects. In particular, the analysis should address whether arrangements for CBD/CDD project implementation come at the expense of local government capacity development.*

Results-based CAS Methodology and Use of Existing Guidelines. Management believes that its recent guidelines for results-based CASs and the process of corporate review of CASs and CAS Completion Reports have now established a strong basis to learn lessons of past interventions and set out the Bank's proposed interventions within a medium-term results framework. All CASs are now required to be based on a CAS Completion Report that evaluates the development impact of past interventions and derives lessons for the design of future interventions. Moreover, all CASs are required to identify country-owned development goals that the Bank will support. In the CAS, country teams choose what they view as the most effective mix of instruments to deliver CAS outcomes. In turn, these outcomes are expected to contribute to achieving country's development goals. In the new format, teams must adequately demonstrate why they have chosen a given set of instruments. In addition, CASs go through an extensive corporate review process that provides guidance to CAS teams on possible weaknesses and deficiencies in analyzing and diagnosing development challenges and the choice of instruments to address these challenges. As part of this review, CAS teams will be asked to explain how operations and instruments, notably including CDD operations, will contribute to achieving CAS outcomes.

Local Government Capacity Development. One of the mandatory issues of discussion in the context of the review of the new generation of results-based CASs (along with governance and results) is capacity development, including local government capacity development. There is growing evidence that greater community participation improves local government capacity, particularly when operations are designed as part of decentralization efforts. In the mid-1990s, there was a concern that support for decentralized initiatives could undermine local government capacity. As a result of this concern, CDD operations have evolved to include the explicit objective to empower communities so that they work with local government and serve as accountability mechanisms to improve local governance (see examples from Zambia and Indonesia above). As evidenced by an increasing number of CASs focused on governance that rely on combinations of CDD operations and decentralization support, Management believes that current guidance meets the objectives set out by OED.

> ***Recommendation 3.*** *For any new CBD/CDD project, the Bank should analyze (using existing processes, such as social assessments) whether it is building on indigenously matured initiatives or attempting to begin a CDD program in a country and then tailor the intervention to local capacity; and the Bank should also selectively undertake rigorous impact assessments upon completion of its ongoing CBD/CDD projects to learn for the future.*

Social Assessments. Management agrees that it is always important to understand the local institutional and social context, though that understanding may not always need to arise from a formal social assessment. Management notes that social assessments are undertaken for many projects and supports their strategic use where there are important knowledge gaps. However, in certain situations such as natural disasters or post-conflict settings, speed of response is critical and these knowledge gaps would need to be filled in parallel with project implementation. In addition as part of the implementation of the social development strategy recently reviewed by the Bank's Board of Executive Directors, social analysis is increasingly moving upstream to the policy and CAS level, which heightens the impact and lowers the cost. On the specific issue of identifying whether a country (not the Bank—the Bank supports the client country) is building on an indigenously matured initiative, that information is normally available as part of appraisal documentation.

Indigenously Matured Initiatives. It is generally true for all projects that they do better when building on indigenously matured initiatives and when design reflects local capacity. The key operational question is what type of intervention to support in low capacity countries, traditional top-down interventions that rely on ministries for implementation or projects that also build on local community participation and community control over decisions? Management, therefore, does not interpret OED's recommendation on tailoring to local capacity to mean that CDD or "CBD/CDD" operations should necessarily be the exception in these settings. An important aspect of the Bank's role is to support innovation in our client countries. Thus, Management believes that it is important to offer to support client governments that request assistance with community development, even when the client has little experience in working with communities. Further, in conflict or recent post-conflict settings where local institutions are very weak—including both formal government structures and informal non-government institutions—Bank efforts to support reconstruction and fight poverty may still best be served by CDD operations and evidence suggests that these types of operations do better in fragile environments than alternative approaches.

Rigorous Impact Assessments. Management notes that, as outlined in Annex II, it has supported or facilitated impact assessments for a large number of client-country CDD operations. Further, through the auspices of its Development Impact Evaluation (DIME) initiative, it is promoting more rigorous impact evaluation across the portfolio. The Office of the Chief Economist is particularly committed to increasing the number of operations that are subject to careful impact evaluation and DEC resources support a number of such studies, including several ongoing impact evaluations of CDD operations. Management is committed to expanding further its evaluation work, especially of social impacts related to enhanced social capital, enhanced local capacity and empowerment.

Management Action Record

OED Recommendation	Management Response
The Bank should provide operational guidance for the application of Bank safeguard policies and fiduciary oversight of CBD/CDD projects and for the strengthening of cost-benefit analysis and M&E systems; and should commission an audit of the fiduciary aspects of a representative sample of CDD projects for submission to the Board within a year.	Management believes that current operational guidance is adequate. Concerning the specific sub-set of CDD operations, Management is already providing operational guidance on safeguard and fiduciary systems, along with training and special reviews. Management is committed to a review of its control framework under IDA14 and considers this as the highest priority use of its resources in this area. However, Management will conduct a review of the audits of an independently selected representative sample of CDD operations by the end of the year following which it will determine what course of action to take, including, as needed, updating current fiduciary guidelines for CDD operations Management concurs with regard to the importance of M&E systems; however, its commitment for action is related to impact evaluation (see Recommendation 3 below).
Future CASs should show how they have analyzed and addressed linkages not only between various CBD/CDD projects to be undertaken in the country but also between CBD/CDD and relevant non-CBD/CDD projects. In particular, the analysis should address whether arrangements for CBD/CDD project implementation come at the expense of local government capacity development.	With the mainstreaming of the results-based CAS during FY05, all CASs are now required to follow a results-based approach. CASs are to be based on a CAS Completion Report that evaluates the development impact of past interventions and derives lessons for the design of future interventions. The Bank analyses the most effective mix of instruments to deliver CAS outcomes and through that analysis demonstrates why the proposed set of instruments was chosen. CDD operations need to meet this test. In addition, CASs go through an extensive corporate review process that provides guidance to CAS teams on possible weaknesses and deficiencies in analyzing and diagnosing development challenges and the choice of instruments to address these challenges. Hence, Management believes that its program of mainstreaming results-based CASs fulfills this recommendation. Management finds that many of its most innovative new operations are designed to combine decentralization initiatives with CDD operations to improve local governance. These programs are based on the operational lessons that empowered local communities that are able to hold local government accountable for service delivery, improve local government capacity to deliver effective and demand-responsive services. Management believes that current guidance and assistance to staff meet the objectives of the OED recommendation and does not plan further steps.

Management Action Record (continued)

OED Recommendation	Management Response
For any new CBD/CDD project, the Bank should analyze (using existing processes, such as social assessments) whether it is building on indigenously matured initiatives or attempting to begin a CDD program in a country and then tailor the intervention to local capacity; and the Bank should also selectively undertake rigorous impact assessments upon completion of its ongoing CBD/CDD projects to learn for the future.	Management agrees that social assessments are valuable tools that are widely employed in CDD operations. It also agrees that CDD design will depend on whether the operation is building on an indigenously matured initiative or is responding to a request from a client that does not have such an initiative. Management believes that this is already the case—the importance of tailoring support for CDD operations to local capacity is already a priority. Therefore, Management does not plan further follow-up with regard to this recommendation. (Management notes that CDD is an important approach in post-conflict settings where "indigenously matured initiatives" are often absent and is an important tool in implementing its operational policy on Development Cooperation and Conflict—OP2.30.) Management notes that borrower governments supported by the Bank are already undertaking many impact evaluations of CDD projects. Several sophisticated evaluations that meet the highest academic standards are currently underway. Given the technical challenges of doing those evaluations well, Management is pleased to note that the Chief Economist and DEC will lead the effort to conduct a meta-evaluation of these impact assessments that result. That assessment is planned for FY07.

Annex S.I: Management Concerns with Scope and Methodology

Management's concerns over the conclusions and recommendations of this review result from issues around the scope of the OED inquiry. Though Management tracks CDD operations and those that involve community participation, OED chose to establish its own portfolio of operations for this review. As a result of this decision, operations that OED examined, both in its portfolio review and its specific cases, differ from those that Management tracks and guides. Specifically, operations OED cites when drawing conclusions about "CDD" are not CDD operations in Management's view. OED based its evaluation on a word-search in project documents and refined the set using OED staff judgment as to whether an operation should be included in the portfolio it examined. Management's tracking of CDD operations is based on Task Team Leaders designating their projects as CDD, subject to review by Regional Management. Given their extensive, in-the-field experience working with client governments to identify and appraise operations, Management believes that operational staff are best placed to identify operations that take a CDD approach.

Beyond these difficulties of scope and definition, Management also questions OED's evaluative methodology, particularly concerning its field work. An important illustration is its treatment of a Brazil operation in Rio Grande do Norte, which is the only Management-recognized CDD operation for which OED conducted field work. First, there are important questions regarding the control group in the OED study. The OED selection of control municipalities and community associations was based on their not having benefited from the Rural Poverty Alleviation Project I (RPAP). However, RPAP is only one of a series of CDD rural development projects the Bank supports in Rio Grande do Norte. The control group included municipalities and community associations that had been involved in these previously Bank-financed CDD-based rural development projects in Rio Grande do Norte. OED's "control" communities had specific municipal councils. Only those municipalities that had participated in CDD operations had these municipal councils. Second, the household survey methodology, on which most of the conclusions are based, had an important built-in negative bias concerning the beneficiary communities. The beneficiary groups defined by OED included households that were not beneficiaries of the operation. The OED study used towns and villages to sample beneficiaries and these generally do not coincide with beneficiary associations. Third, the OED review excluded key non-income measures of poverty (notably, health benefits, savings in time because of more accessible and reliable water supply, and reduction to vulnerability to drought) and asset accumulation from its analysis of program impact. It also introduced negative biases in the measure of impacts by excluding from the analysis the kind of activities more directly linked to income generation (the productive subprojects). Fourth, the program OED selected for comparison purposes differed fundamentally in design and objectives (top-down, large infrastructure investments with no empowerment objective) from the RPAP whose beneficiaries were the subject of OED's study. Finally, the OED review could have drawn more broadly on the literature covering the whole time span of the program. This issue is important because a crucial element of Brazil CDD program is its evolution over time, learning from experience.[19]

Annex S.II: List of CDD Operations with Impact Evaluations (completed and ongoing)

1. Albania Development Fund
2. Armenia Social Investment Fund
3. Armenia Social Investment Fund 2
4. Benin Social Fund
5. Bolivia Social Investment Fund
6. Brazil Rural Poverty Reduction Project
7. Cambodia Seila/Rural Investment and Local Governance Project
8. Ethiopia Women's Development Initiative Project
9. El Salvador Community-Managed Schools Program (EDUCO)
10. Honduras Social Investment Fund
11. India Andhra Pradesh District Poverty Initiative Project
12. Indonesia Support for Conflict-Ridden Areas (SCRAP)
13. Indonesia Urban Poverty Project 2 (UPP2)
14. Indonesia Kecamatan Development Project (KDP1, KDP2, KDP3)
15. Indonesia KDP and Conflict
16. Indonesia Decentralized Agriculture and Forestry Extension Project (DAFEP)
17. Laos Poverty Reduction Fund Project
18. Malawi Social Action Fund (MASAF)
19. Moldova Social Investment Fund
20. Nepal Rural Water Supply Project
21. Nicaragua Emergency Social Investment Fund (FISE1)
22. Pakistan Aga Khan Rural Support Project (AKRSP-Kwaja Study)
23. Pakistan National Rural Support Program (DEC Study)
24. Panama Rural Poverty and National Resources Project
25. Peru Social Fund (FONCODES)
26. Philippines KALAHI-CIDSS
27. Philippines ARMM Social Fund
28. Senegal PNIR (Projet National d'Infrastructures Rurales)
29. Burkina Faso 2nd National Services Development Project (PNDSA2) and Senegal PSAOP (Programme d'Appui au Secteur Agricole et aux Organisations Paysannes)
30. Sierra Leone GoBIFO and IRCBP
31. St. Lucia Poverty Reduction Fund
32. Thailand Social Investment Fund
33. Tanzania Social Action Fund
34. Vietnam Northern Mountains Poverty Reduction Project (NMPRP)
35. Vietnam Community Based Rural Infrastructure Project (CBRIP)
36. Zambia Social Investment Fund (ZAMSIF)

ANNEX T: CHAIRMAN'S SUMMARY: COMMITTEE ON DEVELOPMENT EFFECTIVENESS (CODE)

On August 31, 2005 the Committee on Development Effectiveness (CODE) reviewed the revised draft Management Response to *The Effectiveness of World Bank Support for Community -Based and -Driven Development: An OED Evaluation* as agreed at the first CODE meeting (June 22, 2005) on this topic. On July 27, 2005 a CODE informal roundtable meeting was held so CODE members may better understand some of the issues raised in the OED evaluation, taking into consideration more recent experience. Written statements by some members were circulated before the meeting.

Background. On June 22, 2005 CODE reviewed *The Effectiveness of World Bank Support for Community Development: An OED Evaluation* (the Report) and draft Management Response (MR), for which an interim "Green Sheet" was issued on July 13, 2005. Generally, the Committee perceived that community development (CD) operations had the potential to effectively help and empower the poor, but it also took note of the report's cautionary findings. At the same time, several members and speakers had difficulty drawing a clear position on the report and MR given the disagreements between OED and Management on some points including the definitions used and the scope and methodology of the evaluation, as well as some of the conclusions. Accordingly, as suggested by a member, an informal roundtable meeting was organized on July 27, 2005 to enable CODE members to gain a better understanding of the issues raised in the OED evaluation, based on current experience, both positive and negative, of community-driven development (CDD) operations. At the earlier CODE meeting, it was agreed that the MR needed to be revised and further considered by CODE before completing the discussion on this topic. To remove any ambiguity regarding the scope of the review, OED changed the title of the report to *The Effectiveness of World Bank Support for Community-Based and –Driven Development.*

Revised Draft Management Response (MR). Management concurred with the findings that CDD and CBD operations achieve better results than other operations that do not involve community participation. Management also agreed with OED that sustainability, monitoring and evaluation, and local leadership are important issues for the Bank's work on CDD, as highlighted in the revised MR. The revised MR elaborated on how some concerns raised by OED are being addressed in recent CDD operations while commenting on other issues including: (i) some of the analysis concerning safeguards and fiduciary aspects of CDD; (ii) interpreting the OED recommendation to approach CDD with greater care; and (iii) potential misunderstanding of the Bank's role in CDD operations, which are owned and implemented by countries and not by the Bank. Management also continued to express concerns about the definitions used and the scope and methodology of the evaluation. Given the lengthy process to review this OED evaluation, Management highlighted some key lessons learned including: (i) importance of discussing the issue of scope and definition at an early stage when the Approach Paper of evaluations are presented; (ii) consider a standing committee to discuss methodological issues; and (iii) need for care in ensuring balanced communication of both OED and Management views.

OED Comments. OED welcomed the revised MR. OED was happy to note Management's affirmations that it was already acting on many of the issues raised in the evaluation, which it will monitor and report on results. OED restated the importance of a fiduciary audit of a sample of projects, which should be representative and independently selected. On the issue of scope of the evaluation and specific interest in a review of only CDD operations, OED stated that it is very difficult to separate CBD and CDD elements in a project to enable an evaluation of only CDD initiatives. OED expressed confidence in its methodology and the rigor of its work, which had been reviewed by internal and external experts.

Overall Conclusions and Next Steps. Following extensive discussions, including those at the earlier CODE and informal roundtable meetings, the Committee recognized the important contribution of CDD operations to empowering and helping the poor and it generally supported scaling-up Bank assistance in response to country demand. At the same time, the Committee noted the OED report's cautionary findings, which called for greater vigilance in designing CDD operations. The points highlighted included issues of sustainability and need for exit strategies; fiduciary matters; environment and social safeguards; monitoring and evaluation; building on indigenously matured initiatives; parallel structures and local government and community capacities; and cost-benefit analysis. The Committee welcomed the revised MR and was generally satisfied with the changes. Members noted the more positive tone of the MR, although some members commented that it could be further adjusted and also made suggestions to clarify specific aspects, which Management agreed to consider in the final MR.

Members appreciated Management's acceptance to undertake a fiduciary review of a representative sample of CDDs that are selected independently. In proceeding with disclosure of the OED evaluation report according to the approved OED disclosure policy, the Committee emphasized the importance of balanced communication, including the possibility of placing the summary of CODE discussions upfront instead of as annex to the OED report. OED will consider in a few years the possibility of a more focused evaluation on CDD operations as proposed by some members. Finally, given the lengthy review process for this OED evaluation, Management and OED were requested to explore possible procedural improvements to be considered by the Committee in due course.

The following main issues were raised during the meeting:

Substantive Issues Raised in the OED Evaluation. Members commented on some of the issues raised in the OED evaluation, which had been discussed at previous CODE meetings:

a. ***Sustainability, Aid Dependency, and Exit Strategies.*** In considering sustainability beyond the issue of aid dependency, several speakers stressed the importance of incorporating exit strategies in the design of CDD projects, and suggested that the MR address this matter further. Aid dependency was considered a general issue, not specific to CDDs. Management noted that CDD projects include strategies for exiting communities and that it works closely with client Governments to learn which are most effective. Management also noted that OED's sustainability ratings for the CBD/CDD portfolio review results not only on community-level sustainability but also on the sustainability of funding mechanisms for CBD/CDD approaches, mechanisms that are susceptible to classic problems of aid dependency.
b. ***Fiduciary Audit.*** Ensuring appropriate utilization of funds, especially in the context of local initiatives and systems was considered critical in the design of CDD operations. OED recommended a fiduciary audit of a representative sample of CDD operations be undertaken. Management assured the Committee that under the Bank's operational framework, all operations supported by the Bank are subject to audits by independent auditors. It proposed to undertake a review of the audits of a representative sample of CDD operations selected independently; initially, the revised MR proposed a fiduciary review of five large CDD operations by the end of the year, and on the basis of the review findings determine whether

to recommend to Internal Auditing Department (IAD) an audit of CDD operations. Members welcomed Management agreement to consider a representative sample of CDD operations, which are independently selected. Management noted QAG data that indicate that CDD does better than other operations on financial management.

c. ***Environment Safeguards.*** Some members sought assurance that adequate guidelines were in place, referring to Annex Q of the OED report. A member noted the difficulty of compliance in conflict and post-conflict situations where country systems may be very weak. Management clarified that Annex Q referred to CBD and CDD projects, and not just CDD operations, including issues such as medical waste that are not normally relevant for CDD operations.
d. ***Building on Indigenously Matured Initiatives.*** A few members stated that the Management response should clarify particular circumstances where Bank support to new initiatives may be merited, given OED's findings of greater success with indigenously matured initiatives. Some members noted that in post-conflict countries and LICUS, there may be merit in supporting new initiatives. Management noted that there is evidence that CDD does better than other types of operations in these difficult circumstances.
e. ***Building Local Government and Community Capacities.*** Several members highlighted the importance of strengthening local government and community capacities, and requested elaboration on how to prevent parallel structures detracting from this aim. A member supported the combination of "bottom-up" and "top-down" approach to development, but suggested that the MR clarify how CDD operations should embody the two approaches. Management agreed to clarify further in the MR how CDD operations currently work on strengthening community and local and national government capacity, where relevant.
f. ***Monitoring and Evaluation (M&E).*** Noting Management and OED agreement on importance of M&E, some members sought assurance that staff is adequately equipped to strengthen impact evaluation, track quantitative and qualitative results, and to support countries' M&E capacities. Management noted that many quantitative and qualitative evaluations are already being carried out and agreed that ensuring government and Bank capacity in this area is important.
g. ***Cost-Benefit Analysis.*** While cost-benefit analysis may not be possible in some cases, a few members stressed the need for stronger institutional commitment in this area. They suggested that Management could provide further guidance in this area as well as clarify in the MR the Bank's role given clients' capacity constraints. Management agreed to address this issue more fully in the MR, noting that all operational manuals for CDD operations contain guidance on how to carry out economic analysis. Management will continue to monitor to ensure that guidance remains appropriate and its use will be covered under M&E.

Communication and Disclosure. Speakers acknowledged the importance of OED independence, but also emphasized that there should be balanced communication of all views, including of Management's response. In disclosing evaluations in accordance with the approved OED disclosure policy, some speakers proposed that the summary of CODE discussions be placed at the beginning rather than as annex, particularly for potentially controversial reports.

Lessons Learned. Some members noted that Management continued to have concerns about the definition, scope, and methodology of the OED evaluation. A member commented that there should be Management and OED agreement on the objectives of the evaluation upfront, while OED, as an independent evaluation entity, may be best placed to make the final decision on methodology. It was pointed out that the scope of this evaluation was explicitly outlined in the Approach Paper. Management noted that, while it had communicated its difficulties with the scope and methodology to OED informally, it had erred in not formally commenting in the Approach Paper. In this connection, speakers agreed with Management that one key lesson emerging from reviewing this OED evaluation was the need to pay more careful attention to the Approach Paper for each evaluation. They stated that any significant divergence between Management and OED should be brought to CODE'S attention at an early stage. A few speakers also supported Management's suggestion to explore the possibility of a standing committee to discuss methodology issues; OED stated that it already has in place a thorough system for vetting its methodology by external experts which could be shared with CODE members as and when necessary. OED independence was considered important, but the need to ensure OED's accountability was also raised. Some members suggested a follow-up evaluation more narrowly focused on CDD operations in the near future; OED agreed to consider the possibility in a few years time.

Chander Mohan Vasudev,
Chairman

ENDNOTES

Executive Summary

1. Management notes that CDD operations are clearly distinguished by their giving communities control over decision making and resource allocation.

2. Management notes that it tracks: (1) participation in operations; and (2) community-driven development operations. It finds these two categories as being more operationally useful than the very diverse sample that OED has put together for the purpose of this review.

OED notes: The Bank's tracking of participation is not limited to community participation. Since it also covers participation of all stakeholders at both the project and macro levels, it does not permit the separate tracking of all CBD/CDD nor does it allow for an analysis of participatory issues relevant at the community level that could help inform the design of future CBD/CDD operations (in each situation where the Bank considers fostering community development, it needs to draw from relevant experience from both CDD and CBD projects).

3. Management notes that, when discussing weaknesses, the table does not compare its set of CDD/CBD operations with other Bank operations.

4. Management notes that there have been a number of rigorous evaluations done of operations that involve community participation, which is close to the definition OED created for this review. For example, Rawlings, Sherburne-Benz and Van Domelen 2004, *A Cross-Country Analysis of Community Investments*, Washington, D.C, The World Bank, synthesizes six careful empirical analyses of social funds, each of which was published in the *World Bank Economic Review*. In addition, management notes that a large proportion of the most rigorous evaluation work under way concerns CDD impact. Given the relatively recent Bank operational support to CDD, there has been little opportunity for careful before and after evaluation to be completed.

OED notes: The evaluation draws from this document (listed in references as World Bank 2003d), the full title of which is: "Evaluating Social Funds: A Cross-Country Analysis of Community Investments"; also known as "Social Funds 2000." This study is based on data collected more than 5 years ago and reviews only the experience of social funds—a specific subset of CBD/CDD projects.

5. Management notes that Rawlings, Sherburne-Benz, and van Domelen 2004, cited above by management, provides rigorous evidence that community management of investments offers significant potential for cost savings. That report also provides careful analysis of the benefits of these types of projects.

OED notes: The study cited by management refers to social funds only—a specific subset of CBD/CDD projects—and is based on field work in six countries.

Chapter 1

1. The "community" in a Bank-supported project is considered a "unified, organic whole." Since the group of people in a "community" live in a particular area, share a common interest (water users associations, herders, and the like), and are governed by a set of norms, its members are assumed to be in the best position to identify their most pressing needs and problems. The assumption suggests that there are common problems that can be solved through community consensus. While this may be true, it neglects community members' differences and power relationships, the conflicts, and the diversity of interests that determine day-to-day behavior and that affect the effectiveness of participatory approaches. The poor themselves are rarely a homogenous group; they live in different geographic areas and face different kinds of deprivations, and each seeks a personalized way of reducing poverty (Schneider 1999). For more on community see Annex A.

2. Initially, six "ways" of involving communities in Bank-supported interventions were defined, though later the Bank's Social Development Department adopted a more intuitive fourfold classification (information sharing, consultation, collaboration, empowerment). Although it is not stated, presumably both categorizations were derived from the work of Arnstein (1969), who created an eight-rung ladder of citizen participation.

3. The CDD Anchor in its recently established CDD database (see Chapter 2), also includes projects that involve community control in the development and implementation of their donor-supported development plans, as well as projects that focus primarily on information sharing, consultation, and collaboration.

4. Management notes again that the definition used by OED is closest to that of participation and that there are benchmarks for evaluating participation, specifically those laid out in the *Participation Sourcebook*.

5. Management notes that it tracks: (1) participation in operations, and(2) community-driven development operations. For operational relevance, management believes that the review would have been more useful had it been based on either or both of the categories that management tracks.

6. Management notes that, given the Review's definition of CBD/CDD, there is a larger set of impact evaluation evidence to rely on. For example, Rawlings, Sherburne-Benz and van Domelen 2004, cited by management above, reviews a set of high-quality empirical studies on community participation and its impact.

Chapter 2

1. The Anchor's CDD database also includes information on CBD projects.

2. Over two-thirds of the projects in the sample of 84 devote more than 75 percent of project cost to CBD/CDD. Since community participation is a process issue, it has the potential to affect project outcomes even when it forms a small part of the project cost.

3. Management notes that there is often a detailed description of participatory processes in the project appraisal documents. In addition, these processes are discussed in great detail in project and field manuals.

Chapter 3

1. Using the Bank's primary sector coding.

2. This finding is supported by a Bank study on the performance of community-level user groups carried out in the context of three Bank-supported interventions in India. The study questioned whether user groups as currently designed and implemented can achieve long-term sustainability as independent organizational entities. According to the study, past experience with various government and NGO initiatives has habituated user groups to let final responsibility for the groups' management rest with an external authority (Alsop and others 2002).

3. Moore (2001) examines the use of the concept of empowerment in multilateral development agencies, including the World Bank, and finds that while the notion of empowering the poor was important in framing the discussion on poverty reduction in these institutions, the lack of a clear definition could lead to different interpretations of the concept of empowerment. The review finds two distinct implicit definitions of empowerment within the reports in these institutions: the underlying proposition of one definition is that improving the material status of poor people is empowering because it weakens the social, economic, and political dependence and provides the poor with greater freedom and autonomy; the underlying proposition behind the second definition is that insofar as empowerment contributes to collective organization of the poor, it can also contribute to political action and may imply political confrontation.

4. It is important to acknowledge that it is much more difficult to meet and measure the qualitative goals than the quantitative goals. For example, household survey data analysis from Benin found that communities' access to school infrastructure, supplies, and equipment increased because of the Bank-supported projects, though this did not necessarily mean improvement in access to education services, which is also determined by, among other things, availability of teachers. (See Annex P and section on sustainability in Chapter 4 for an explanation.) Moreover, part of the improvement in capacity is expected to come about through the participation of the communities in the planning, design, and construction of the infrastructure. As a result, in the short duration of a Bank-supported intervention, when achieving visible results is seen as an indicator of progress on implementation, progress toward qualitative goals tends to receive less attention, not only from the

Bank, but also from the country.

Management notes that rigorous cross-country studies, not cited in this review, found that schools funded with community inputs have more and better teachers than those that were funded in the traditional top-down manner. Further, in the case of Benin, all schools funded by the project had teachers.

5. "Participation can make development assistance more effective. But it works best for groups that are already able to help themselves" (Da Cunha and others 1997).

6. The literature and earlier OED evaluations also consider the dairy experience in India among the few examples of successful scaling up of sustainable rural development (Krishna and others 1997; Uphoff and others 1998; Candler and Kumar 1998).

7. SEWA has had some Ford Foundation support but no major external assistance. The Orangi Pilot project received support from several donors, including the World Bank (see Uphoff and others 1998; Krishna and others 1997 for details).

8. Requested and funded by the Aga Khan Foundation.

9. Since in Uttar Pradesh the comparator communities had no program, whereas in Madhya Pradesh the comparator was communities with the same activity, also supported through a participatory approach, but by the government, it is not surprising that results are more significant in Uttar Pradesh than in Madhya Pradesh.

10. Management notes that other reviews have found quite different and more positive results from those cited here.

11. "But certain cultural settings are better suited to local participation and collective action than others. Participation works best when it is based in, rather than in opposition to, existing organizations. In Northeast Brazil, regional tradition and existing social, economic, and political structures pose strong challenges to horizontal social organization and thus to popular mobilization and participatory development. Although certain democratizing trends have weakened traditional authorities, prior organization still poses challenges, which must be recognized and systematically addressed in policy planning and in project design and implementation" (Costa and others 1997).

12. It is worth noting that household data also show that the poor in project communities in Madhya Pradesh reported a significantly greater increase in trust, association life, and mobilization skills than the relatively better-off (see Annex N).

13. The Bank staff survey found that only 40 percent of the respondents were satisfied or very satisfied with their Regional management's understanding of the objectives and design of CBD/CDD interventions. This suggests that Bank management may not completely understand what is needed for CBD/CDD to succeed. This may also explain why Bank procedures have not yet been fully adapted to CBD/CDD.

14. It is worth noting here that the literature suggests—and earlier OED work on social fund projects confirms—that having the elite and the local leaders in the decision-making position does not necessarily constitute a problem in and of itself. In fact, the literature shows that the involvement of the elite could also be helpful in some ways. The important issue is not so much how to avoid elite domination, but how best to use the power and energy of the elite to serve the poor (Narayan 1995). One way of doing so, perhaps, would be to create appropriate mechanisms to ensure, before a subproject is funded, "that the ideas of the leader are also the most important ones for the community as a whole" (OED 2002b, p. xxvii). As Platteau and Gaspar (2003) argue, so long as the intervention of the elite leads to an improvement in the situation of the poor, the latter are likely to be thankful to their leaders.

15. Management notes that it did not concur with the analysis and conclusions of OED's social funds evaluation.

16. "The danger is not going far enough, and being satisfied with any partial progress," as Ostrom (1999) puts it, "creating dependent citizens rather than entrepreneurial citizens reduces the capacity of citizens to produce capital." The costs of development assistance will also inevitably increase—it is not costless to establish new organizations." The "stages" theory also notes that "progression is not taken to be inevitable, with outcomes being regression (going back to the previous stage), stagnation or arrested development (remaining at one stage), and extinction (organizations may fail or terminate)" (Pretty and Ward 2001).

17. A recent Bank study (Alsop and others 2002) based on fieldwork in three states of India also found that members' perceptions of the purpose of user groups differ from the perceptions of project designers and implementers.

18. In his study of 60 villages in the state of Rajasthan in India, Krishna (2001) shows that no matter how high the level of social capital, it needs to be marshaled strategically and directed toward incentives available within the broader institutional and environment.

19. Management notes that rigorous evaluations on which Rawling, Sherburne-Benz, and Van Domelen, 2004, cited above, is based show that the bottom two deciles of the income distribution benefit more than higher deciles.

OED notes: Of the five social funds for which data are presented in the study cited by management, four social funds (Honduras, Nicaragua, Peru, Zambia) had a neutral or only mildly progressive distribution of beneficiaries at the household level, and the fifth social fund (Armenia) had a regressive distribution (see pages 64–65, table 3.3 and figure 3.3 of the management-cited study); this lack of progressivity is of concern because social funds aim to reach poor communities and households using a variety of targeting mechanisms.

20. A recent study by the Institute for Social and Economic Change in India, which carried out fieldwork in the States of Karnataka and Uttaranchal, found significant elite capture of benefits in participatory watershed projects (Rajasekhar and others 2004).

21. In the context of irrigation schemes in Tanzania, Koopman and others (2001) find that while landowners were the main beneficiaries, they did not shoulder a greater share of the costs. Instead, the net costs borne by tenants were significantly higher, for they were not only required to put in as much free labor as landowners, but also ended up paying higher rents, because the project increased the value of land.

22. The expression "participatory spaces" (Cornwall 2002) is used here to identify the various types of community organizations, formal and informal, created to enable the participation of project beneficiaries in the process of making decisions.

23. The literature also notes reasons for the lack of participation of the poor. Participation places additional demands on community members, which are likely to be particularly problematic for poorer households (Pantoja 2000; Garcia and Way 2003). As Baland and Platteau (2002) point out, the poor often lack incentives to take part in collective undertakings, as these violate their survival constraints. As the authors explain, poverty tends to shrink the time horizon, because it forces people to attach considerable importance to their present income opportunities. Consequently, the poor are likely to resist any type of collective activity that requires them to forgo present income opportunities—even if it permanently increases future incomes. This argument is echoed by Weinberger and Jutting's (2001) quantitative analysis.

24. The literature review carried out for this evaluation distinguishes between formal inclusion, which concerns the extent to which community members are able to enter decision-making arenas, and substantive inclusion, which captures the extent to which different participants are able to exert influence over decisions. For example, poor people may opt not to speak up against the views and positions put forward by more powerful members of the community but, rather, conform to them (Kolavalli and Kerr 2002, p. 225). As Linden (1997) points out, keeping a low profile is an essential survival strategy of poor people. In the context of patronage, the poor are highly dependent on their leaders, and are hence unwilling to antagonize them (Kumar 2002).

25. Rajasekhar and others (2004) found that the activity preference across the local organizations was to a large extent influenced by the level of contributions. The study reports: "The well-off farmers needed certain type of activities to be undertaken. Under the framework of beneficiary contribution having important say in the activity, the well-off farmers contributed more and also obtained more from the groups. This was, thus a case of 'elite capture,' which had negative impact on the processes that the [local organizations] had to engage in."

26. The literature also shows that inadequate attention to issues such as inequality within a community can also affect targeting outcomes of CDD interventions, because economic and social heterogeneity can increase the risk of elite capture (Elbers and others 2004) Governments rarely have information on the level of inequality in communities.

27. For example, in the context of the Indian Panchayat Raj system in Karnataka, Vyasulu and Vyasulu (1999) found that women attained high levels of formal inclusion. At the gram panchayat level, well over 40 percent of elected representatives were women. However, many elected women were surrogates for husbands and fathers who could not contest because of the reservation, while others had been put in place

by the wealthy and powerful for their malleability.

28. For example, a socioeconomic impact study was carried out in connection with the Borgou Pilot project in Benin. The OED assessment for the project questioned the credibility of the ERR rates reported by that study. In Brazil, a review of an often-quoted impact study by van Zyl and others (2000) revealed that the study had not compared project communities against controls. In addition, the study report provided no information on the number of respondents in the three different kinds of project communities, and no indication of how many subprojects had been financed per community. Further, there are several shortcomings in the cost-benefit analysis reported.

29. That report notes that, "Although social funds were typically more efficient than other national programs in term of overhead expenditures, their investment unit costs tended to be more efficient only where there was significant input and control by communities." (World Bank 2003d)

30. Kent and Rimarachin's (1994) study on public works in Peru found that community contribution ranged from 7 to 47 percent, and was on average 20 percent of total project costs. Isham and Kahkonen (2002) found that community contribution to water service projects in Sri Lanka was 43 percent of total construction costs—well above the required 20 percent.

31. Management notes that the background work for Rawlings, Sherburne-Benz and Van Domelen 2004, cited above by management, found that community management of investments offers significant potential for cost savings, often on the order of 25–40 percent, even after taking into account the full value of community contributions.

32. Econometric analysis by Kerr and others (2000) finds that participatory watershed projects in India performed better than technocratic and top-down projects. The authors also find that a combination of participation and sound technical input performed best of all. Similarly, Kahkonen's (1999) review of the literature maintains that community-managed water and sanitation projects worked better than government-managed schemes.

Chapter 4

1. The capacity of the Bank to support a CBD/CDD approach is addressed in Chapter 5.

2. The OED assessment of the Matrouh Project found that the important issue of what impact the ongoing adjudication of Bedouin lands is going to have on the poor and on rangeland management systems was ignored. Further, the Egypt country study found that in the Sohag Project, while the community process elements were quite well covered, QAG noted that the larger policy issue of subsidized interest rates was inadequately addressed, related fiscal issues were not well covered, institutions had not been adequately appraised for capacity, and the risk that the project could undermine the development of alternative credit sources had not been adequately assessed.

3. Bank management notes in response that the new national CDD project in Benin (approved by the Board in October 2005) is fully taking the decentralization framework into account and intends to build local government's capacity to implement the CDD approach.

4. Management notes that communes did not exist until one year after the Borgou Project became effective.

5. The majority of the councilors interviewed in Rio Grande do Norte had not received any training by the RPAP or the follow-on and ongoing RPRP. From the NGO focus group session it emerged that a training event for municipal councilors had been organized in the state capital in the past. Some NGO representatives criticized this form of training for it only allowed the participation of few councilors per municipality and was a one-time event, and not a systematic training program.

6. It is worth noting that the latest ongoing CDD projects in Northeast Brazil are attempting to promote greater integration of existing programs to improve the impact of public resources available for poverty reduction. However, it is too early to say how successful this effort will be.

7. Three models of implementation are being used in community-based projects in Philippines: The government agency model has a line ministry or local government as the executing agency for the project. It is responsible for the design and implementation, procurement, financial management, monitoring, and evaluation. The project is often carried out by a project management unit within the agency, and executed by local offices of the ministry in conjunction with local authorities and communities. In the social fund model, an autonomous agency of government makes grants directly to beneficiary communities or individuals. In

the community-driven development model, the communities themselves decide which projects to undertake and are responsible for their execution. The Comprehensive Integrated Delivery of Social Services (CIDSS) component of SEMP 1 and the proposed SEMP 2 and the proposed "Kalahi" Project are examples of this model. (Source: "Community-Driven Development: A Case study of the Philippines." East Asia Region Workshop June 12–13 2002.)

8. The rapid multiplication of national NGOs in response to the availability of funds from the international community is also an issue that has been raised in the literature (Platteau and Gaspart 2003; Chabal and Daloz 1999).

9. It is important here to distinguish between NGOs and grassroots community organizations, which may have different motivations for working with communities. However, the country studies were not able to research the role of these organizations.

10. Van de Walle and Johnston (1996) note in the context of lack of aid coordination, "a conservative estimate for a typical African country is that 600 projects translates into 2,400 quarterly reports a year submitted to different overseeing entities; and more than 1,000 annual missions to appraise, monitor and evaluate. Each mission asks to meet with key officials, and each will ask the government to comment on its reports. Is it any wonder that the most common complaint voiced by officials interviewed in the case studies is that aid imposes too many administrative burdens?"

11. For northeast Brazil, specifically, the van Zyl study reports that 89 percent of the sample of 3,633 subprojects funded by the RPAP in 1997–98 were found to be operational in the year 2000.

12. Management notes the evidence presented in the background research for Rawlings, Sherburne-Benz and Van Domelen 2004, cited earlier by management. That work found that "impact evidence showed that the facilities in which social funds invest can be at least as sustainable as similar facilities if not more so. The majority of the infrastructure appeared to be well constructed and operating adequately and levels of maintenance were equivalent or better than comparators."

13. OED's Impact Evaluation of Basic Education in Ghana (OED 2004b) also found that the downside of community financing of schools is that it leads to disparities in resource availability, because poorer communities have less resources to contribute in comparison with richer communities. Further, a review of community support for Basic Education in Sub-Saharan Africa also found that support for recurrent expenditures poses sustainability problems. According to the report, "Schools need a predictable flow of income to meet their recurrent expenditures, yet communities are often unable to provide this. This is especially the case among poor communities, who are often vulnerable to external shocks, and whose income is irregular" (Watt 2001, p. 29).

14. See Annex I for an explanation on project-supported municipal councils in northeast Brazil.

15. It is worth noting that only 18 percent of the respondents to the Bank Staff Survey agreed with the statement that community maintenance contributions are sufficient to sustain infrastructure investment for Bank-funded CBD/CDD projects (Annex L).

16. The Ethiopia Pastoral Community Development Project (fiscal 2003) and the Nigeria Community-Based Poverty Reduction Project (fiscal 2001) are examples.

17. Among the infrastructures implemented in a village in Kalale commune of Benin's Borgou region was an agricultural storage facility financed through the Borgou Pilot Project. Ten percent of the total project cost was to be put into an account for repairs or other maintenance. When asked whether the funds needed to be replenished when they were used, the village leader told OED they did not. When asked if there was anything left of the 10 percent funds, he also said no, though it had only been two years since the subproject had been completed. When asked what the community would do now if something were to happen to the storage facility he was not at all worried and said that they would seek new funds. In this particular village several Bank projects and other donor interventions had been implemented, so it would be reasonable for the village committee to assume that they could just go to another donor when the need arose.

18. A recent study on the role of local organizations in water supply and sanitation in the states of Karnataka and Uttaranchal notes that the possibility of obtaining resources from the government toward the maintenance of water supply projects could mean that local organizations do not have an incentive to mobilize resources from users (Rajasekhar and Veerashekhararappa 2004).

19. Further, OED's social fund evaluation found the technical quality of social fund infrastructure to be variable across countries and between sectors. The findings of the recent self evaluation of social funds were similar in that respect (World Bank 2003d).

20. "Ensuring that positions are filled, that staff report for work, and that they are responsive to all their clients is a major challenge. ...Incentive payments might encourage professionals to work in remote areas, but they can be expensive....Even when positions are filled, staff absence rates can be high" (World Bank 2004d, pp. 22–23).

21. Thus the ICR for the Cambodia Social Fund acknowledges "sustainability was not set up as one of the main objectives because of the project's primary concern with the rapid and cost effective delivery of subprojects. Another reason why sustainability concerns were not more integrated into project operational activities was the assumption that a demand driven identification process would ensure community ownership and that line agencies would take over operations and maintenance of subprojects."

22. The case study on Indonesia's Kecamatan Development Program for the Shanghai Conference (May 2004) points out: "Two limitations of the KDP model are particularly worth underscoring since they can to some extent be overcome. The first is that technically difficult activities or activities that involve recurrent costs are not easily addressed through the KDP system as it is currently designed. Examples, of such necessary activities include large-scale health provision, providing teachers for schools, or any kind of infrastructure network planning" (World Bank 2004b). If maintaining the services from schools through CDD interventions is a challenge for Indonesia, it is an even bigger challenge for countries like Benin and Nepal.

23. A significant number of focus groups (50 percent of the female focus groups and 40 percent of the male focus groups) in that state expressed an interest in receiving further training.

Chapter 5

1. Staff skills within the institution have also become more diversified, and today Bank staff come from a variety of academic disciplines and varied institutional experiences.

2. For a CDD intervention covering eight states in northeast Brazil, construction of small dams was barely mentioned at appraisal and no effort was made to set down guidelines for dam safety and to study the cumulative input of a large number of small dams. However, a *Social Development Note* (World Bank 2001c) mentioned that over a thousand such dams were built under this program.

3. For example, in Nigeria the internal controls are reported to be weak or inoperative and provide negligible assurance that the funds are being used entirely for their intended purposes. In Senegal, even though the scope of NGO involvement has increased substantially, the CFAA notes that the supervisory capacity of NGOs' oversight bodies is very weak. Fiduciary sector work in Pakistan has reported that compliance with existing internal controls and procedures have been inadequate and the financial reports and financial accounts have often been untimely or incomplete.

4. There is considerable evidence in the literature on mismanagement of aid transfers that occur in class or caste-based societies (Platteau and Gaspart 2003; Bardhan 2002; Conning and Kevane 2002).

5. "As compared to other policy areas, performance in developing countries is in general weakest in public sector governance. And within public sector governance, it is weakest with respect to transparency, accountability, and control of corruption. And the weaknesses are the most pervasive precisely in countries where stronger institutional capacities are needed to manage development interventions that will spur progress toward the MDGs—poor countries" (World Bank-IMF 2004).

6. At the Fiduciary Forum 04, managers recognized the need to translate diagnostic into action. "Too often we do excellent work on Country Financial Accountability Assessments and Country Procurement Assessment Reports, and then the country team checks these off [its 'to-do' list] and says, 'Okay, that's done,' when the real work actually starts afterwards" (Fiduciary Forum 04, Managing Risk Realizing Opportunity).

7. Internal documents from the midterm review of the Andhra Pradesh District Poverty Initiatives Project noted that an independent review of financial and procurement processes had been completed. The review found that progress had been made, but it also confirmed some recurring weaknesses. Specifically, compliance remained inadequate and the processes in place provided limited assurance that the project funds had been used for the intended purposes.

8. The fieldwork done for the Indonesia Kecamatan Development Project found that while the majority of people who lost small amounts of land to roads and other infrastructure did not seem overly concerned, a few were not happy. Since in virtually all cases land values rose substantially because of the infrastructure in question, it would be difficult to argue that anyone ended up worse off than they were before the project. However, there is no clarity in the Bank's resettlement policy on whether loss of land requires compensation, even when land values go up more than the value of land lost—that is, whether relative loss or loss comparing the with- and without-project scenario matters. In any event, the OED mission found the appraisal text on compensation for lost land confusing and likely to put pressure on affected households not to seek compensation.

9. File:///C:/Documents%20and%20Settings/wb251042/Local%20Settings/Temporary%20Internet%20Files /Content.IE5/1WDNJU3F/300,29,World Bank Staff)

10. "Compartmentalization within major aid organizations of the expertise and responsibilities to support administrative reforms, sectoral assistance programmes and community development projects, produces fragmented and competing interventions that do not address and even retard the systemic changes needed to advance decentralization" (Romeo 2003).

Annex B

1. A detailed explanation is presented in the CDD evaluation discussion paper available at http://www.worldbank.org/oed/cbdcdd/documents/discussion_paper.pdf.

Annex C

1. From the World Bank community-driven development Web site <http://lnweb18.worldbank.org/ESSD/sdvext.nsf/09ByDocName/ProjectPreparationImplementationKeyDesignPrinciples> accessed January 2005.

Annex D

1. The projects reviewed were: Albania: Second Community Works Project (P077297); Cameroon: Community Development Program Support Project (P073629); Honduras: Community Based Education Project (P007397); India: Andhra Pradesh District Poverty Initiatives Project (P045049); Philippines: Kalahi - CIDSS Project (P077012); and Yemen: Third Social Fund for Development Project (P082498).

2. These are undertaken to validate the findings of project Implementation Completion Reports.

3. The literature on social funds is excluded from this review, as it has been the subject of a recent OED evaluation (OED 2002b).

Annex E

1. As of September 2004. A detailed explanation of the methodology for identifying the universe of CBD/CDD is presented in the document "CDD: A Study Methodology" available at http://www.worldbank.org/oed/cbdcdd/documents/discussion_paper.pdf. This document was shared with workshop participants and was also posted on the above Web site for comments. While there was discussion at the workshop around the methodology adopted for identifying the universe, no alternative approaches were offered to identify the universe. Nor did any of the Regions provide an alternative list of projects.

2. The list of projects identified in the post-2000 period by the word search was compared with the list produced by the CDD Anchor. Some post-2000 projects in OED's universe were absent from the CDD Anchor's list and some were additional to the list. All these projects were reviewed for their appropriateness; some were dropped from the list of 833 projects that was available at the design stage and others were added to give a final total of 847 projects.

Annex F

1. A detailed explanation of the methodology for identifying the sample of CDD is presented in the document *CDD: A Study Methodology*: http://www.worldbank.org/oed/cbdcdd/documents/discussion_paper. pdf.

Annex G

1. OED ratings are based on OED reviews of ICRs, 25 percent of which are subsequently revisited through OED field assessments. OED ratings are analyzed by exit year since OED rates each project on only on exit.

2. OED rates outcome on a six-point scale: 6 = highly satisfactory, 5 = satisfactory, 4 = moderately satisfactory, 3 = moderately unsatisfactory, 2 = unsatisfactory and 1 = highly unsatisfactory. These ratings are presented in most reports, including the *Annual Re-*

port on Portfolio Performance and *Annual Report on Development Effectiveness*, on a two-point scale by summing the top three ratings (4 to 6) as satisfactory and summing the bottom three ratings (1-3) as unsatisfactory. While a small percentage of projects is "not rated," to keep the denominator constant for all three ratings (outcome, sustainability, and institutional development impact), calculations for percent satisfactory projects are based on the denominator equaling all closed investment lending during the specified period.

3. Post-conflict countries with a CBD/CDD project exiting during 1994–2003 include Angola, Burundi, Cambodia, Colombia, Congo, Democratic Republic of, Djibouti, Eritrea, Ethiopia, Guatemala, Indonesia, Macedonia, former Yugoslav Republic of, Mozambique, Philippines, Rwanda, Sierra Leone, Sri Lanka, Tajikistan, Timor-Leste, Uganda, and the West Bank and Gaza.

4. Regional analysis is restricted to Regions with more than 25 projects.

5. The non-CBD/CDD portfolio has been performing below CBD/CDD portfolio for both Africa and Latin America and the Caribbean, however, decline in the performance of non-CBD/CDD portfolio in the Latin American and Caribbean Region over the two phases has been only 2 percentage points, and the increase in the Africa Region portfolio has been 7 percentage points.

6. Sectoral analysis is restricted to Sector Boards with more than 25 CBD/CDD projects.

7. OED rates sustainability on a four-point scale: 4 = highly likely, 3 = likely, 2 = unlikely, 1 = highly unlikely, plus non-evaluable. Calculations for percent "likely" or better (includes both "highly likely" and "likely.") ratings in this section are based on all closed projects including projects rated non-evaluable and uncertain. Excluding "non-evaluable" pushes percentages upwards by 7 percentage points for CBD/CDD projects and by 5 percentage points for non-CBD/CDD projects in phase 2. The reasons to keep the non-evaluable in the denominator are twofold: first, the evaluation wanted to keep the denominator constant for all three OED ratings, namely outcome, sustainability and Institutional impact; second, non-evaluable rating is given to projects largely because of poor quality of the ICRs, which makes it difficult for an evaluator to make any concrete assessment on the likely hood of sustainable benefits from the project. The evaluation wanted to capture this "negative" aspect as well for all projects—CBD/CDD and non-CBD/CDD projects.

8. OED rates ID impact on a four-point scale: 4 = high, 3 = substantial, 2 = modest, and 1 = negligible. The percentage of projects with "substantial" ID impact includes both "substantial" and "high" ratings.

Annex I

1. In Vietnam, officials picked multiple choices, unlike the other three countries, where officials picked one primary choice of central, regional/provincial, municipal/local, communities, NGOs, other donors, others, and do not know.

2. This was also raised in interviews with stakeholders at various levels in Benin.

Annex J

1. Note that we are not here talking of the costs of the investments but of the costs to all players of getting to the point of implementing and then supervising that investment.

2. It is reasonable to expect that these costs will decline over time.

3. A Study of Rural Hill Potentials and Service Delivery Systems, by SAPROS and IFAD, April 2002, IFAD.

4. Sample sizes from 110 households up to 154 households.

5. Often there is little detailed evidence to back up the claims of savings. Making a fair comparison between provision of infrastructure through different means is a complex calculation calling for allocation of a number of fixed costs that are difficult to allocate.

6. The opportunity cost curve of household time may be concave, with modest amounts of time spent in meetings having quite small opportunity costs but, as the time increases, having quite substantial costs through impact on labor peaks related to the agricultural calendar. There is some anecdotal evidence that the costs to the poor are greater because they can least afford the lost labor.

Annex L

1. Multivariate analysis indicates that respondents from the East Asia and the Pacific and Latin America and Caribbean Regions were more likely to express dissatisfaction with coordination within the Bank across sectors as compared to all other respondents (table L.5).

2. Multivariate analysis indicates that respondents from the Europe and Central Asia Region, and sociologist/anthropologists were less likely to agree with the fact as were respondents who had participated in larger number of CBD/CDD projects. Interestingly, managers (sector level and above) were more likely to agree that implementation costs per dollar lent for CBD/CDD projects are higher than more traditional projects (table L.5).

3. Multivariate analysis indicates that economist were more likely to indicate disagreement; and respondents from Europe and Central Asia more likely to indicate agreement (table L.5).

4. Multivariate analysis indicates that respondents who had participated in larger number of CBD/CDD projects were more likely to disagree with this statement (table L.5).

5. Multivariate analysis indicates that respondents from Africa and Latin America and the Caribbean were more likely to disagree with the fact that NGO-supported interventions generally achieve a better CBD/CDD outcome than Bank interventions (table L.5).

Annex M

1. AgeFIB became inactive in fiscal year 2004; and the ICR presented it as a CDD intervention, though from the appraisal document it appeared to be a CBD project.

2. AgeFIB and PILSA were implemented in other regions of Benin also.

3. While the first two types of investments were chosen because together they accounted for 60 percent of investments financed by the RPAP in Rio Grande do Norte, the second and third type were chosen because eligible PAC communities had mainly these types of investments

4. The on-going RPRP had restricted the number of municipalities targeted under the RPAP because some were financially able to meet the needs of their communities. These municipalities could not therefore be appropriate comparator for this study.

5. Differences between the comparator community that had benefited from the reformulated NRDP and the other two comparator communities were tested using the same model discussed on page 109, under "Multivariate Analysis" (specification without interactions). In this model the project dummy represented the community that had benefited from the reformulated NRDP. Only two significant differences were found. Respondents in the community that had benefited from the reformulated NRDP reported a significantly smaller increase in their participation in political events, and a significantly grater increase in ownership of medium consumer durables, which was driven by greater increase in ownership of satellite dishes.

6. The draft questionnaire is in available on the Web site http://www.worldbank.org/oed/cbdcdd.

7. Benin was the only country for which weights were not used due to a lack of information on community population.

8. The interactive variable for women in project areas was included for the projects in Benin and Uttar Pradesh, as these targeted women explicitly (Annex N).

9. A likelihood ratio test was performed in order to test the validity of the restricted model and this was rejected in favor of the unrestricted model, which includes three separate dummy variables for the three types of implementation modalities. The three dummy variables were differently associated with changes in: (a) in associational life, (b) circle of friends, (c) access to information and (d) mobilization skills.

Annex N

1. "CDD empowers poor people (...) Targeted community-driven approaches devolve control and decision making to poor women and men. This empowers them immediately and directly. (...) the speed and directness with which CDD empowers poor people is rarely matched by other institutional frameworks for poverty reduction. (...) Control over decisions and resources can also give communities the opportunity to build social capital (defined as the ability of individuals to secure benefits as a result of membership in social networks) by expanding the depth and range of their networks." (http://lnweb18.worldbank.org/ESSD/sdvext.nsf/09ByDocName/BasicConceptsPrinciplesWhyCDD).

2. As already mentioned in Annex M, the bivariate analysis for the Brazil project reports only the response rate of FUMAC communities, which account for 60 percent of respondents in project communities.

3. In Madhya Pradesh, village forest committee (VFC) or the forest protection committee (FPC) were created, which comprised of one male and one female

member from each household in the village. In Uttar Pradesh the project created two distinct committees, the Site Implementation Committee (SIC) and Water User Group (WUG), which played distinct role. While the SIC decided on broader project management issues, the WUG decided on water usage and water rates of a particular boring around which it was formed. In Brazil, a Community Association needed to be legally constituted for the community to take part in the project. The Community Association was responsible for selecting the subproject, submitting a proposal, and if successful for implementing and maintaining the subproject. In Benin, a Comite de Concertation (CC) was set up in each community and was given primary responsibility for monitoring project implementation at the field level.

4. The idea that decision-making forums are neutral and that by entering them people can meet on a level playing field has been criticized by a number of scholars because it ignores that differences in the distribution of power and resources among community members impinge on the process of collective decision-making (Leach and others 1999; White 1996; Molyneux 2002).

5. Attendance at meetings for project selection was lower in PAC and FUMAC-P communities, where only 18 and 28 percent of the respondents respectively attended.

6. In PAC and FUMAC-P communities a much smaller share of respondents reported speaking at the meetings for project selection, respectively 10 and 14 percent.

7. In Brazil, a significantly greater number of CA members reported owning durable goods (car, motorcycle, freezer, and satellite dish) and large animals (ox and cow) prior to subproject implementation than did non-members. CA members also reported significantly greater mobilization skills and participation in political and socio-cultural events prior to subproject implementation than did non-members. In Madhya Pradesh, a significantly greater number of members of forest committees reported owning land and large animals (ox and cow) prior to subproject implementation than did non-members. Committee members were also better educated than non-members, and reported greater mobilization skills, social network and participation in traditional and non-traditional events prior to subproject implementation than did non-members. In Uttar Pradesh, SIC members were better educated than non-members, and reported greater mobilization skills and social network prior to subproject implementation than did non-members. A significantly greater number of SIC members also owned oxen prior to subproject implementation than did non-members.

8. As Kumar and Corbridge (2002) point out, village elites are likely to nominate themselves as representatives in their role of gatekeepers of development interventions. In other cases, participatory projects choose to work through village chiefs or community leaders, for these are seen as legitimate and appropriate institutions of community representation (Kumar and Corbridge 2002; Ribot 1998; Gibson and Marks 1995). In addition, communities generally elect the most prominent members and those with political connection with power-holders, as they are believed to be the only ones in the position to attract benefits to the community (Linden 1997; Platteau and Gaspart 2003).

9. Around 40 percent of the 84 CBD/CDD projects in the sample included an extensive dissemination campaign on project information, while another 40 percent had only some focus on dissemination, and the remaining 20 percent had no major focus on dissemination.

10. The share of respondents in PAC and FUMAC-P communities who were unaware of the cost of the Bank-funded subproject was higher than in FUMAC communities—respectively 92 and 91 percent.

11. Based on her fieldwork in Northeast Brazil, Tendler (2000) writes that "information ... [was] surprisingly low even in the Brazilian programs."

12. The same is true for respondents in FUMAC-P communities.

13. The variable that captures changes in respondents' mobilization skills is a composite variable. See tables M.9–M.12 for details on how this variable was created in each of the four project areas.

14. In Brazil, FUMAC-P communities in Brazil are negatively associated with changes in associational life, while no significant association was found between the latter and PAC communities.

15. As defined by the World Bank Social Capital Web site http://www1.worldbank.org/prem/poverty/scapital/index.htm.

16. The variables that capture changes in trust and associational life are composite variables. See tables M.9–M.12 for details on how these two composite

variables were created in each of the four project areas.

17. In Uttar Pradesh the positive association between the project dummy and changes in trust is driven by respondent's greater trust in village members and village organizations.

18. In Brazil, although no association was found between the project dummies and changes in trust, respondents in all three types of project communities reported a significantly smaller increase in trust in the municipal government than did respondents in comparator communities.

19. The Village-Level Participatory Approach included participatory rural appraisal and other partnership efforts that enable communities to coordinate and execute their own rural development project with assistance from extension agents and financial resources from a variety of programs.

Annex O

1. This information is based on an in-depth review of 13 projects from the random sample of 54 targeted projects in the sample of 84—two from fiscal years 1989–93, five from fiscal 1994–98, and six from fiscal 1999–2003.

2. In Benin, the Bank's social funds project (AgeFIB) targeted poor rural and peri-urban communities, with a special focus on women and unemployed youth, and in the Community-based Food Security Project (PILSA) pre-identified problem areas were targeted to ensure that assistance would be provided to the most disadvantaged segments of the rural population.

Annex P

1. As productive subprojects are normally investments that interest CA members in particular rather than communities as whole (though the latter can benefit indirectly form such investments), we only considered responses from CA members for the analysis of sustainability of irrigation subprojects.

Annex Q

1. The safeguard policies—covering environmental assessment, natural habitats, pest management, involuntary resettlement, indigenous peoples, forests, safety of dams, cultural property, projects on international waterways, and projects in disputed areas—provide a mechanism for integrating environmental and social concerns into development decision making.

2. The response rate on the questionnaire was 32 percent.

3. PPARs are prepared for selected projects by the Operations Evaluation Department, whereas ICRs are prepared for all projects by the Regions.

Annex S

1. The standard World Bank definition, available on the CDD Web site (http://www.worldbank.org/oed/cbdcdd), states that CDD is an approach that "gives control over planning decisions and investment resources to community groups and local governments."

2. *The Effectiveness of World Bank Support for Community-Based and -Driven Development: An OED Evaluation*, July 11, 2005.

3. *An OED Review of Social Development in Bank Activities*, Operations Evaluation Department, World Bank, February 17, 2004.

4. OED notes that this is likely due to the fact that management's CDD portfolio covers only projects approved from FY 00 onwards.

5. *Approach Paper: Evaluation of the World Bank's Support for Community Driven Development (CDD)* (CODE2003-0052), July 31, 2003.

6. OED notes that the Approach Paper (para. 6) also said that "Since most of the current CDD projects have evolved from the Bank's experience with CBD projects, the evaluation will review both CBD and CDD interventions."

7. The title of the OED report first referred to CDD, that was changed later to "community development," before changing it again recently to "CBD/CDD."

8. OED notes that it found in its investigation that most projects evaluated contained both CBD and CDD components and there are very few 'pure' CDD projects. Management notes that this is not surprising given the fact that OED's sample was designed to capture projects with both CBD and CDD components (see Annex E of the report).

9. *An OED Review of Social Development in Bank Activities*, Operations Evaluation Department, World Bank, February 17, 2004.

10. *Evaluating Social Funds: A Cross-Country Analysis of Community Investments*, L.B. Rawlings, L. Sherburne-Benz, J. Van Domelen, World Bank, 2004.

11. Ibid.

12. OED notes that the list in Annex II includes impact evaluations which are still ongoing and thus have not been "carried out" yet.

13. OED notes that it did not find any evidence in the documentation which it had access to that economic analysis was carried out for most individual sub-projects.

14. *Getting an Earful: A Review of Beneficiary Assessments of Social Funds*, D. Owen, J. van Domelen, World Bank, 1998.

15. Olken, Benjamin, *Monitoring Corruption: Evidence from a Field Experiment in Indonesia*, NBER, November 2004.

16. OED notes that its own reviews do not show that CDD operations do better on safeguard and fiduciary aspects than other operations.

17. OED notes that its database shows no significant difference in overall Bank performance between CBD/CDD operations and overall Bank-supported operations.

18. OED notes that its own reviews do not show that CDD operations do better on fiduciary aspects than other operations. Management notes that QAG reviews of the sample of operations OED developed for this report highlight no particular concern about CBD/CDD operations.

19. OED emphasizes that it has reviewed the methodology on the project very carefully and stands by its conclusions.

REFERENCES

Agarwal, B. 2001. "Participatory Exclusions, Community Forestry, and Gender: An Analysis of South Asia and a Conceptual Framework." *World Development* 29(10):1623–48.

———. 2000a. "Conceptualizing Environmental Collective Action: Why Gender Matters." *Cambridge Journal of Economics* 24(3):283–310.

———. 2000b. "Group Functioning and Community Forestry in South Asia: A Gender Analysis and Conceptual Framework." WIDER Working Paper 172, UNU/WIDER, Helsinki.

Agrawal, A., and C.C. Gibson. 1999. "Enchantment and Disenchantment: The Role of Community in Natural Resource Conservation." *World Development* 27(4):629–49.

Alsop, Ruth, Disa Sjoblom, Ceema Namazie, and Pawan Patil. 2002. "Community-Level User Groups in Three World Bank–Aided Projects: Do they Perform as Expected?" Social Development Papers 40. World Bank Environmentally and Socially Sustainable Development (ESSD) Network, Washington, D.C.

Anani, Kofi. 1999. "Sustainable Governance of Livelihoods in Rural Africa: A Place-Based Response to Globalism in Africa." *Development* 42(2):57–63(7).

Arnstein, S.R. 1969. "A Ladder of Citizen Participation" *Journal of the American Planning Association* 35(4): 216–24.

Arrow, K., R. Solow, P.R. Portney, E.E. Leamer, R. Radner, and H. Schuman. 1993. "Report of the NOAA Panel on Contingent Valuation." *Federal Register* 58: 4601–14.

Baland, J-M, and J-P Platteau. 2002. "Collective Action on The Commons: The Role of Inequality." In J-M Baland, P. Bardhan, and S. Bowles, eds., *Inequality, Collective Action and Environmental Sustainability*, papers presented at the Inequality Cooperation and Sustainability Workshop, Santa Fe Institute, September 21–23, 2001. <http://discuss.santafe.edu/sustainability/discuss/msgReader$3> accessed March 2005.

Bardhan, P. 2002. "Decentralization of Governance and Development." *Journal of Economic Perspectives* 16(4): 185–205.

Beck, Tony, and Cathy Nesmith. 2001. "Building on Poor People's Capacities: The Case of Common Property Resources in India and West Africa." *World Development* 29(1):119–33.

Bennett, Lynn, Mike Goldberg, and Pamela Hunte. 1996. "Ownership and Sustainability: Lessons on Group Based Financial Services from South Asia." *Journal of International Development* 8(2): 271–88.

Binswanger, H., and S. Aiyar. 2003. "Scaling up Community-Driven Development: Theoretical Underpinnings and Program Design Implications." World Bank Policy Research Working Paper 3039. Washington D.C.: World Bank.

Blair, Harry. 2003. "Civil Society and Pro-Poor Initiatives at the Local Level in Bangladesh." Draft, February 28. Department for International Development, UK. <http://idpm.man.ac.uk/cprc/Conference/conferencepapers/Blair%20Harry%20draft%2003.03.03.pdf> accessed March 2005.

———. 2000. "Participation and Accountability at the Periphery: Democratic Local Governance in Six Countries." *World Development* 28(1): 21–39.

Brock, K., A. Cornwall, and J. Gaventa. 2001. "Power, Knowledge and Political Spaces in the Framing of Poverty Policy." Institute of Development Studies Working Paper 143. Brighton, U.K.: IDS. <http://www.ids.ac.uk/

ids/bookshop/wp/wp143.pdf>accessed March 2005.

Candler, W., and N. Kumar. 1998. *The Dairy Revolution: The Impact of Dairy Development in India and the World Bank's Contribution*. Operations Evaluation Department Study Series. Washington, D.C.: World Bank.

Chabal, P., and J.P. Daloz. 1999. *Africa Works: Disorder as Political Instrument*. Oxford: James Currey.

Chambers, R. 1995. "Paradigm Shifts and the Practice of Participatory Research and Development." In N. Nelson and S. Wright, eds., *Power and Participatory Development Theory and Practice*. London: Intermediate Technology.

Cleaver, F. 1999. "Paradoxes of Participation: Questioning Participatory Approaches to Development." *Journal of International Development* 11(4): 597–612.

———. 1998. "There's a Right Way to Do It – Informal Arrangements for Local Resource Management in Zimbabwe." *Waterlines* 16(4).

———. 1997. "Gendered Incentives and Informal Institutions: Women, Men and the Management of Water." Discussion Paper Series 2, No. 3, Development and Project Planning Center. University of Bradford, U.K.

Coady, David, Margaret Grosh, and John Hoddinott. 2004. *Targeting of Transfers in Developing Countries Review of Lessons and Experience: Regional and Sectoral Studies*. Washington, D.C.: World Bank and IFPRI.

Collinson, M.P. 1982. *Farming Systems Research in Eastern Africa: The Experience of CIMMYT and Some National Agricultural Research Services, 1976–81*. International Wheat and Maize Improvement Center. Nairobi: CIMMYT.

Conning, J., and M. Kevane. 2002. "Community-Based Targeting Mechanisms for Social Safety Nets: A Critical Review." *World Development* 30(3): 375–94

Cornwall, A. 2003. "Whose Voices? Whose Choices? Reflections on Gender and Participatory Development." *World Development* 31(8):1325–42.

———. 2002. "Making Spaces, Changing Places: Situating Participation in Development." IDS Working Paper 170. Brighton, U.K.

Costa, Alberto, C.G. Conrad, P. Kottak, and Rosane M. Prado. 1997. "The Sociopolitical Context of Participatory Development in Northeastern Brazil." *Human Organization* 56(2).

da Cunha, Paulo Vieira, and Maria Valeria Junho Pena. 1997. "The Limits and Merits of Participation." World Bank Policy Research Working Paper 1838. Washington, D.C.

Dahl-Ostergaard, T., D. Moore, V. Ramirez, M. Wenner, and A. Bonde. 2003. "Community-Driven Rural Development: What Have We Learned?" Inter-American Development Bank Sustainable Development Department Technical Paper Series. Washington, D.C. <http://www.iadb.org/sds/doc/RUR-COWI-E.pdf> accessed March 2005.

Das Gupta, M., H. Grandvoinnet, and M. Romani. 2000. "State-Community Synergies in Development: Laying the Basis for Collective Action." World Bank Policy Research Working Paper 2439. Washington, D.C.

de Clercq, Francine. 1994. "Putting Community Participation into Development Work: The Difficult Case of Winterveld." *Development South Africa* 11(3).

Desai, V. 1996. "Access to Power and Participation." *Third World Planning Review* 18(2): 217–42.

Development Committee. 2004. "Global Monitoring Report 2004. Policies and Actions for Achieving the MDGs and Related Outcomes." DC2004-0006. Joint Ministerial Committee of the Boards of Governors of the Bank and the Fund on the Transfer of Real Resources to Developing Countries. Washington, D.C.

Devereux, Stephen, and Kay Sharp. Forthcoming. "Trends in Poverty and Destitution in Wollo, Ethiopia. *Journal of Development Studies*.

Elbers, Chris, Peter F. Lanjouw, Johan A. Mistiaen, Berk Ozler, and Ken Simler. 2004. "On the Unequal Inequality of Poor Communities." *The World Bank Economic Review* 18(3).

Einhorn, Jessica. 2001. "The World Bank's Mission Creep." *Foreign Affairs* 80(5): 22.

Estrella, Marisol, and John Gaventa. 1998. "Who Counts Reality? Participatory Monitoring and Evaluation A Literature Review." IDS Working Paper 70. Brighton, U.K.

Forster, R. 1998. "GTZ's Experience with Mainstreaming Primary Stakeholder Participation." Paper presented at the International Conference on Mainstreaming and Up-Scaling of Primary Stakeholder Participation—Lessons Learned and Ways Forward. Washington D.C., November 19–20, 1998.

Garcia, X.M., and S-A. Way. 2003. "Winning Spaces: Participatory Methodologies in Rural Processes in Mexico." IDS Working Paper 180. Brighton, U.K.

Gibson, C., and S.A. Marks. 1995. "Transforming Rural Hunters into Conservationists: An Assessment of Community-Based Wildlife Management Programs in Africa." *World Development* 23(6):941–57.

Greiner, L.E. 1972. "Evolution and Revolution as Organizations Grow." *Harvard Business Review* 50 (July-August): 37–46.

Grootaert, C. 1998. "Social Capital: The Missing Link?" World Bank Social Capital Initiative Working Paper 3. Washington, D.C.

Gueye, B. 1999. "Whither Participation? Experience from Francophone West Africa." Drylands Issue Paper 87. International Institute for Environment and Development. Dryland Program <http://www.iied.org/docs/drylands/dry_ip87eng.pdf> accessed March 2005.

Gugerty, Mary Kay, and Michael Kremer. 2000. "Outside Funding of Community Organizations: Benefiting or Displacing the Poor?" National Bureau of Economic Research Working Paper 7896. Cambridge, MA.

Handy, C. 1985. *Understanding Organizations*. Harmondsworth: Penguin.

Hentschel, J. 1994. "Does Participation Cost the World Bank More? Emerging Evidence." World Bank Human Resource Development and Operations Policy (HRO) Working Paper 31. Washington, D.C.

IBGE (Instituto Brasileiro de Geografia e Estadística). 2003. Perfil dos Municípios Brasileiros: Gestão Publica 2001, Rio de Janeiro. <http://www.ibge.gov.br/home/estatistica/economia/perfilmunic/2001/munic2001.pdf> accessed March 2005.

Isham, J., and S. Kähkönen. 2002. "Institutional Determinants of the Impact of Community-Based Water Services: Evidence from Sri Lanka and India." *Economic Development and Cultural Change* 50(3): 667–91.

Isham, Jonathan, Deepa Narayan, and Lant Pritchett. 1995. "Does Participation Improve Performance? Establishing Causality with Subjective Data." *The World Bank Economic Review* 9(2):175–200.

Jenkins, R., and A.M. Goetz. 1999. "Accounts and Accountability: Theoretical Implications of the Right-to-Information Movement in India." *Third World Quarterly* 20(3):603–22.

Jones, Emma, and SPEECH. 2001. " 'Of Other Spaces' Situating Participatory Practices: A Case Study from South India." IDS Working Paper 137. Brighton Sussex, U.K.

Kähkönen, S. 1999. "Does Social Capital Matter in Water and Sanitation Delivery? A Review of Literature." World Bank Social Capital Initiative Working Paper 9. Washington, D.C.

Kent, B.R., and J. Rimarachin. 1994. "Rural Public Works Construction in the Andes of Northern Peru." *Third World Planning Review* 16(4):358–74.

Kerr, J., with G. Pangare, V.L. Pangare, and P. George. 2000. "An Evaluation of Dryland Watershed Development Projects in India." EPTD Discussion Paper 68. Washington, D.C.: IFPRI.

Khwaja, A.I. 2003. "A Note on Measuring Empowerment—An Economist's Perspective." Kennedy School of Government Harvard University. Paper presented at the Workshop on "Measuring Empowerment: Cross-Disciplinary Perspectives," World Bank, Washington, D.C., February 4–5, 2003.

———. 2000. "Can Good Projects Succeed in Bad Communities? Collective Action in Public Good Provision" Harvard University. Paper presented at the Annual Bank Conference on Development Economics, May 2, 2001.

Kleemeier, Elizabeth. 2000. "The Impact of Participation on Sustainability: An Analysis of the Malawi Rural Piped Scheme Program. *World Development* 28(5): 929–44.

Kolavalli, S., and J. Kerr. 2002. "Scaling up Participatory Watershed Development in India." *Development and Change* 33(2): 213–35.

Koopman, J., and R. Kweka, M. Mboya, and S.W. Wangwe. 2001. "Community Participation in

Traditional Irrigation Scheme Rehabilitation Projects in Tanzania: Report of a Collaborative Research Project." Ministry of Agriculture and Cooperatives, Irrigation Section, Dar es Salaam, Tanzania.

Korten, D.C. 1980. "Community Organization and Rural Development: A Learning Process Approach." *Public Administration Review* 40(5): 480–511.

Krishna, A. 2004. "Partnership Between Elected Local Governments and Community-Based Organizations: Exploring the Scope for Synergy." Social Development Papers, Community Driven Development, Number 52/February.

———. 2003. "Falling into Poverty: The Other Side of Poverty Reduction." Special Article, *Economic and Political Weekly*. Hitkari House, Mumbai, India.

———. 2002. *Active Social Capital. Tracing the Roots of Development and Democracy*. New York: Columbia University Press

———. 2001. "Moving from the Stock of Social Capital to the Flow of Benefits: The Role of Agency." *World Development* 29(6): 925–43.

Krishna, A., N. Uphoff, and M. Esman (eds.). 1997. *Reasons for Hope: Instructive Experiences in Rural Development*. West Hartford, CT: Kumarian.

Krishna, A., M. Kapila, M. Porwal, and V. Singh. 2003. "Falling into Poverty in a High-Growth State: Escaping Poverty and Becoming Poor in Gujarat Villages." Special Article, *Economic and Political Weekly*. Hitkari House, Mumbai, India

Krishna, A., M. Kapila, S. Pathak, M. Porwal, K. Singh, and V. Singh. 2004. "Falling into Poverty in Villages of Andhra Pradesh: Why Poverty Avoidance Policies are Needed." Special Article, *Economic and Political Weekly*. Hitkari House, Mumbai, India

Krishna, A., P. Kristjanson, M. Radeny, and W. Nindo. 2004. "Escaping Poverty and Becoming Poor in 20 Kenyan Villages." *Journal of Human Development*, 5(2): 211–26.

———. 2002. "The Challenges of Community Participation in Forest Development in Nepal." OED Working Paper Series. Washington, D.C..

Kumar, N. 2003. "Community-Driven Development: Lessons from the Sahel—An Analytical Review." OED Working Paper Series. Washington, D.C.

Kumar, N., N. Saxena, Y. Alagh, and K. Mitra. 2000. *India: Alleviating Poverty through Forest Development*. Evaluation Country Case Study Series, Operations Evaluation Department. Washington, D.C.: World Bank.

Kumar, Sanjay, and Stuart Corbridge. 2002. "Programmed to Fail? Development Projects and the Politics of Participation." *The Journal of Development Studies* 39(2) 830–51.

Leach, M., R. Mearns, and I. Scoones. 1999. "Environmental Entitlement: Dynamics and Institutions in Community-Based Natural Resource Management." *World Development* 27(2): 225–47.

Leipziger, Danny, Marianne Fay, Quentin Woden, and Tito Yepes. 2003. "Achieving the Millennium Development Goals—A Multi-Sectoral Approach Revisited." World Bank Policy Research Working Paper 3163. Washington, D.C.

Linden van der, J. 1997, "On Popular Participation in a Culture of Patronage; Patrons and Grassroots Organization in a Sites and Services Project in Hyderabad, Pakistan." *Development* 9 (1): 81–90.

Lipton, Michael. n.d. "Rural Poverty Reduction: The Neglected Priority." Work at the Poverty Research Unit, Sussex University, for the International Fund for Agriculture Development's Report on Rural Poverty.

Manor, J. 1999. *The Political Economy of Democratic Decentralisation. Directions in Development*. Washington D.C.: World Bank.

Mansuri, G., and V. Rao. 2004. "Community-Based and -Driven Development: A Critical Review." *World Bank Research Observer* 19(1): 1–39.

Meinzen-Dick, R.S., K.V. Raju, and A. Gulati. 2002. "What Affects Organization and Collective Action for Managing Resources? Evidence from Canal Irrigation Systems in India." *World Development* 30(4):649–66.

Minot, N., and B. Baulch. 2004. "Poverty Mapping with Aggregate Census Data." MSSD Discussion Paper 49. Washington, D.C.: IFPRI. <http://www.ifpri.org/divs/mtid/dp/papers/mssdp49.pdf> accessed March 2005.

Molyneux, M. 2002. "Gender and the Silences of Social Capital: Lessons from Latin America." *Development and Change* 33(2):167–88.

Moore, Mick. 2001. "Empowerment at Last?" *Journal of International Development* 13(3):321–29.

Moore, Mick, and Anuradha Joshi. 1999. "Between Cant and Corporatism: Creating an Enabling Environment for the Poor." *IDS Bulletin* 30(4). Brighton, U.K.

Narayan, Deepa. 1995. *The Contribution of People's Participation Evidence from 121 Rural Water Supply Projects*. Environmentally Sustainable Development Occasional Paper No. 1. Washington, D.C.: World Bank.

Narayan, Deepa, and Lant Pritchett. 1997. "Cents and Sociability: Household Income and Social Capital in Rural Tanzania." World Bank Policy Research Working Paper 1796. Washington, D.C.

Nelson N., and S. Wright (eds.). 1995. *Power and Participatory Development Theory and Practice.* London: Intermediate Technology.

North, D.C. 1991. *Institutions, Institutional Change and Economic Performance. Political Economy of Institutions and Decisions*. Cambridge, U.K.: Cambridge University Press.

Oakley, Peter, and others. 1991. *Projects with People: The Practice of Participation in Rural Development*. Geneva: ILO.

OED (Operations Evaluation Department, World Bank). 2004a. *Monitoring and Evaluation: Some Tools, Methods and Approaches*. Washington, D.C.: World Bank.

———. 2004b. *Books, Building and Learning Outcomes: An Impact Evaluation of World Bank Support to Basic Education in Ghana*. Operations Evaluation Department Study Series. Washington, D.C.: World Bank.

———. 2003c. *An OED Review of Social Development in Bank Activities.* Operations Evaluation Department. Washington, D.C.

———. 2002a. *IDA's Partnership for Poverty Reduction: An Independent Evaluation of Fiscal Years 1994–2000.* Operations Evaluation Department. Washington, D.C.: World Bank.

———. 2002b. *Social Funds: Assessing Effectiveness*. Operations Evaluation Department Study Series. Washington, D.C.: World Bank.

———. 2002c. *The Next Ascent: An Evaluation of the Aga Khan Rural Support Program, Pakistan*. Operations Evaluation Department Study Series. Washington, D.C.: World Bank.

———. 2001. "The National Agricultural Research Project, the National Agricultural Extension Project, the National Livestock Services Project, the Agricultural Diversification Project, and the Agricultural Sector Investment Project "(sector overview). Project Performance Assessment Report. Report No. 22439, Operations Evaluation Department. Washington, D.C.

———. 1999a. *Nongovernmental Organizations in World Bank-Supported Projects*. Operations Evaluation Department. Report No. 19061. Washington, D.C.: World Bank.

———. 1999b. *Agricultural Extension Projects in Kenya—An Impact Evaluation*. Report No. 19523. Washington, D.C.: World Bank.

———. 1998. *The World Bank's Experience with Post-Conflict Reconstruction*. Operations Evaluation Department Study Series. Washington, D.C.: World Bank.

Ostrom, E. 1999. "Social Capital: A Fad or a Fundamental Concept?" In P. Dasgupta and I. Serageldin, eds., *Social Capital: A Multifaceted Perspective*. Washington, D.C.: World Bank.

Overseas Development Institute. 1996. "The Impact of NGO Development Projects." Briefing Paper 2/96. <http://www.odi.org.uk/publications/briefing/2_96.html> accessed March 2005.

Pantoja, E. 2000. "Exploring the Concept of Social Capital and its Relevance for Community-Based Development: The Case of Coal Mining Areas in Orissa, India." World Bank Social Capital Initiative Working Paper 18. Washington D.C.

Picciotto, Robert. 1992. "Participatory Development Myths and Dilemmas." Participatory Development Working Paper 930. Washington D.C.: World Bank.

Pimbert, M., V. Bainbridge, S. Foerster, K. Pasteur, G. Pratt, and I.Y. Arroyo. 2000. "Transforming Bureaucracies: Institutionalizing Participation and People Centered Processes in Natural Resource Management: An Annotated Bibliography." London: IIED. <http://

www.iied.org/docs/sarl/AnnotBib20001.pdf> accessed March 2005.

Platteau, Jean-Philippe. 2003. "Institutional and Distributional Aspects of Sustainability in Community-Driven Development." Paper prepared for the Fifth Biennial World Bank Conference on Evaluation and Development, Evaluating Development Effectiveness: Challenges and the Way Forward. Washington D.C., July 5–16, 2003.

Platteau, J-P, and F. Gaspart. 2003. "The Risk of Resource Misappropriation in Community-Driven Development." *World Development* 31(10):1687–1703.

Pretty, Jules. 1998. "Sustainable Agricultural Intensification: Farmer Participation, Social Capital and Technology Design." Paper Prepared for the World Bank's Rural Week, Washington. D.C.

Pretty, Jules, and Hugh Ward. 2001. "Social Capital and the Environment." *World Development* 29(2) 209-227.

Pritchett, Lant, and Michael Woolcock. 2004. "Solutions When the Solution is the Problem: Arraying the Disarray in Development." *World Development* 32(2): 191–212.

Pronk, Jan P. 2003. "Aid as a Catalyst: A Rejoinder." *Development and Change* 34(3):383–400.

Rajasekhar, D., and Veerashekharappa. 2004. "Role of Local Organizations in Water Supply and Sanitation Sector." A Study in Karnataka and Uttaranchal States, India. Institute for Social and Economic Change. Bangalore, India.

Rajasekhar, D., D.V. Gopalappa, and Madhushree Sekhar. 2004. "Role of Local Organizations in Watershed Development." A Study in Karnataka and Uttaranchal States, India. Institute for Social and Economic Change. Bangalore, India.

Rao, V., and A.M. Ibáñez. 2003. "The Social Impact of Social Funds in Jamaica: A Mixed-Methods Analysis of Participation, Targeting, and Collective Action in Community-Driven Development." World Bank Policy Research Working Paper 2970. Washington, D.C.

Ravallion, Martin, and Gaurav Datt. 1996. "India's Checkered History in the Fight against Poverty: Are There Lessons for the Future?" *Economic and Political Weekly* 31 (Special Number):2479–86.

Renata, Elad L. and Jack E. Houston 2002. "Seasonal Labor Constraints and Intra-household Dynamics in the Female Fields of Southern Cameroon." *Agricultural Economics* 27:23–32.

Ribot, J.C. 2001. "Integral Local Development: 'Accommodating Multiple Interests' through Entrustment and Accountable Representation." *International Journal of Agricultural Resources, Governance and Ecology* 1(3/4): 327–50.

———. 1998. "Decentralization, Participation and Accountability in Sahelian Forestry: Legal Instruments of Political-Administrative Control." Institute of International Studies. Berkeley Workshop on Environmental Politics. Working Paper WP00-5-Ribot. <http://repositories.cdlib.org/iis/bwep/WP00-5-Ribot> accessed March 2005.

———. 1995. "From Exclusion to Participation: Turning Senegal's Forestry Policy around?" *World Development* 23(9):1587–99.

Romeo, Leonardo G. 2003. "The Role of External Assistance in Supporting Decentralization Reform." *Public Administration and Development* 23: 89–96.

SAPROS & IFAD. 2002. *Nepal—A Study of Rural Hill Potentials and Service Delivery Systems*. Sapros:Kathmandu, Nepal.

SAPROS & World Bank. 2000. *Delivery of Rural Development Services, A Comparative Assessment of Alternative Institutional Arrangements with a Focus on the Terai*. Sapros: Kathmandu, Nepal.

Schady, Norbert R. 2000. "Picking the Poor: Indicators for Geographic Targeting in Peru." World Bank Policy Research Working Paper 2477. Washington, D.C.

Schneider, H. 1999. "Participatory Governance for Poverty Reduction." *Journal of International Development* 11(4):521–34.

Schou, Arild. 2002. "Popular Participation in Decentralised Service Delivery and Social Funds." NIBR Working Paper 124. Oslo.

Schroeder, Larry. 2000. "Social Funds and Local Government: The Case of Malawi." *Public Administration and Development* 20:423–38.

Schultz, Theodore W. 1964. *Transforming Traditional Agriculture*. New Haven, CT: Yale University Press.

Sen, Amartya. 1999. *Development as Freedom*. New York: Alfred A Knopf.

Serrano, R. 1996. "Who Knows What's Best for the Poor? Demand-Driven Policies and Rural Poverty in Northeast Brazil." Thesis, MIT.

Shepherd, A. 1998. "Participatory Environmental Management: Contradiction of Process, Project and Bureaucracy in the Himalayan Foothills." In J. Blackburn and J. Holland, eds., *Who Changes? Institutionalizing Participation in Development*. London: Intermediate Technology.

Tendler, Judith. 2000. "Why Are Social Funds So Popular?" In Shahid Yusuf, Simon Evenett, and Weiping Wu, eds., *Local Dynamics in an Era of Globalization: 21st Century Catalysts for Development*. Oxford, U.K.: Oxford University Press.

———. 1997. *Good Government in the Tropics*. Baltimore and London: The John Hopkins University Press.

———. 1989. "What Ever Happened to Poverty Alleviation?" *World Development* 17(7): 1033–44.

Thompson, John. 1995. "Participatory Approaches in Government Bureaucracies: Facilitating the Process of Institutional Change." *World Development* 23(9):1521–54.

Tripp, Aili Mari. 2001. "Non-Formal Institutions, Informal Economics, and the Politics of Inclusion." Discussion Paper No. 2001/108. World Institute for Development Economics Research/United Nations University. New York.

Turton, C., and J. Farrington. 1998. "Enhancing Rural Livelihoods through Participatory Watershed Development in India." *Natural Resource Perspectives* 34, London: ODI.

UNDP (United Nations Development Program). 2004. *Human Development Report 2004: Cultural Liberty in Today's Diverse World*. <http://hdr.undp.org/reports/global/2004/> accessed March 2005

Uphoff, N., and C.M. Wijayaratna. 2000. "Demonstrated Benefits from Social Capital: The Productivity of Farmer Organizations in Gal Oya, Sri Lanka." *World Development* 28(11): 1875–90.

Uphoff, N., M. Esman, and A. Krishna. 1998. *Reasons for Success. Learning from Instructive Experiences in Rural Development*. Bloomfield, CT: Kumarian.

van de Walle, N., and T.A. Johnston. 1996. "Improving Aid to Africa." Policy Essay No. 21. Baltimore: Overseas Development Council.

van der Linden, J. 1997. "On Popular Participation in a Culture of Patronage; Patrons and Grassroots Organization in a Sites and Services Project in Hyderabad, Pakistan." *Environment and Urbanization* 9(1):81–90.

van Donge, Jankees. 2003. *Nurtured from above and Growing from the Roots: Social Funds and Decentralization in Zambia and Malawi*. The Hague: Institute of Social Studies. <http://www.devstud.org.uk/publications/papers/conf03/dsaconf03vandonge.pdf> accessed March 2005.

van Zyl, J., L. Sonn, and A. Costa. 2000. "Decentralized Rural Development, Enhanced Community Participation and Local Government Performance: Evidence from the Northeast Brazil." Unpublished paper.

Vyasulu, P., and V. Vyasulu. 1999. "Women in Panchayati Raj: Grassroots Democracy in India. Experience from Malgudi." Paper presented at the Meeting on Women and Political Participation: 21st Century Challenges, UNDP, New Delhi, March 24–26, 1999. http://magnet.undp.org/events/gender/india/VYASULU3.htm

Wagel, S., and P. Shah. 2003. "Case Study 2—Porto Alegre, Brazil: Participatory Approaches in Budgeting and Public Expenditure Management." *Social Development Note* 71, World Bank. <http://www.worldbank.org/participation/sdn/snd71.pdf> accessed March 2005.

Walter, Ian, Rafael Del Cid, Fidel Ordoñez, and Florencia Rodríguez. 1999. "Ex-Post Evaluation of the Honduran Social Investment Fund." Report for the World Bank. <http://wbln0018.worldbank.org/HDNet/HDdocs.nsf/socialfunds/49898ac982b7c7de852568e2005d75ce/$FILE/FHISexecsummary.pdf> accessed March 2005.

Wassenich, Paul, and Katherine Whiteside. 2004. "CDD Impact Assessments Study: Optimizing Evaluation Design Under Constraints." *Social Development Papers* Number 51, February.

Watt, Patrick 2001. "Community Support for Basic Education in Sub-Saharan Africa." World Bank Africa Region Human Development Working Paper Series. Washington, D.C.

Weinberger, K., and J.P. Jutting. 2001. "Women's Participation in Local Organizations: Conditions and Constraints." *World Development* 29(8):1391–1404.

White, S.C. 1996. "Depoliticising Development: the Uses and Abuses of Participation." *Development in Practice* 6(1):6–15.

Wilks, Alex. 2001. "Overstretched and Underloved: World Bank Faces Strategy Decisions." Bretton Woods Project. Washington, D.C.

Williams, G. 2003. "Toward a Re-politicisation of Development: Political Capabilities and Space of Empowerment." Paper presented at the conference Participation: From Tyranny to Transition? Exploring New Approaches to Participatory Development," University of Manchester, Manchester, February 27–28,

World Bank. 2004a. "Community-Driven Development in Local Government Capacity Building Projects: Emerging Approaches in Africa." *Social Development Notes* No. 86 (November). Washington, D.C.

———. 2004b. "Case Study Summaries for Reducing Poverty Sustaining Growth, Scaling Up Poverty Reduction." A Global Learning Process and Conference, Shanghai, May 25–27, 2004.

———. 2004c. "Negotiating Social Change in Rural Nepal: Crosscutting Gender, Caste and Ethnic Dimensions of Empowerment and Social Inclusion. Measuring Empowerment and Social Inclusion Study: Phase I Report, Social Development." Draft.

———. 2004d. *World Development Report 2004:. Making Services Work for Poor People*. Washington, D.C.

———. 2004e. "Community-Driven Development in Urban Upgrading." *Social Development Notes* No. 85 (February). Washington, D.C.

———. 2003a. "The Role of Selectivity in Enhancing IDA Effectiveness: A Progress Report." IDA/R2003-0199. Washington, D.C.<http://siteresources.worldbank.org/IDA/Resources/MTRselectivityERS.pdf> accessed March 2005.

———. 2003b. *PRSP Sourcebook*. Washington, D.C.

———. 2003c. "Review of Bank Supervision of CDD Operations in the EAP Region" (Draft). EAP, VPU. <http://lnweb18.worldbank.org/ESSD/sdvext.nsf/09ByDocName/ReviewOfBankSupervisionOfCDOperationsInTheEAPRegion-RevisedDraft/$FILE/EAPCD-SupervisionRevisedRptMar2003.pdf> accessed March 2005.

———. 2003d. "Evaluating Social Funds: A Cross-Country Analysis of Community Investments." Regional and Sectoral Studies. Washington, D.C.

———. 2003e. "Community-Driven Reconstruction as an Instrument in War-to-Peace Transitions." CPR Working Paper No. 7, August. Social Development Department ESSD Network. <http://lnweb18.worldbank.org/ESSD/sdvext.nsf/60ByDocName/Community-drivenReconstructionasanInstrumentinWar-to-PeaceTransitions/$FILE/SDP43-CPRWP07Aug21.pdf> accessed March 2005.

———. 2002a. "A Tale of Two Projects: Community-Based Reconstruction in East Timor and Rwanda." *Social Funds Innovation Update* 2(4). Human Development Network-Social Protection Unit, Social Funds Thematic Group. Washington, D.C.

———. 2002b. *Empowerment and Poverty Reduction: A Sourcebook*. <http://siteresources.worldbank.org/INTEMPOWERMENT/Resources/486312-1095094954594/draft.pdf> accessed March 2005.

———. 2002c. "Sleeping on our Own Mats: An Introductory Guide to Community Based Monitoring and Evaluation." Africa Region, Rural Development II. Washington, D.C.

———. 2001a. "Decentralization and Governance: Does Decentralization Improve Public Service Delivery?" *PREM Note* Number 55. Washington, D.C.

———. 2001b. "World Bank Strategic Framework" January 24. Washington, D.C.<http://siteresources.worldbank.org/EXTABOU-

TUS/Resources/strategic.pdf> accessed March 2005.

———. 2001c. "Empowering the Poor through Decentralization: Brazil Rural Poverty Alleviation Program." *Social Development Note* No. 51. Washington, D.C.

———. 2000. "The Community Driven Development Approach in the Africa Region: A Vision of Poverty Reduction Through Empowerment." Washington, D.C.

———. 1996. *The World Bank Participation Sourcebook*. Environmentally Sustainable Development Network. Washington, D.C.

———. 1995. "Designing Community Based Development" (by Deepa Narayan). Environment Department Paper No. 007. Participation Series. Washington, D.C.

World Bank and IMF 2004. "Global Monitoring Report 2004: Policies and Actions for Achieving the MDGs and Related Outcomes." Background Paper, Development Committee (Joint Ministerial Committee of the Boards of Governors of the Bank and the Fund) on the Transfer of Real Resources to Developing Countries. Washington, D.C.

Wunsch, James S. 2001. "Decentralization, Local Governance and 'Recentralization' in Africa." *Public Administration and Development* 21: 277-88.

Yukio, Ikemoto. 2001. "Poverty Alleviation Policies and Ethnic Minority People in Vietnam." Institute of Oriental Culture, University of Tokyo. <http://www.st-edmunds.cam.ac.uk/vhi/sen/papers/ikemoto.pdf> accessed March 2005.